DEADLY DANCE

THE
CHIPPENDALES
MURDERS

DEADLY DANCE

THE CHIPPENDALES MURDERS

by

K. Scot Macdonald
and
Patrick MontesDeOca

Kerrera House Press

Cover Image © Enzo Giobbe

Macdonald, K. Scot and MontesDeOca, Patrick
Deadly Dance: the Chippendales
Murders/K. Scot Macdonald—1st Edition
p.　　cm.
ISBN: 978-0-9916653-2-7
Kerrera House Press
Culver City, CA
www.KerreraHousePress.com

First Printing: 2014
Printed in the United States of America

10　9　8　7　6　5　4　3　2　1

For photographs related to *Deadly Dance* visit
KerreraHousePress.com.

This book would not have been possible without the cooperation of many people who discussed events they would have liked to have forgotten, including Val and Tom De Noia, Marie De Noia-Aronson, Michael Geddes, Bruce Nahin, Janet Hudson, Steve Clymer, Jim Henderson, William Mott, David Drucker, and Ray Colon. Thank you.

Thanks also to Enzo Giobbe for permission to use the cover image.

Although every effort was made to discover what truly happened, in such a complex story there are undoubtedly still mistakes. Any such errors are mine and have been made with no malice or intent to harm any living person—or the memory of a loved one.

On the last day of his life, Tuesday, April 7, 1987, 46-year-old Nicholas "Nick" John De Noia stopped by his office on the fifteenth floor of 264 West 40th Street in Manhattan to pick up some business papers. Since 1981, De Noia had been working for Steve Banerjee, founder and owner of Chippendales, first as choreographer and then producer of the company's male exotic stage show. Banerjee had gone to great lengths to convince the reluctant New Jersey native to take the job because De Noia was an excellent choice. His extensive credentials included production of a play at Washington's famous Ford's Theater, five Emmys for excellence in television, including one for a series of children's fairy tales for NBC called the *Unicorn Tales*, and experience on Broadway.

By seeking to match the demanding artistic standards of Broadway, the lean, muscular De Noia transformed the Chippendales show from a bunch of muscle-bound jocks strutting and often stumbling around on stage into a professional, Vegas-style production with well-honed choreography, extravagant costumes and high-tech special effects that made the show an event of a lifetime for every lust-filled woman who attended. Although a Chippendales emcee described De Noia as "equal parts Julius Caesar, P. T. Barnum, the Marquis de Sade, and Bob Fosse," the dancers loved him because the show became a phenomenal success and the Chippendales dancers became international sex symbols.

By the mid-1980s at a time when the average American household was bringing in $770 a week, the New York *Daily News* reported that Chippendales tour profits had hit $80,000 a week. Some nights the beefcake show made $25,000. Based on a November 13, 1984 deal with Steve Banerjee scribbled on a paper restaurant napkin, Nick De Noia received half the profits from the tour shows. He was quickly becoming a wealthy man and, as a result of his many media appearances, had become known as Mr. Chippendales.

That Tuesday afternoon in 1987 in New York, De Noia was on his way to Indianapolis where the Chippendales were scheduled to perform. Just after 3:30 p.m., De Noia, in blue jeans and an open-necked, dark dress shirt with a white grid pattern, looked up from his desk to see a Hispanic male walk into his office. The man was in his late thirties, neatly dressed in a dark tan, waist-length jacket and blue jeans. He might have been the man who had called a short time before to make a 4:30 appointment for an audition, but not only was he far too early for the appointment, he was also clearly no dancer. At 5' 7" and 145 pounds, he was far shorter and smaller than the dancers De Noia hired. He also looked ill, his cheekbones protruding against his taut, pockmarked skin.

"Are you Nick De Noia?" The man's tone suggested this was not a question De Noia could refuse to answer.

"Yes," De Noia acknowledged.

"You're a dead man then," the stranger said, pulling a 9 mm automatic handgun out of his waistband and leveling it at De Noia's face.

De Noia rose from behind his desk. The choreographer smiled as if it was a joke, before a look of "sheer panic" crossed his face. The stranger pulled the trigger and fatally shot De Noia once just below the left eye.

Chapter 1
Reaching for the American Dream

On November 19, 1973, with a borrowed $1,000, an Indian-American partner, and a recent Loyola Marymount University Law School graduate handling the legal aspects of the deal, Somen Banerjee signed an agreement to rent with an option to buy a failing nightclub in the Palms district of West Los Angeles: the Round Robin.

The moribund Round Robin was at 3739 Overland Avenue just south of Palms Boulevard where the road narrowed and small, run-down businesses crowded the road before the street widened again at Venice Boulevard. The area was on the verge of being seedy, dotted with garages enclosed by rusted chain-link fences and two-bedroom, single-story houses with sun-bleached paint, some of which had been converted into small businesses and hole-in-the-wall restaurants. The street was pot holed, its sidewalks cracked.

Outside, Overland lacked streetlights. Inside, the club was dimly lit. The Round Robin boasted a tiny dance floor, which was usually empty. The crummy combo that masqueraded as a band probably drove more people away than they attracted.

It was so quiet that Banerjee's new attorney, Bruce Nahin, was studying for the bar exam at the club because it was quieter than a library.

Banerjee's future looked bleak. In the first two weeks running the club, he and his partners went more than $5,000 into the red. Banerjee worked hard to attract business. He changed the club's name to Destiny II, hung out a mammoth sign proclaiming that the club was "Under New Management," and held a grand opening. Since there were always more men than women at nightclubs, the key was to lure women into the club and the men, like lions after lambs, would follow, so he offered no cover charge and two free drinks to all the ladies. It all helped, but not enough.

The new name, Destiny II, was meant to denote Banerjee's new future. When he arrived in Los Angeles, he had bought a Mobil gas station, his first destiny; the club would be his second. Whatever his destiny, he had already come a long way.

Somen Banerjee was born into the fourth generation of a family of printers on October 8, 1946 in what was then Bombay and is now, under a more accurate pronunciation system, Mumbai, India. He emigrated from the West Indian port city to Canada and then to the United States in 1969, ending up in Los Angeles. Like many immigrants to the United States, he adopted a Westernized name: Steve. Like most immigrants, the newly renamed Steve was competitive, with a phenomenally high need to achieve and a belief in the American dream that put most native-born Americans to shame. Within a couple of years of arriving in the City of Angels, he had bought a Mobil gas station in posh Playa del Rey, just north of LAX on the shores of the Pacific. He had far greater dreams, however, than just owning a gas station. America was the land of opportunity and he planned to seize every opportunity that came within his reach.

Steve Banerjee was far from the stereotypical gas station manager. Although he carried 160 pudgy pounds on a 5' 9" frame, Steve dressed for success. He wore large, at-the-time stylish glasses, colorful button-down Oxford shirts with silk ties and dress slacks. Adding to his out-of-place appearance at the gas station was his attitude, which betrayed at every opportunity his belief that his present work was far beneath what was going to be his true station in life. He was brusque with customers, showing his resentment when they even just asked for the restroom key. He read business journals and studied the work of his favorite designers and filmmakers, Giorgio Armani, Calvin Klein and Steven Spielberg, all the while dreaming of making it big in America. He acquired the Round Robin with thoughts of turning it into a posh backgammon club, reflecting his image of himself as a fashionable gentleman of means. When he adopted the name Steve, he also retained his given name of Somen, probably because in his native Bengali, Somen is pronounced "show-men." The sound of his name matched his dream of succeeding as a club owner.

Even as the club struggled, Steve met a man who would become his closest friend: Ralph Augustine "Angel" Colon, whom Steve would know as Ray. In 1975, when he met Steve, Ray was 5' 8" and 155 pounds, with dark brown hair, clear hazel eyes, and a panther tattoo on his upper right arm. Since he had relocated from the East Coast, he also sported a deep California tan. He drank two or three beers a day, but later said he never had an alcohol or drug problem. He had a laid-back demeanor that overlay an intense personality, which seemed to emanate from him like a simmering aura. His physicality included an underlying menace that never seemed to dissipate entirely, even when he was laughing. Ray seemed like the type of man who would live up to the motto: no better friend, no worse enemy.

Born September 15, 1944 in the Bronx, Ray grew up in Astoria, Queens and then Long Island. He was raised Catholic by his mother, whom he later said was "really great." Under his mother's influence, he was an altar boy and attended grade school at Our Lady of Mount Carmel in Astoria. His mother worked as a guard at Pilgrim State Mental Hospital in New York, before moving to California late in life. His father was "a good man, who was unable to show affection," Ray would later recall. He did not develop a close relationship with his father until he was about 25. His father worked at various times as a restaurant maitre d', in the catering business and as an apartment manager. Ray had two sisters, the elder, Cynthia Laterra, lived in Seldon, New York, and the younger, Cecelia Alvarez, lived on the Westside of Los Angeles in Culver City and worked as a receptionist at a law firm. He also had a younger brother,

Gilbert, who lived east of Los Angeles in San Bernardino, California. By 1975, Ray and Gilbert had not been in close contact for more than a decade. Ray disliked his brother's tattoos and his apparent propensity for fathering children whom, Ray felt, he then abandoned.

Between October 1962 and December 1964, Ray served in the US Air Force, attaining the rank of Airman 3 while stationed in Amarillo, Texas. While in the service he earned his GED, but he also got into trouble. He took a *Playboy* magazine addressed to another individual from a mail slot and read it while on duty. He was charged with tampering with the mail and transferred to a job he disliked. He said he requested and was granted a General (Under Honorable Conditions) Discharge. Records show that he was charged with three counts of forgery in Amarillo in 1964, which may have contributed to his discharge, although it is unclear whether he served any prison time at that point.

In 1964 Ray married Jeannie Pettigrew and then flirted with architecture, studying at Westwood State University in Canyon, Texas. Neither his architecture career nor his marriage lasted. His records from Westwood State were held due to an outstanding debt and he divorced Jeannie in 1966. After the divorce, he felt "emotionally low," so he saw a psychologist. The psychologist gave him some tests and said Ray wasn't "dumb"—at least that was the part Ray remembered decades later. Ray did not return for any further visits.

Ray moved west in the early 1970s and in 1973 married Vicky Trainer in Santa Monica, which resulted in another divorce in 1975. Ray later said the marriage was one of convenience based on a friendship. Trainer wanted to regain custody of her son and thought she would have a better chance of doing so if she was married, so Ray obliged. Once she had custody of her son, she and Ray divorced. On May 5, 1976, Ray married Barbara Barnes, a registered nurse at St. John's Hospital in Santa Monica. She was 14 years his junior and his third wife.

Throughout his life, Ray's first love was music. He had started a band when he was 14 and toured the Southern states. In Los Angeles he cut a couple of albums and sold some singles, later claiming he worked with Mark Gordon, whose other acts included Tony Orlando, The Fifth Dimension, and Thelma

Houston. He touched fame and fortune, but never grasped either. He started writing songs for other singers and groups, and then went on to produce, becoming president and co-owner of a small recording company in Hollywood, Hi-Spot Productions.

On a warm afternoon in 1975, after being stranded with car trouble and forced to take a bus, Ray stopped at Destiny II to have a cold drink on his way home. The club was just a few blocks from the apartment Ray was renting in the Overland Palms complex. In the empty club, Steve Banerjee approached Ray to tell him about some of the club's many specials. Steve soon learned that Ray was in the music business and asked Ray for advice about the club's band. The band had been under contract when Steve bought the club, so he had little choice but to keep them, even though they were lousy. Ray told Steve the band had to go.

When Steve asked what he should do for music after he fired the band, Ray told him, "Hire the Beatles. They'll pack 'em in." Then Ray turned serious and suggested turning the club into a discotheque. The mid-1970s were the golden age of disco. Disco groups such as The Bee Gees, The Jackson 5, Gloria Gaynor, and the Village People dominated the pop charts. Ray advised Steve to put a few lights in the ceiling and buy a first-class sound system. He predicted that in two months the new equipment would pay for itself.

Steve wanted to take Ray's advice, but Steve's partner, Cash Charandy, opposed breaking the band's contract and worried about what the club would do for entertainment. Without a band, Destiny II was just another bar in a city with a million bars, clubs and taverns ranging from the Roxy and the Troubadour to the Whisky a Go Go and the latest on the block, the Improv, which opened in 1975. Based on Ray's advice, Steve's proposal to fire the band and buy a top-of-the-line sound and light system to play disco music floored Steve's cautious partner. They were already out of pocket the money to buy the club, had been losing money since the day they opened, and now Steve wanted to pour more money into the failing club. Charandy wanted to back out of the deal and cut their losses, but Steve, the gifted salesman, convinced his partner to take one more chance to ignite Destiny II with a disco makeover.

Ray's advice was worth its words in gold. After the make-over, Destiny II was soon doing a respectable, even brisk business. Disco was where the money was. By the end of 1975, the new dance-oriented pop music had become a recognized genre with feature articles, regular columns and record charts in the music press. Two years later, John Travolta's *Saturday Night Fever*, a movie about a troubled Brooklyn youth who spends his evenings at a disco, would become a huge commercial success and spawn the bestselling sound track of all time.

Although disco was an emerging phenomenon, Steve's promotional skills also helped Destiny II's improving fortunes. Flyers advertised a gimmick every night the club was open: no cover on Monday nights; ladies received a free drink Tuesday night until 11 p.m.; $2 cover on Wednesday and Thursday nights with all well drinks—made with the cheapest liquors, such as Scotch, bourbon and rum—$1.50 until 11 p.m.; and Friday and Saturday the cover charge was only $3 at a time when many clubs charged double that or more. Steve would try anything to get patrons in the door and their money in his till.

At the club, an NFL-sized doorman guarded the entrance, his services definitely required now that a long line of beautiful women and flashily dressed men waited impatiently to get in every night. Flashing, multi-colored lights and the pulsating rumble of Van McCoy's "The Hustle," the Bee Gees's "Jive Talkin'" and other disco hits thundered through the open glass doors behind the giant doorman in his designer suit. Beside the entrance, lights flashed out of the darkness within through a wall of floor-to-ceiling windows, providing those waiting outside with tantalizing glimpses of the hedonistic world within. Women wore Lycra stretch hot pants, mini dresses and clinging Spandex tops to accent their curves. Big waves, perms and rough cuts were "in," while mood rings adorned fingers. Guys wore satin jackets, open-necked shirts with the collars turned up and shining gold medallions on their exposed, tanned chests. The medallions were sometimes obscured by shoulder-length hair, although perms were also popular among the men. Shiny polyester Quina shirts with pointy colors were prized possessions. Platform shoes made even the shortest man stand tall in his bell-bottom pants. Women wore flowing Halston dresses. Gold lame, leopard skin and tight jumpsuits glowed in the ultraviolet lights of Steve's new top-of-the-line light system, which reflected off mirror balls hanging from the ceiling. It was all the epitome of style in fashion conscious 1975 Los Angeles.

Destiny II's success alleviated, but did not end Steve's battles with his cautious partner. When Steve suspected that a door-man was skimming from the cover charges, Steve wanted to fire him immediately. Charandy gave the doorman the benefit of the doubt. A new doorman might be even worse, Charandy warned. Whereas Charandy trusted their employees, Steve trusted no one. Steve counted the receipts every night and kept track of every penny that came in the door. Steve verbally assaulted waitresses who accidently dropped drinks and often fired them on the spot. He blew up at bartenders who gave free drinks to pretty women, even as his partner said to let it go. After all, many clubs gave free drinks to hot women who would keep packs of men around paying for liquid courage to try to pick up the pretty girls.

Furious at his partner's management style and cautious nature, Steve bought Charandy out and became sole owner of Destiny II. Given later events, selling out was probably the smartest business decision Cash Charandy ever made. Soon after, someone burgled Destiny II. Steve kept the club's operating funds in a safe in the locked liquor room behind the bar. Someone used a sledgehammer to smash a hole large enough for a man to crawl through in the wall behind the bar into the liquor room and then assaulted the back of the safe with a hammer or an ax. The safe was the fireproof type and had a relatively thin back, which collapsed under the intruder's attack. The burglar emptied the safe.

The police sent two detectives to investigate and a seething Steve accused Charandy. The burglars had known exactly where to break a hole through the wall to come out next to the safe. The detectives said they would investigate.

After they left, Steve called Ray and threatened to kill his ex-partner for committing the burglary. Suspecting that a doorman he had recently fired might have conspired with Charandy to burgle Destiny II, Steve threatened to fire the entire staff. With no evidence, Ray asked how Steve could have any idea who was behind the theft, but Steve was certain. Ray counseled forgetting about the burglary and moving on, but Steve was adamant. Ray calmed Steve down, but then Steve asked Ray to find someone to ask around to find out who was behind the crime. Ray wondered why Steve had chosen him for such a request, but Steve knew people.

Although he had enjoyed some success in the music business, Ray's record producing did not pay the bills. So, on the basis of his childhood ties from New York, he was also a member of a crew that worked for a member of the Los Angeles Mafia: Rocky Delamo.* Although Ray denied it, the FBI later believed Ray had connections via Rocky to the New York-based Bonanno or Gambino crime families. Even though it had been nicknamed the "Mickey Mouse Mafia," the LA mob was as serious and deadly as its East Coast counterpart. Ray and his crew provided muscle for Rocky, who, like Ray, was a transplanted New Yorker. They convinced debtors to meet their interest payments or weekly vig (short for *vigorish* from Yiddish or Russian slang, which originally meant the bookmaker's cut of a bet). Ray and his crew also shook down drug dealers and enforced discipline within the organization. In one case Ray later recalled, Ray and his crew put a bullet through the left hand of an accountant who worked for Delamo. The accountant had been skimming a little off the top each week. Delamo would have had him killed, but the accountant was gifted at his job. With a bullet through his left hand, the right-handed accountant could still work for Delamo and, the mob boss was certain, the number-cruncher would never again skim money from anyone. Although he worked for a Mafia member, Ray was not a made member of La Cosa Nostra. He was not even of Italian descent, let alone a son of Sicily, usually a requirement for joining the criminal organization. Ray was mostly of Puerto Rican ancestry.

Even with his background, Ray diplomatically declined Steve's request to investigate the burglary. As the weeks passed, Steve mentioned the burglary less often and with it, his demand that Ray find someone to investigate the crime. In the future, Ray would find Steve's requests far more difficult to ignore.

In interviews Ray often changed names. Most names have been changed back to the real names. Names that remain changed are indicated by an * the first time each appears in the narrative.

Chapter 2
The Birth of Chippendales

In his constant quest to make Destiny II ever more popular, Steve conceived the idea of lowering the price of well drinks to a dime—the price of a first-class stamp in 1975—and then at 11 o'clock when everyone was comfortably settled in for the evening, raising the prices back to full price. "The dime drinks will fill the place," he said, "and the normal price will fill the till."

Just as Steve predicted, the promotion was a smash. Dime well drinks emptied the bottles behind the bar, but filled the cash register, especially after 11 o'clock, when customers, well irrigated on cheap drinks, were beyond caring what they paid to keep the liquor flowing. The bartenders poured with both hands and still couldn't keep up with demand. The waitresses loved the promotion. They made more in tips than they did on their hourly wage as they hustled between the bar and their tables in endless, frenetic circuits. Assembly line drinking had arrived at Destiny II.

When customers began to grumble about the change from dime to full-price drinks at 11 o'clock, Steve, always one to give the customers what they wanted as long as it paid, sold drinks for a dime until 11 and then raised the price to a quarter, then to a dollar and so on, every half hour until closing. The gimmick worked. The customers stopped grumbling and the cash poured in.

Steve and his close friends, including Ray and his attorney Bruce Nahin, regularly met at Steve's house to plot new ways to make Destiny II even more successful. The three-story house at 151 Napoleon Street stood just above the beach in Playa del Rey. It was on a quiet street across from an easement for the airport, which was naturally landscaped with purple sage, California lilac and blazing stars. The house faced southwest, offering stunning views down the coast to Rancho Palos Verdes and across the broad, sandy beach to the boundless Pacific.

At one such meeting, Steve decided to hire a designer to redo his office at Destiny II. The designer added a fireplace with a wide, dark-wood mantle, and replaced the standard office furniture with a carved, wood table, two ornate sofas and high-backed wing chairs. The office looked more like an English club deep in the heart of London than the office of a nightclub owner on LA's Westside. Maybe it was his Indian background with the subcontinent's legacy of British Imperial rule or maybe it was the symbols and trappings of wealth and success that the redesigned office portrayed but, in either case, Steve loved his new den.

The redesign of his office started Steve thinking in terms of raising the level of class of Destiny II from a popular, yet common nightclub into a unique, first-class establishment. Steve's new designer would deliver the opulent ambience, which would attract the wealthy patrons who would contribute even more to Steve's overflowing coffers. For this, the fifth remodel of his club with as many name changes since he bought it, Steve was going first class all the way: the trendiest interior decorator, the most expensive furniture and the finest materials.

Part of the reason Steve kept remodeling the club, even thought it was already a success, was that clubs at that time in Los Angeles changed their name and décor with frightening frequency as they tried to keep old customers and attract new ones. But part of the reason was related to Steve's view of business, which was the same as that of the character Gordon Gekko in the 1987 movie, *Wall Street*. Almost a decade before

Michael Douglas's Gekko said, "It's not a question of enough, pal. It's a zero-sum game. Somebody wins, somebody loses," Steve kept a vigilant eye on the competition because he too saw the world as a zero-sum game. Steve told Ray, "I have to stay ahead of the competition or they'll eat me alive."

Steve kept the club open during the remodel to keep costs down. In March 1978, after six weeks of frantic renovations amid bewildered but curious customers, the remodeled club held its grand re-opening. On opening night, Steve's promotional skills and advertising paid off as young, well-dressed customers with thick wallets flocked to the club. A procession of BMWs, Mercedes and Porsches kept the valets, their pockets jingling with generous tips, running to keep up. Above the door was a new sign in old English script: CHIPPENDALES.

Inside, for $20 customers found themselves in a different world. The bar was a dark wood with a surface polished to a mirror sheen. Food was served—at first a full menu, but later just *hors d'oeuvres* purchased frozen wholesale and microwaved. Just as it had been in Destiny II, the parquet dance floor was in front, where disco music throbbed and multicolored lights flashed. In the back, ornate Chippendale tables held teak backgammon boards and onyx chess sets. Players lounged in the cushioned splendor of hand-carved, antique Chippendale chairs. The furniture was named for Thomas Chippendale, an 18th Century English master cabinet and furniture maker known for his mid-Georgian, elegant designs. Steve's attorney, Bruce Nahin, suggested the new name for the club and said it would be legal to use it. Chippendales was like no other club in Los Angeles and, contrary to Steve's worries about the competition eating him alive, Chippendales devoured the competition.

Soon after the Chippendales remodel, Steve, who often visited other clubs for ideas to grow his already booming business, saw a strip show for women at a biker bar in Redondo Beach. The bar was packed with women who went wild for the male strippers. Inspired, Steve decided to bring a similar, if higher class show to Chippendales.

With no cautious partner to slow him down, Steve immediately published newspaper ads for male dancers. The first ads attracted more than 200 applicants for 10 dancer and 10 waiter/

bartender positions, even though the waiters and bartenders would work solely for tips and the dancers would only be paid $30 a night. Steve's preference was for dancers who were not yet 25 and were at least 6' with a muscular body and long hair. He wanted them clean-shaven and with no body hair, especially any that would show around a g-string.

Steve selected a troupe of hunky, confident jocks, although most could barely dance. Dancers or not, in the late spring of 1978 Chippendales introduced "A Male Exotic Dance Night for Ladies Only." Conveniently forgetting where he got the idea, Steve proclaimed it the first such show in the United States. With flyers distributed all over Los Angeles to beauty salons, women's clothing stores and jewelers, Chippendales quickly went from being a style of furniture to being synonymous with hot and exciting male strippers. By the early 1980s, Chippendales was the hottest nightclub in Los Angeles and women were hot to trot to its door. Anyone who was anyone went to Chippendales: Hollywood stars, professional athletes, Playboy playmates from Hef's nearby Holmby Hills mansion, and the sons and daughters of the Beverly Hills elite. Cher, Brooke Shields and Hugh Hefner himself partied at the popular club.

Steve's instructions to his staff emphasized the importance of attracting and keeping the wealthy clientele or, as Steve called them, the "Money Crowd." His written instructions to his staff stated, "Good looking, well connected, fashionable professionals, businessmen, etc., should be given a VIP card.... People pulling [up] in fancy cars and limo's are to be treated extra special. Get them a VIP card." His focus was on pampering his wealthy customers with the finest care. He stressed "hosting a customer with charm, poise, diplomacy, humor, and above all a warm hospitality that will make him or her feel special. Special to be at Chippendales—to be back—recommending this place to others...You must make all our guests feel excited to be here, make them forget their daily grind, give them a group of people to party with."

The low, single-story building at 3739 Overland Avenue with the neon Chippendales sign was nondescript from the outside. But in the early 1980s, as the sun set, Steve would dispatch one of his Adonises out to the street to lure in business as women drove home from work along busy Overland. Inspired by the Playboy bunny's white collar and cuffs with a black bow tie, Steve's Chippendales dancers wore skin-tight black pants with their chests bared, accented by white cuffs to better display muscular arms, and a white collar with a black bow tie. The barker, as he would have been called if he had worked for a circus, wore the same outfit as the dancers as he enticed the ladies inside.

Outside the club, well before opening time, a line of women two blocks long waited to enter the only place in town where they could see male strippers in an upscale, safe environment. The class Steve demanded started at the door, where bare-chested doormen wore the trademarked Chippendales' white cuffs and black bow-tie attire. They looked like a butler should in every woman's most erotic dreams. Identically attired valets met cars in the covered driveway. They had written instructions from Steve to "positively open [the car] door for ladies." Every customer had to be greeted with a smile.

Once inside the club's glass doors, the women could do whatever they wanted, free from the fear that any man would take advantage of them. Until 10 p.m. it was women only and every woman was treated like a queen in this X-rated wonderland. No male customers were permitted inside during the show. Even the drinks were aimed at females: Cosmos; Manhattans; gin and tonics with a maraschino cherry; and strawberry daiquiris topped with a dollop of whipped cream. The drinks flowed as fast as the tanned, muscular waiters could bring them to the hot-and-bothered clientele. The club would quickly fill to capacity and beyond, with women packed onto tiered platforms at tiny tables clustered around the compact dance floor.

The tension and excitement built to a crescendo until the show began, releasing the tension and turning the club into a mad house. Muscle-bound men with glistening oiled bodies danced for the women to the chart-topping disco music of the BeeGees, K.C. and the Sunshine Band, the Village People, and Andy Gibb. Each dancer had a theme: Zorro, Superman, a James Dean-style tough guy, a room service waiter, and a fireman. Some of the dancers lip-synched to the music. Women in various stages of inebriation crowded around the dancers as the hunks approached the edge of the dance floor.

Whenever a dancer bent down to kiss a patron, called a "tip 'n kiss," she would invariably throw her arms around the dancer's neck. When the dancer tried to straighten up to move on, the woman would hang on as if she was clinging to a life preserver in a typhoon. The dancer would then lift the woman with their neck until she let go. It was like a weight machine at the gym, except this machine screamed for more and paid for the pleasure of it. The dancers made $75 to $125 a night on "tip 'n kisses" alone. Many of the dancers developed extremely muscular necks, which they nicknamed "Chippendales' necks."

Yet for all the money involved, the accent was always on class. As Steve said in an interview, the dancers' job was "to charm the ladies. Most of the ladies do not get that in everyday life. It's something they strive for, but it just isn't there and that is what we look to create" at Chippendales. Charm might have been the goal, but lust scored.

At first, Steve had thought that women would leave after the show. Although he would have made a nice profit if they had, almost none did. They stayed at Chippendales to drink and party. At 10 p.m. the doors opened to the men, who lined up for blocks all the way to Palms Boulevard to get into a club full of horny, inebriated women. After the show, most of the women were ready and willing to do anything, anywhere after ogling Adonises for hours. If you couldn't get laid at Chippendales, you had to look like Quasimodo on a bad hair day. In the post-Pill, pre-AIDS world of the late 1970s and early 1980s, there was sex in the bathroom stalls every night at Chippendales. The dancers could have any woman in the club they wanted. Doing it with a Chippendales dancer was a mark of distinction, a trophy that reversed the age-old belief that men hunted women. One emcee heard that a large woman with hair bleached blonde and big teeth offered a dancer $500 to snort a line of cocaine off his penis. He turned her down. Such a rejection was a rarity. In a television interview, one patron said she went to the club with her friend and her friend's mother. She saw the mother leaving the club after the show with one of the dancers, easily half her age. The mother later admitted giving the dancer a blow job in his car; a notch on her bedpost and grist for the female gossip circuit.

Steve paid Ray Colon $500 a week to help manage the show, so Ray was at the club almost every night. He saw people screwing everywhere, from the bathroom stalls and the tables to cars and neighbors' lawns. Once Ray even saw a couple screwing on the dance floor amidst dozens of other dancing couples. Every drug known to man was being ingested, shot or snorted. Attorney Bruce Nahin lived what he later called the "sex, cocaine and rock 'n' roll" lifestyle, coming close to becoming addicted to cocaine before a police officer friend and meeting his future wife straightened him out. Steve tried to control all of the excesses, but some of his staff were the very ones committing the most outrageous acts. The temptations were too great for anyone to abstain. Bacchanalian delights reigned.

It was a classic American success story: immigrant makes good. Sex, drugs and disco—all for profit. Chippendales raked in tens of thousands of dollars every night. Steve had a three-foot safe at his Playa del Ray beach house packed to capacity with cash. It was the go-go 1980s, when excess was in, "greed was good" according to *Wall Street*'s Gordon Gekko, and flaunting your wealth on television's *Lifestyles of the Rich and Famous* was a mark of success. Chippendales exemplified the attitude. Even so, the club garnered gallons of bad ink in the press and loads of unwanted attention from the authorities.

The publicity was particularly poisonous when on August 14, 1980, Canadian-born 1980 Playboy Playmate of the Year, Dorothy Stratten—her name changed from Dorothy Ruth Hoogstraten to appeal more to the panting male public—was found dead in her West Los Angeles home near the body of her estranged husband, Paul Snider. Both bodies were nude. Police concluded that Stratten met Snider to discuss an amicable divorce. Not wanting to lose Stratten, Snider raped and murdered Stratten, then mutilated the body, before committing suicide with a Mossberg 12-gauge shotgun. Adding to the media attention was the fact that Stratten wanted to divorce the controlling Snider in part because she was having an affair with director Peter Bogdonovich while they were shooting her first film, a romantic comedy called *They all Laughed* (released in 1981).

Most upsetting for Steve, the media reported that Snider worked for Chippendales. Snider had produced a female mud wrestling show for a few months at the club, but it had lost money and Steve cancelled the contract. After the murder/suicide, Steve was livid, desperately worried about the potential damage to the image of his upscale club. Ray told Steve to relax and let the tempest pass, especially since Chippendales was only tangentially involved. Steve still fumed and worried, but in time the media stopped linking Snider and the murder/suicide to Chippendales.

Besides Playmates and murder/suicides, Steve faced a host of other problems. The police put female undercover officers in the club. If they saw a patron even touch a dancer, they closed Chippendales for the night. Steve could do little about it, even though he hired security guards to defend the stage. It would have taken a legion of lion tamers to keep the female audience at bay when the oiled Chippendales hit the dance floor. With no stage, the dancers had to fight their way through the female horde even to just reach the dance floor and, unlike most men at strip clubs who just watched, women considered the show at Chippendales a contact sport. Touching, grabbing and fondling were de rigueur. The screaming women would even tear the clothes off the gyrating dancers in their desperate quest for a souvenir, any souvenir.

Parking was also a major problem, especially since Chippendales only had 30 spots on its property. Patrons parked on Overland and every street within easy, and often not so easy, walking distance, as well as in the driveways and parking lots of apartment complexes, at a 7-Eleven and at other nearby businesses. Customers complained to the business owners about the lack of available parking in the early evening as lines formed for the club. The business owners and neighbors then complained to the police who wrote citations without mercy. The tickets hurt Steve's business as customers began to balance the hassle of finding parking and, even if they found a spot, discovering a parking ticket on their windshield after an evening at the club, against the allure of Chippendales. More and more, the club lost out to other clubs with less ambiance and male nudity but far less of a parking ticket threat.

On top of the parking problems, the California Department of Alcohol Beverage Control cited the club for gender discrimination for not allowing men into the club until after the strip show. Steve explained his admittance policy in court; "We have to create some kind of atmosphere for a show, and the minute you let gentlemen in, that inhibits women and they can't act the way [they would] if there's women only. This is a social thing, the way they were raised. They act certain ways in front of men...They [ordinary men] spoil the reaction and the look."

Besides gender discrimination, Steve also faced racial discrimination lawsuits. Steve often stood near the front door in the shadows outside as he checked-out approaching customers. He would whisper to the doormen not to allow blacks, Hispanics, Iranians, and anyone else who was not white and looked like they belonged on the cover of *GQ* or *Vogue* into his club. In his official written instructions to door personnel, he wrote that gang members, "pimps," "real slick drug culturists," and "Gypsies" should not be admitted. He asserted in the instructions that "Gypsies" would "ruin the place in a month." He then went on to provide a checklist for how to identify "Gypsies": "All males in a group of two or more. Dark complexion with a fast New York or Phillie accent. Out-of-state license plate. Dress in a suit and tie which doesn't match when they open their mouth. Tells all kinds of lies (i.e., they are from the CBS News Dept. in New York)." He also cautioned, "Don't make a mistake by turning some nice people away by thinking they are gypsies either. In case of doubt ask nicely about Gypsies...they are proud and will let you know that they are, and at that say good-bye." Steve did not draw the line at just discriminating against minorities. He also wrote that "No one with the armed forces or [in] sailor's uniform" should be admitted because, he wrote, "We tried that in the past and it just did not work." Steve thought that everyone shared his prejudices, so he did not want anyone to know that he—an Indian—owned the club. Therefore, he made his attorney, Bruce Nahin, who owned only 10 percent of the club, his Chief Administrative Officer.

Steve believed the fallacy that minorities and the poor bring drugs, fights, crime, and prostitution. His belief was the fundamental error of equating color and lack of wealth with crime. Greed, not need, leads to crime, as Steve was later to repeatedly prove.

Apparently aware that what he was doing was illegal, Steve devised a system of membership cards so, he thought, he could legally bar whomever he wanted from his club. Gold cards entitled the holder to enter Chippendales without waiting and with as many guests as the cardholder wished. Blue cards had slightly fewer privileges. A blue cardholder might have to wait a short time to get in on crowded nights. Steve handed out the cards free to those he wanted in his club: wealthy whites, attorneys, doctors, sports figures, and business people. He even sent some cards out cold to people on "prestigious" mailing lists he purchased. But he told minorities and others he considered undesirable that the cards cost anywhere up to $1,000. In depositions, Steve denied that the issuance of the cards had any relation to race or ethnicity.

Steve's admittance policies were ironic because his long-time head of security was black and the designer who had created the look of Chippendales was not only black, but also gay. It was also ironic that Steve was an Indian, a distinct and tiny minority in the United States, yet he sought to bar other minorities from his club. As any psychologist knows, often the people most protective of the bastions of privilege are the most recent members of the club. Steve had come to America to make his fortune and part of his vision of success was fitting in; being as White, Anglo-Saxon and Protestant as possible.

Mirroring his white-and-wealthy admittance policy, you not only had to be handsome to work at Chippendales, you also had to be white, save for a few rare exceptions. Steve later explained his hiring policies in court; "We are setting a certain look and the average gentleman from the street, they do not have that kind of look and that is the reason they don't get hired here."

Even though Steve only hired the men he wanted, his relations with his employees were always tense, largely due to his personality. Steve had always been demanding, but with the success of Chippendales, his confidence soared and he demanded ever more from his employees. He gave a tongue lashing to anyone who put a toe within a foot of the line, let alone anyone who stepped over the line. Steve even fired his brother, Shubrat "Shubo" Banerjee, who had served as chairman of Chippendales for a brief tenure in 1978. The staff began to hate Steve, complaining to Ray Colon, even though they knew Steve and Ray were close friends.

One night Steve and the club's deejay started yelling and gesturing at each other in the deejay booth like two gorillas in a cage constructed to house only one primate. Steve stormed out of the booth and made straight for his advisor and confidante: Ray. Steve spewed forth a slew of curses and complained that the deejay was always hustling women and didn't concentrate on spinning records.

By now Ray had learned how to handle Steve's eruptions. The club-owner needed time to let off steam, so Ray let him rant and ordered Steve a drink. Ray suggested that Steve fire the deejay. Steve grudgingly conceded that the customers loved the skirt-chaser. Then keep him and let him chase the beauties, Ray said, as long as the customers keep coming.

Over the following months Steve hired and fired the deejay, and then rehired him again when business suffered and customers demanded their favorite record-spinner back. One week the DJ would be gone, the next week he would be back. It was an on-going battle for years. Ray never saw an employee fired so many times, except maybe the managers Steve would hire, fire, re-hire, and then fire again. Compared to Steve, George Steinbrenner was a piker. In fact, Steve offered Ray the manager job once, but Ray said, "Thanks, but no thanks. I don't want to lose our friendship." Friendship had its limits and no friendship could survive Steve as a boss.

Chapter 3
Crime with Amateurs

Even as he fought the authorities over parking and gender discrimination, Steve found time for romance. He met Irene Katherine Tychowsky at Chippendales in early 1978. A pretty girl in her early twenties, she had brown hair and an impressive body every straight male noticed. She worked as a registered nurse during the day and a Chippendales cashier at night. Steve asked her out and they were soon a couple. In 1980 they moved in together. Love seemed to be in the air, but Steve's romance did not distract him from business for long, if at all.

The club evolved, with wooden benches installed along the walls and near the dance floor to allow even more customers to ogle the strip show. Video monitors were hung from the ceiling to show music and R-rated videos of buffed men before the show. Home VCRs were just becoming common in the late 1970s, so R-rated videos were still a novelty for many of the club's female customers. The Chippendales product line expanded to include T-shirts, thongs, playing and greeting cards, sweatshirts, black bow ties, hats, calendars, and videos. The money kept Steve's safe full, but he always wanted more.

On December 3, 1978, Steve called and asked Ray Colon to meet him at Chippendales. Ray often picked up women at the club and had come close to divorce over the nights he had spent at the female-filled Chippendales. After Barbara served him with divorce papers one night at the club, Ray had stayed away from the club for months. Ray did not want to lose his wife, so he was reluctant to meet Steve at Chippendales. Steve said he had something important to talk about and insisted they meet. Finally, Ray gave in and said he could stop by for a few minutes. Even though for years Steve had asked Ray for advice, reminiscent of a Mafia Don's *Consigliore*, in an odd twist on the relationship, Steve always seemed able to convince Ray to do what he wanted, even if it meant risking Ray's marriage. To Ray, loyalty was everything; he met Steve.

From behind his antique desk at Chippendales, Steve made small talk. Since Barbara would be home from work soon, Ray pushed Steve to say what he wanted. Steve hesitated, but finally said he had a big problem and that Ray was his only hope, since he was his best friend. Steve said he would not even discuss what he was about to talk about with anyone, not even his brother. Ray still had no idea where Steve was heading. After more talk about their friendship, Steve explained that two clubs had just opened: Osco's on La Cienega and Moody's in Santa Monica. Steve said they were major problems. Ray had heard of them, but did not see a problem. Steve complained that the police and fire department were already hurting his business by ticketing every illegally parked car near the club and repeatedly closing Chippendales for overcrowding. Ray found it hard to feel sorry for the increasingly wealthy club owner with the Playa del Rey beach house and a Mercedes in the garage.

Steve complained that some of his best customers were now going to Osco's and Moody's. He was losing valuable customers and loads of money. After doing so well, Chippendales was suffering. Steve said something had to be done. Ray listened to Steve complain and then, glancing at his watch and believing it was a straightforward business problem with a solution to be found in marketing or advertising, idly asked if there was anything he could do.

Steve met Ray's eyes. He hesitated. Then Steve said he wanted the rival clubs burned down.

Ray later said he was shocked, although given his background with Rocky, Ray's shock may have been far more due to hearing such a suggestion from an apparently respectable businessman, than due to the suggestion itself. In any case, Steve misunderstood Ray's hesitation. Steve explained that he did not expect Ray to burn down the clubs himself. Steve just wanted Ray to find someone who could do it. Baffled by why Steve would risk committing a serious crime just to maintain his cash flow, which was not exactly hurting even with the increased competition, Ray later said he tried to dissuade Steve. Arguing that he had worked hard to build Chippendales into a success, Steve said he wouldn't stand idly by as other clubs stole his hard-won customers.

Steve took an envelope out of a drawer and tossed it on the desk between them.

"There's $7,000," Steve said. He told Ray to find someone to commit the arsons, pay them however much he wanted, and Ray could keep whatever was left over.

Ray stared at the envelope. He had seen more money than that in a plain manila envelope before, but never just sitting there waiting to be taken for nothing. He certainly needed the money. The Feds had recently arrested Rocky and much of the LA Mafia, leaving Ray out of one of his jobs—the most profitable one. Worse, his partner in Hi-Spot Productions had clipped $70,000 from the company to spend on a bimbo he was trying to bed. Hi-Spot was bankrupt. On top of those disasters, Ray had left Chippendales so he could keep Barbara, which meant losing the $500 a week Steve had been paying him to help manage the show. To try to make ends meet, Ray now managed the Overland Palms Apartments, where he had been renting. Just a few blocks up Overland from Chippendales, the complex consisted of four, two-story buildings on either side of a narrow driveway. The sun-faded apartments had no landscaping and needed paint. Ray also worked at Citizen's Personal Safety Service in West Los Angeles as a DUI and traffic school instructor. Neither position paid much, so he and Barbara mainly lived on her nursing income. Ray stared at the $7,000 just waiting to be picked up.

Ray asked Steve what would happen if he couldn't find anyone to do it. Steve replied that he would forget it, since he didn't
trust anyone else enough to ask.

Ray still did not reach for the envelope. He had never committed arson before. He had hurt people for Rocky, but in his
mind that had been different. They had all, for various reasons,
deserved what they got. The accountant whom Ray had shot in
the hand had been skimming money from Rocky's books. Debtors Ray and his crew had roughed up had refused to pay their
weekly *vig*. In some twisted way, Ray believed that what Steve
was asking him to do wasn't honorable or fair. The other clubs
were legitimate businesses competing fairly with Chippendales
and, from what Ray had seen at the consistently packed Chippendales, the other clubs had been losing badly. Why punish
the owners of the other clubs for striving to achieve the American dream, just as Steve had been doing when he bought Destiny II and transformed it into Chippendales?

Steve picked up the envelope and held it out to Ray. The
whole thing made no sense to Ray, but cash had a sense all its
own. Ray decided he was about to make an easy $7,000. He
could take the money and, as he later said, "Not do shit." It
wasn't like Steve was Rocky. Given how much Chippendales
was bringing in every week, the club owner probably wouldn't
even remember a paltry $7,000. Arson was just a crazy thought
Steve had hatched. In a week he would be begging Ray to forget the whole thing. It would be the easiest $7,000 Ray had ever
made.

Ray reached over and took the envelope.

Ray later said he did nothing about the arson plan. The days
turned into weeks and the weeks into months. Steve was busy
running his club and probably thought that finding an arsonist
took time. Steve did not mention their conversation about the
rival clubs again and Ray assumed the silence would last, but
he knew deep down that it would not. Steve had not created
and run a thriving business by forgetting things; big or small,
legal or illegal.

Finally after several months, one afternoon in early 1979 a
seething Steve called Ray and demanded to know what he was
trying to pull. Ray claimed he was working on it. Steve didn't

believe him. Steve said he had asked Ray for help because he trusted his old friend and thought that Ray could get the job done. If he couldn't, Steve said, Ray should give him his money back. Reluctantly, Ray admitted that he didn't have the money to give back. He had spent it. Ray remembered Steve saying that he better do the job or their friendship would be "null and void. After that, who knows what might happen."

Ray exploded. He was not used to being threatened. He demanded to know who the hell Steve thought he was talking to. Steve suddenly became calm and reasonable. Steve explained that all would be well between them if Ray just did the job. He said that if Ray had needed $7,000 he should have just asked for it. But, Steve stressed, they had made a deal and he asked, "You keep your word, don't you Ray?"

If Ray said no, he had to come up with $7,000 at a time when the average US household's annual income was $17,000. Given his financial situation, the $7,000 may as well have been $7 million.

Ray told Steve he would complete the arson contract. Not knowing any arsonists, Ray consulted one of his closest crew mates. Keeping the different parts of his life separate, Ray never socialized with wiseguys, especially anyone outside his crew, except for one old friend: Leon Defina.* Defina was Ray's only real friend in his crew. Tall, muscular and a flashy dresser, Defina just missed being handsome. He chased women at every opportunity and often caught them, at least for a brief time before the next woman caught his roving eyes. A small-time thug, he had happened onto a good thing: his partnership with Ray. Colon kept Defina out of trouble, providing a cautionary brake that the impulsive Defina completely lacked. Defina provided the muscle and violence that Ray avoided. Although Ray later claimed that he had shot the accountant's hand and roughed up Rocky's debtors, it seems far more likely that Defina actually pulled the trigger and threw the punches, albeit on Ray's instructions. Ray always seemed to be the button man, arranging the violence, but not actually committing it.

Once Ray had laid out his arson situation to his friend, Defina concluded that it was obvious that the party involved—whom Ray left unnamed—was not going to forget about the money. Defina asked how much juice the guy had. It was a much more serious situation if the party in question had connections to the Mafia or to anyone else willing to commit a felony for a few greenbacks. Ray didn't know whether Steve knew anyone else with Mafia connections, but he did know that Steve had money and with money he could probably find someone to deal with Ray for welching on the arson contract.

With deadly seriousness, Defina asked his friend, "You want I should take him out?"

They had been members of the same crew for years and were closer than brothers; most brothers didn't have information to put the other in jail for longer than most people lived. Unlike Ray, who hesitated to arrange arson for Steve, Defina would kill for Ray.

Ray declined.

Fearing Steve would hire someone else to come after him if he didn't arrange the arson, Ray decided he had to complete the job. However, Ray didn't want to get his crew or, worse, the Mafia involved. They would arrange the arsons, then blackmail Steve until they owned the club and Steve had a dime left in his pocket. Then they would take the dime. Ray asked Defina if he knew a couple of street people "with big balls and tiny brains" who were not connected in any way.

Defina suggested Jerry Molina,* who hung out at a 7-Eleven at Palms and Overland. Jerry was young and had balls, but a tiny brain, Defina explained. He gave Ray a description of Jerry and his running mate, Paul.*

Defina flicked ashes off his cigarette and Ray later recalled him saying, "I don't have to tell you, a lot can go wrong when you work with amateurs."

Ray decided to check out the target before looking up his would-be arsonists. Outside a nightclub/restaurant in Santa Monica, a neon sign proclaimed Moody's in bright blue light. Ray walked through the crowded restaurant looking for the club. Where was it? Finally he spotted a narrow stairway. Ray descended to the club in the basement. The dance floor was packed with young customers spinning and twisting to disco music under flashing, multi-colored lights. Compared to Chippendales, Moody's was smaller, less classy and had to be far less profitable. Ray couldn't see why Steve saw any threat at all from Moody's. It was like McDonald's worrying about a hole-in-the-wall greasy spoon housed in a plywood shack in the parking lot across the street; ludicrous.

Even so, Ray surveyed the club with the eye of an arsonist, which he was not, although he had plenty of experience scouting venues for other types of illegal jobs. Moody's did not look promising for a clean arson. With no windows or exits from the club other than the narrow stairway up to the restaurant, any fire when the club was full of customers would transform the basement into a crematorium. Ray later said that arranging arson was bad enough, but arranging mass murder was out of the question. The job would have to be done after business hours, so the club would be empty.

Ray left Moody's and slid into his Oldsmobile Toronado. He drove east along four-lane Santa Monica Boulevard, dropped down to Pico and then turned right down Overland. He passed over the Santa Monica Freeway and then up and over a hill toward Chippendales. It was ironic that the arsonists Steve had been looking for hung out almost on his doorstep: the 7-Eleven Defina had mentioned was on the corner of Palms and Overland, just two blocks north of Chippendales.

In a neighborhood of two-story apartment buildings, 1930s-style bungalows and small businesses, the 7-Eleven was a well-lit haven for teenagers looking for trouble. As Ray pulled up, two teenage boys leaned in the windows on either side of a compact car. Two young women in the car, their hands full of sodas and chips, were trying to brush off the young Romeos.

Ray guided his coupe into the lot, parked and got out. The girls started their car and pulled out. Ray sized up the two would-be Lotharios and gestured at them to come over. The youths swaggered over, trying to look cool. Ray asked their names. Jerry was more than 200 pounds, with short hair and a premature potbelly. He looked 18 going on 40. He wore a T-shirt and jeans, sporting tattoos on his flabby arms. Paul was 150 pounds, if he had change in his pockets, and had light-brown, shoulder-length hair and dark eyes. He looked like he would snap in a stiff breeze.

Ray brushed past their youthful bravado to state that he had a job for them, if they could handle it. The pair said they could handle anything, if the price was right. Ray had found Steve his arsonists.

A few days later Ray was parked on a side street just off Santa Monica Boulevard overlooking Moody's. Jerry's bulk filled the seat beside him and Paul bounced around in the back seat like a cricket on speed. It was 3 a.m., March 6, 1979.

Ray had noted that Moody's had no burglar alarm, just bars over the windows for security. Jerry had a short crowbar that Ray had asked him to bring hidden under his shirt. Paul, eager and excited, said that he had brought some extra tools, just in case. He showed Ray a wrench, pliers and a screwdriver. With Defina's admonition about working with amateurs echoing in his mind, Ray warned Paul not to leave any of the tools behind.

Ray stayed in the car as lookout. If he saw anything that might be a threat, he would blink the car's lights. If there was serious trouble, such as the cops, he would give one long honk on the car's horn to distract them, hopefully giving Jerry and Paul a chance to get away.

Jerry took a full red gas can from the floor, its irritating fumes permeating the car, and got out, followed by Paul, carrying his precious tools. The pair crossed the street and ran across the parking lot toward the darkened restaurant/club. They reached the back door and, checking that no one was in sight, tried to pry open the metal door with the crowbar. They failed. Paul suggested trying to break the doorknob off and forcing their way in that way. Jerry nodded and Paul pounded on the door-knob with his wrench.

Hearing the clanging all the way across the parking lot and street as if a foundry was in full operation, a startled Ray wondered what the hell his amateurs were doing. He looked up and down the street for signs of trouble. Nothing moved. No one was in sight.

The clanging stopped.

Frightened by the racket, Jerry had grabbed the wrench from Paul. Jerry tried to twist the doorknob off. This tactic also failed. It was hard enough getting a grip on the knob with the pliers, let alone snapping the knob off. Jerry gave up and looked around, desperate. His eyes lit up when he spotted a hose. He told Paul to use the crowbar to make an opening in the metal grill in the bottom of the door.

As Paul attacked the grill—more noise—Jerry picked up the hose and looked around. He spotted what he was looking for; the gas meter. Using Paul's wrench, he opened the side valve on the meter. The hiss of gas told him the valve was working. Jerry stuck one end of the hose onto the valve. He fed the other end through the hole Paul had pried in the door's grill. Jerry ran over to a dumpster and collected a wad of yellowed newspapers. He crumpled them up loosely against the door, poured gas on the papers, and pulled out his lighter. Then he told Paul, "Run!"

Paul sprinted back toward the car as Jerry lit the newspapers. The newspapers smoked, then caught fire. Jerry took off running. Ray watched as the pair ran toward him, backlit by the flickering flames. Ray started the car. The second the arsonists scrambled in, he slammed the gas pedal down to make their get away.

Thirty minutes later over an early restaurant breakfast, Ray castigated his accomplices. Jerry started to defend himself, but Ray cut him off, telling him in a harsh whisper that he had hired them to burn the building down, not blow up half the city. Since they hadn't heard an explosion yet, Ray prayed that someone had extinguished the fire before the gas ignited.

The trio fell silent. Jerry took a mouthful of fried egg, while Paul nibbled on a piece of bacon. Ray sipped his coffee, wishing the whole awful night would just go away. Defina had been right; when you work with amateurs anything could happen.

Sullen, Paul asked if they would still get paid for their night's antics. Ray said, "No way." The young thugs looked crestfallen. Ray relented and paid them each $100, but said, "Do yourself and every other schmuck who lives in the city a favor and leave burning down buildings to the professionals."

Ray should have heeded his own advice.

Later that morning, Steve called Ray, waking the arson arranger after his late night's work. Steve wanted to know what had happened. He had just heard on the radio about a fire at Moody's— it had caused no serious damage.

Ray heard traffic noises and asked Steve if he was calling from his car phone. Steve demanded to know what difference it made where he was calling from. Ray said anyone could be listening in, but Steve didn't care. His anger had overtaken his reason, as well as any sense of caution. Steve yelled at Ray that their friendship was over, but then demanded that Ray meet him at his office. Ray said he couldn't. Steve threatened to come over to Ray's apartment.

Tired and fed up, Ray mocked the pudgy club owner, "You gonna beat me up?"

Backing down, but still adamant, Steve said he had to talk to Ray and finally, as usual, Ray agreed to meet him.

Soon after, Ray sat across from Steve in his office at Chippendales. Ray was exhausted. His shoulders slumped and his head throbbed from a headache, which six aspirin had failed to alleviate. His day had started poorly at Moody's, worsened with Steve's call and could only get worse meeting the hot-tempered club owner. Steve slammed his fist down on his antique desk and screamed that it had been five months since Ray took his $7,000 and nothing had been accomplished. Moody's was still in business. Steve said he was certain Ray knew people and, if he really wanted to, he could arrange to burn down Moody's. Ray countered that he had done his best. Their argument built to a shouted crescendo, but ended abruptly when Steve unexpectedly told Ray to forget about Moody's—for now.

In the shocked silence as Ray processed this change in plans, Steve said he would give Ray another chance to prove his loyalty and friendship.

"How?" Ray asked, warily. What new crime would $7,000 buy?

Steve wanted Ray to check out two clubs: Osco's on La Cienega and Bentley's in Santa Monica. They were the newest hot spots and Steve wanted them burned down. Steve sounded as matter-a-fact about his fiery plans as if he was requesting white wine instead of red with dinner. Leery, but still owing Steve $7,000, Ray reluctantly agreed to look into the possibility of burning down the rival clubs.

Reluctant to now commit two arsons, Ray spent several months stalling and with time Steve appeared to forget about his arson plans. Ray's life, however, was about to change. In an ironic twist, having lost his underworld job working for the imprisoned Rocky in 1981, Ray earned a certificate in Police Officer Standard Training (POST) with what he later claimed was a grade of A at El Camino College in El Camino, California. No transcript is available to verify his claim. With his certificate, he became a reserve police officer in Palm Springs.

The change in profession irked Steve, who thought that Ray believed he had become too good to associate with Steve. Ray rarely visited Chippendales anymore, but he arrived at the club one evening with some police colleagues who had learned that Ray knew Steve. The officers wanted to come to the club after the male exotic dance show when the women were riled up and men were allowed inside. Ray had stalled, but had finally relented. Steve arrived at their table and welcomed the officers. Steve told them that he used to see Ray more often, but now that Ray was a cop Ray thought he was too good to associate with a lowly club owner. Steve then poured a drink over Ray's head. Steve was laughing as if it was a joke. Ray laughed it off, but he was seething. Their friendship was strained to near the breaking point.

Soon after the drink incident, Irene, Steve's girlfriend, who liked Ray, invited Ray over to their house in Playa del Ray. Ray did not want to go, but Irene insisted. Even Steve's girlfriend could get Ray to do things he later claimed he did not want to do; a born disciple.

After Irene let him in and hugged him, Ray found Steve on a sofa watching television in the living room. As Ray entered the room, Steve stood, hesitated and then offered his hand to Ray before they halfheartedly embraced. Steve offered Ray a drink and laughed when Ray asked for a soda. Steve thought the change from alcohol to soda was because he was a police officer, but Ray said many of his colleagues drank like they owned stock in every liquor company in the country.

Irene had to go to the airport to pick up her sister, who was returning from a trip to visit their parents in Buffalo, New York. Ray rose to leave, but Irene insisted he stay, since Steve was not going. As they heard Irene leave, Steve and Ray watched each other warily like two circling boxers. Finally, Steve broke the tension by asking how Ray liked being a cop. Steve then said that Ray would probably be the first person to arrest someone if they did something wrong.

"Even you," Ray said slowly and evenly, his eyes focused on his old friend.

Steve asked if Ray carried a gun. Ray was evasive, but Steve pressed and Ray admitted that he did. Steve asked to see it. Ray declined, but Steve kept asking and finally Ray reached into the small of his back to remove a 9 mm semi-automatic in a holster tucked in his pant's waistband. Ray pulled the chamber back, popped out a round and removed the clip before he handed the weapon to Steve. The Chippendales owner savored holding the gun, studying every detail and inspecting it from every angle. Then he aimed it at Ray's head.

Steve said he bet that Ray must feel powerful pointing a gun at someone's head. When Ray asked Steve what he was feeling, Steve lowered the weapon and said he was just a businessman. He was not into violence.

Chapter 4
The Coming of De Noia

Even though Chippendales was a local hit and was making a fortune, Steve wanted more. Like all successful businessmen, it was not so much the money that was important to Steve, as it was that indefinable goal called success. Dollars were just a means of keeping score. Steve admired Walt Disney and dreamed of success at a Disney level. For starters, Steve wanted to own the biggest and the best nightclub in Los Angeles. If he could, he probably would have burned down every single competing club. Barring destroying the competition, which had not worked out well so far, one way to dominate the market was to raise the level of professionalism of the Chippendales show. But who could do it?

In late 1981 Steve hired Nicolas "Nick" De Noia, an Emmy award-winning, Broadway choreographer and television producer. A tough, outspoken perfectionist, the energetic De Noia was born in New Jersey in 1941. He wore large glasses, which were fashionable in the 1980s, and had bushy, dark eyebrows and graying, black hair. His straight, white teeth often showed through a big smile.

In his twenties, De Noia had taught at the Charles E. Hughes High School for the Humanities, which was then in a tough area of Manhattan. He produced student plays that earned glowing reviews in *The New York Times*, a paper which rarely, if ever, reviewed high school productions at all. De Noia demanded perfection from his student charges and they delivered. He was tough, but his students loved him, many maintaining a correspondence with him for years after they graduated.

After teaching, De Noia moved into acting. Bearing a passing resemblance to the actor/comedian Steve Martin, De Noia struggled through some bit acting parts, sometimes under the stage name Nick Dennis. His acting career culminated in a lead role in the 1971 movie, *Some of My Best Friends Are...*, about a group of gay friends who meet in a New York bar to discuss the pros and cons of gay life.

De Noia then produced plays, including *Echoes of the Left Bank*, a musical for the famous Ford's Theatre in Washington, DC, in 1971-72. In the mid-1970s, he started Unicorn Tales, a company that produced family-oriented musical and fantasy television shows for children. Some of the shows De Noia produced and directed included *The Magic Hat* (1977), *The Maltese Unicorn* (1978), *Big Apple Birthday* (1978), and *Alex and the Wonderful Doo-Wah Lamp* (1978). He also produced and directed an exercise video, *Muscle Motion* (1983). Besides producing and directing, De Noia wrote an ugly-duckling-into-a-swan children's movie, *The Magic Pony Ride* (1977) and an Italian-immigrant-meets-Pinocchio movie, *The Stowaway* (1977). His television productions won five Emmys for children's programming. He also produced shows for a troupe called Broadway Tonight, which performed on stages across the country and on cruise ships around the world.

Based on his Emmy success, De Noia wanted to try the big time: Hollywood. He moved to Los Angeles and landed a position at Hanna-Barbera Productions, of *The Flintstones, Johnny Quest* and Scooby-Doo fame. Fairly quickly, the driven and demanding De Noia realized he did not like working for someone else, so he went out on his own again.

He was soon approached about a job at Chippendales. His first visit to the club far from impressed him. Paul Snider was producing a female mud wrestling show at the time and after catching a glimpse of it, De Noia walked out, saying, "You've got to be kidding me." This was light years away from his dreams of Hollywood, let alone from his experiences on Broadway.

One of Steve's representatives approached De Noia again and offered him $1,000 a week. De Noia was told Steve just wanted the show polished, so the job would only last a few weeks. De Noia said the mud wrestling had to go. Steve agreed. De Noia demanded complete control over the show. Steve agreed.

Steve chose his producer well. De Noia quickly took control of the Chippendales dancers. Steve's attorney, Nahin, later said Steve was trying to put on a show for girls but, being just a young, heterosexual male, he really didn't have a clue. De Noia, Nahin said, "made the show" by making it a show for women. "For whatever reason, he [De Noia] had his fingers on the pulse of women."

De Noia told the dancers, "I'm your audience. Make me want you." With his dance background, some of the male dancers probably thought that he did. Although Steve told Ray that De Noia was gay, the choreographer had been married to Jennifer O'Neill, the hauntingly beautiful star of *Summer of '42* and spokesperson for an unprecedented 30 years for Cover Girl Cosmetics. They had met when both were represented by the William Morris Agency, a major Los Angeles talent agency. Although the marriage was short, it was sweet, and after their divorce the two remained close. Whatever the truth about his sexual preferences, at events De Noia always had a big-breasted, gorgeous woman on his arm.

De Noia immediately set out to raise the show's level of class. He told his dancers, "I want this to be like the [Paris] *Folies Bergere*, a classy, upscale show. I don't want it to be nasty and rude and crude. I want it to be fun and playful." He insisted that the customers never be called women, always ladies. He ordered the dancers that when they selected a woman from the audience to bring onto the stage as part of the show, to never choose the best looking woman in the audience. They must choose a big, homely, beautiful woman, because that was the sort of customer who needed to be adored the most—and would remember the experience the longest.

During rehearsals with his dancers, the muscular De Noia would scream at his charges as if they were children. He derided them as a bunch of hard bodies moving like a pack of dumbass jocks screwing around in a locker room. Auditions, which previously had only asked would-be Chippendales dancers to strip down to their briefs, now required applicants to do some actual dancing. De Noia emphasized that—besides being handsome—the dancers were performers, whose every move should be graceful and sensuous.

De Noia blended rock, pop and heavy metal music into the production, as well as modern dance elements, including martial arts moves, jazz, gymnastics, ballet, and then-popular break dancing. Choreographers Steve Merrit and Mark Donnelly also joined Chippendales to help De Noia further improve the show. The newly polished show transformed the club from a local hit into a national phenomenon—all because of Nick De Noia.

The shows now started with an emcee, who roared, "Ladies, fasten your seat belts. It's going to be a bumpy night tonight." The music exploded as the emcee continued, "Get out of your chairs, get up on your feet, put your hands together, you're gonna feel the beat. We're feeling alright. We're gonna rock the walls tonight."

The opening act was usually five dancers in jeans and cut-off jerseys showing their six-packs, who stripped down during their act to their g strings as pounding music pulsated throughout the club. A series of set pieces followed, starting with Fantasy Night. "Welcome to Hotel Chippendales, where they satisfy all your needs." Six dancers strode out in bellboy uniforms and proceeded to dance and act like servants in every woman's most erotic dream. A breakfast-in-bed scene often followed, with a dancer simulating climax, lighting a cigarette and blowing a smoke ring. There was a Tarzan scene with a plastic banana used by a dancer as if he was masturbating, with lotion spurting out of the prop, and an *Apocalypse Now* scene with dancers in army fatigues and explosions in the background.

The most famous scene in the show was the shower scene. Five Chippendales dancers, each in a stall, lathered up in their thongs, then showered off, using strategically positioned towels to cover themselves. Even under De Noia's iron control, there were glitches. One night a crew member quit at the last minute and there was no water for the dancers to shower off with—and no towels. The dancers were left to exit the stage as best they could: naked and slathered in soap.

After each scene, the dancers moved around the edge of the dance floor offering kisses for tips. Some dancers overstayed their welcome and, if the show lagged at all because of a pro-longed series of tip-and-kisses, De Noia would pull the dancer aside and "tear him several new ass holes," in the words of a former emcee. The dancers put up with it because De Noia made them stars. Steve put up with it because De Noia made him a fortune.

With greater success, came greater problems. After several long and costly legal battles over many years, in February 1985 Steve agreed to an affirmative action program to avoid a class action lawsuit. To redress the imbalance of his almost com-pletely carnation-white staff, he agreed that 25 percent of all new Chippendales' employees would be African-American. At the time, the club employed 130, only six of whom were black. Steve also agreed that African-Americans would not be denied entrance to the club. Furthermore, he agreed to do at least $500,000 worth of business with African-American mer-chants, and to pay a total of $85,000 to African-Americans, not to exceed $250 to any one individual, who could prove they had been denied entrance to Chippendales because of their skin color. All the fines were just the price of doing business—busi-ness Steve's way.

Steve also had a long-running war with the fire department. One Friday night in February 1983, as a light rain fell outside, an LA City Fire Department Inspector, Ernest Castillo, declared that the crowd of rowdy women at the strip show was too large. Chippendales was authorized to hold 214 customers. When the fearless Castillo closed the club at 9:30 p.m., an estimated 550 disappointed and angry women were forced to file out of the club, leaving behind the objects of their desires—the dancers, as well as their paid-for drinks. With his eye closely on the bottom line, Steve made matters worse when he refused to refund their tickets and instead offered free passes to another show. The wet and frustrated, but well-dressed women hissed and booed, shouting that they wanted their cover charge and the money for their drinks and tips for stage-side seats refunded, but to no avail. Steve never gave money back to anyone.

Probably the most irritated group were 37 legal secretaries who had paid to charter a bus for the trip from Bakersfield. They were offered calendars and free passes to another show, but they had not come 110 miles for hunks in a calendar; they wanted hunks in the flesh.

As fire trucks, police cruisers, customers' cars, and onlookers clogged Overland Avenue, Steve's valets attempted to clear the parking lot, but delays mounted and many of the women waited more than an hour in the cold February rain for their vehicles. At one point, a scuffle broke out between a valet and an irate customer, prompting the police to step in to restore order. The police officers found themselves in a new role as valets to speed up the process of dispersing the dispirited crowd.

Inspector Castillo cited Steve for violating the fire code. Steve would have to appear at yet another hearing, but Chippendales was free to open the following night.

Another evening, as a fireman in helmet, jacket and knee boots strode on stage, the boisterous female crowd chanted, "Take it off! Take if off!" But this time, the fireman was not an exotic dancer. He was a real fireman and the club was closed, yet again, for overcrowding.

Late in 1983, a judge, frustrated by Chippendales near constant violation of the fire code, handed down an injunction that would fine Chippendales $2,500 and put Steve in jail for up to five days for any new infractions. Over the next five years, the club was closed 13 times for overcrowding. Chippendales was on and off probation continually, and through it all the fines increased, reaching $14,000 at one point. Steve was far from deterred. He boasted, "Every time I get cited, I come up with a new product" to cover the fine, from mugs and calendars to lingerie and videos. By the 1980s, Steve was selling more than a million calendars a year and his business brought in $8 million a year, which put such fines in a completely different perspective.

Steve railed against all the attention Chippendales received from the police and fire departments. The Los Angeles Fire Department said Chippendales was inspected more than other clubs because of its record of violating capacity regulations. A fire inspector said they inspected Chippendales almost every weekend because they could be sure that most of the time they would find a violation. Chief Tom McMaster of the Engineering and Research Section of the LA Fire Prevention Bureau said, "When people allow a restaurant [or club] to get that crowded, they're a danger to the public, like a driver going 100 mph on the freeway. Some of the most disastrous restaurant fires in United States' history have been caused by overcrowding." The LA City Attorney, James K. Hahn, said that Chippendales had "repeatedly shown a callous disregard for the safety of patrons."

Steve vehemently disagreed. At first, Steve said, the authorities had claimed that the male revue was lewd, crude and unethical. Women disagreed and packed the club. "From day one," Steve told a reporter, the authorities "felt that if Chippendales became very profitable and successful, places like this were going to be in every city and [on] every block…. and when they realized that we weren't going to close down, it became a vendetta for them more than anything else." Steve moaned to a reporter, "Every time I turn around, I get sued." His partner and attorney, Nahin, agreed, later saying, "The establishment didn't particularly enjoy what we were doing."

Steve believed the city was harassing him by sending inspectors from "the Fire Department one day, the building inspectors after that and then back to the Fire Department." Steve said, the "first year of our operation we were raided by [the] LAPD with their helicopters, [and] 40 officers at least ten times. In '83, after losing several legal battles they deployed the fire dept. We are being harassed every week….Hard Rock Cafe and Spagos are always as crowded as we are."

Steve considered a civil lawsuit against city and state agencies. He said, "The issue is not overcrowding…they're [city officials] saying what people should and should not watch." In his personal notebook, he wrote, "The issue here is a moral one. Ever since the club opened its doors...various branches of city government have relentlessly attempted to close the club. They think a male revue for women is immoral. This male dominated city cannot accept a nightclub primarily for women. If you take into consideration how many eateries and nightclubs are out there and how many fire code violations have been filed in the last five years, you will see a clear-cut case of harassment against us. All we want the city to know is, as long as we have an audience, the show will go on.....The issue is not that of over-crowding, it's censorship."

Whatever the reason for all the attention from the police and fire departments, Chippendales under De Noia's artistic direction was becoming increasingly famous. The Chippendales story, albeit in thinly veiled form, even made it into the movies. In 1982, many scenes for the movie *Ladies Night* were filmed at Chippendales. The film told the story of the owner of a male strip club, played by Dan Haggerty, who is portrayed either as a ruthless gangster or a tough businessman with the proverbial heart of gold. Steve helped bankroll the film and was made an executive producer. Although the story was fiction and the name Chippendales was never supposed to appear in the film, Steve spread money around to the crew in an attempt to get the Chippendales sign in the movie. It was one of the few times he failed to get his way.

Chapter 5
The Banerjee-De Noia Wars

For all their success, the greed-driven Steve and the perfectionist De Noia soon clashed over control and money, especially since De Noia quickly came to consider the show his own private fiefdom. Not the least bit intimidated by Steve's ranting, De Noia argued that it was his show based on their contract and the fact that he had created the new, vastly improved look of the revue. The war between the two men surfaced in clashes big and small.

When a dancer called to say that he was not going to be able to make a rehearsal, De Noia yelled at him for missing the practice. The dancer pleaded that his car's carburetor had died. De Noia was not interested in excuses. He told the dancer that he should have taken a cab. Then the dancer made the grave error of saying that Steve had told him he could miss the rehearsal. De Noia exploded that he didn't give a damn what Steve said. De Noia was running the show and to prove it he would fire the dancer if he wasn't at rehearsal within 15 minutes.

Although control of the revue was often the spark that ignited arguments between Steve and De Noia, money was at the core of their disagreements. Since De Noia had taken over, Steve had made a fortune. De Noia knew it and he wanted more of the profits or he would walk. It was as simple as that. There were a hundred other clubs that would have drained their bank accounts to have the man behind Chippendales' success create a rival male revue. De Noia knew it and Steve knew it.

De Noia sought a way to defuse the escalating war with Steve. He found a club in Manhattan called Magique, whose owners, two brothers, were interested in hosting the Chippendales sensation. In October 1983, De Noia approached Steve with the idea of opening a second Chippendales at Magique. Not wanting De Noia to work for a rival club, Steve agreed.

Within a month of opening Magique was making a fortune. De Noia called it "The most important entertainment for women in the world." On First Avenue at 60th Street and with room for 1,000 women, Magique was far larger than the LA club. When it opened the police had to be hired to keep order at the phenomenally popular club for the first two weeks. De Noia and Chippendales dancers appeared on *Phil Donahue, Sally Jessie Rafael* and other big-name daytime talk shows, turning Chippendales into a national phenomenon.

Even though continental separation should have cooled the abrasive relationship between Steve and De Noia, a mere 2,400 miles of separation had little effect. Steve visited New York to oversee Magique and whenever he came another battle erupted in the rapidly escalating Banerjee-De Noia War.

Steve's attorney, Nahin, as 10 percent owner and Chippendales' Chief Administrative Officer, often acted as go-between, especially in the all-too-common periods when Steve and De Noia refused to talk to each other. Steve would call Nahin to yell at De Noia, ordering Nahin to pass along the rant to the choreographer. De Noia would then call Nahin to scream about Steve, asking Nahin to pass along the message to Steve. Nahin often acted as the swing vote on everything from hiring and firing to show schedules and financial matters. It was a perilous position to be in, something akin to being Poland in 1938 stuck between Nazi Germany and Stalinist Russia. Such a position requiring the utmost tact and diplomacy was at least to some extent related to Nahin's original plans for his life. Born in Los Angeles in 1953, Nahin had planned to become a diplomat, studying political science as an undergraduate at the University of California, Los Angeles. Then, after the 1973 Yom Kippur War, Nahin heard that the Soviet bloc and their allies refused to allow Jews to serve as diplomats to their countries, so Nahin, of Persian-Jewish extraction, changed his plans. He studied law, just as his father had, although his father probably never had a client like Steve Banerjee.

De Noia and Steve would often meet at restaurants so the Chippendales staff would not overhear their verbal battles, even though everyone in the organization knew the two men loathed each other. Things came to a head on November 13, 1984, in a Manhattan restaurant. The two men sat at a booth trying to keep their argument at something resembling a normal conversational volume as other customers glanced over anxiously at the feuding pair.

Steve argued that De Noia was already more than well paid for his services and that De Noia was just trying to bleed him. The choreographer was just doing what Steve paid him for; putting on a show that filled the club. De Noia countered that Steve was making a fortune off his choreography and directing skills at Magique, and he wanted a larger share of the profits. Steve loathed sharing the profits with anyone and was jealous of De Noia's success and notoriety. De Noia, not Steve, had been appearing on national television talk shows and had earned the moniker, Mr. Chippendales.

As with most disputes, both were right to a degree. Steve had created the Chippendales concept and his money had, in partnership with the owners of Magique, funded the profitable new show in New York. De Noia had polished the show to a glossy sheen and taken it to a new level of professionalism and profits. Even so, neither was about to admit that the other had so much as a penny's worth of claim to more of the profits than they were already getting.

De Noia once again threatened to leave and create a rival show somewhere else. Steve knew that De Noia was planning a new review, called US Male, complete with a postage stamp logo, which De Noia would own completely.

Steve threatened to sue De Noia for breach of contract if he left to open a rival show. It was no empty threat. Nahin regularly crisscrossed the country enforcing the Chippendales trademark against clubs that offered Chippendales-like shows. In some cases, Steve's quest to protect the brand bordered on silly. When a New Mexico disc jockey planned to assemble a group of overweight dancers to strut their stuff as a parody act called Chunkendales, he received a letter from Chippendales warning him to cease and desist from any such plan. Steve ensured that Chippendales remained his and his alone.

Finally De Noia made Steve an offer. He would give up his rights to the New York show in exchange for half of any touring profits. Surprisingly, Steve agreed. He grabbed a paper napkin and wrote, "I, Steve Banerjee, full owner and Chairman of the Board of Easebe Corp. [created by Steve in 1975 to manage his businesses] and sole owner of Chippendales Inc., do hereby award to Nick De Noia on this 13th day of November 1984, fifty-percent (50%) of all monies received from touring rights involving the 'Chippendales Dancers' minus any and all expenses. All remaining monies will then be equally shared." Steve signed the napkin with a flourish and threw it at De Noia.

The deal was made. There was no fine print. No legalese. If the Chippendales dancers went on tour, De Noia would get half the profits. Both parties thought they made a good deal. Steve believed he had kept De Noia as an employee, at least for a little longer, in exchange for a worthless concession. The Chippendales dancers did not tour, so there were no profits to divide and, Steve believed, if they ever did, the profits would be small. Steve believed the real money would continue to flow from the clubs in New York and Los Angeles. Steve had plans to open more clubs in other cities. De Noia also believed that he had made a good deal. He thought that if the Chippendales dancers started touring, they would rake in piles of money. Even better, he had finally achieved the impossible: he had wrung a concession from Steve Banerjee.

Chapter 6
Arson, Again

Soon after the November 1984 Napkin Deal, Steve called Ray Colon. Ray had planned to become a regular police officer in Palm Springs, put in his 20 years and retire, but a routine physical revealed that he had polycystic kidneys, a hereditary disease that led to fibrous growths in the kidneys. His father would die just two years later at the age of 52 from the disease, and Ray's sisters suffered from the same condition. Ray's kidneys would probably fail within a few years and he would have to undergo dialysis daily. Unable to meet the physical requirements of the job, his budding career as a police officer was over and, with only a few years in as a reserve officer, his disability pension was minute. Within a few months of his discharge from the force, Ray was back managing the Overland Palms apartments and teaching traffic school, with the occasional robbery of a drug dealer with his old crewmate Leon Defina to supplement his cash flow.

When Steve called, he said he had been sorry to hear that Ray had lost his job and invited Ray to lunch. Ray declined, but

Steve played on their friendship, even saying he thought of Ray like a brother. As usual, Steve convinced Ray to do as he asked.

They had lunch at Hamburger Hamlet in posh Brentwood. Nestled at the base of the Santa Monica Mountains, Brentwood is bordered by the wealthy areas of Pacific Palisades, Bel Air and Santa Monica. San Vicente, Wilshire and Sunset Boulevards are the main east-west thoroughfares, with San Vicente sporting a broad meridian dotted with colorful, sprawling jacarandas. A decade later, O.J. Simpson would be charged but found not guilty of the murder of his ex-wife, Nicole Brown Simpson and waiter/actor Ronald Goldman on Bundy in Brentwood.

Steve and Ray sat in the back of the Hamburger Hamlet as sun streamed through the skylight in the cathedral ceiling. The upholstered benches with wood trim and spindle-backed chairs gave the restaurant a country feel. It was a tense lunch, with neither man saying much as they ate. Ray apologized for not attending Steve's September 29, 1984 wedding to Irene in her hometown of Buffalo, New York, to which Ray had been invited. Ray explained that he and Barbara had wanted to attend, but had been unable to afford the trip. Steve said he understood, but still appeared to resent Ray's absence from his wedding.

It was not until the remains of their meal had been cleared and they were drinking coffee that they really started to talk. Steve said that Chippendales was still the hottest club in town, but he resented other clubs stealing "his business." He also complained about De Noia, but his anger was focused on the rival clubs. He mentioned Bentley's, which Steve said had stolen his idea of using a classy name, and another club called the Pearl Harbor. He appeared to have forgotten his interest in Osco's, which he had mentioned to Ray as a possible arson target after the disastrous attack on Moody's, but Bentley's still made the target list. Even so, like the Japanese in 1941, Pearl Harbor was Steve's prime target.

Steve complained that half his customers were going to the Pearl Harbor, which was in the basement of a Red Onion restaurant in Marina del Rey. Ray suggested that Chippendales' newness was wearing off and competition was bound to increase. Steve did not see it that way. He wanted to stay on top. Once again Steve said he hoped Ray could help him out. This time

Ray knew exactly what Steve wanted: arson. Ray declined, but Steve swore the rival club was crippling Chippendales. Seeing that Ray wasn't buying, Steve leaned back and tried a different tact. He said he had trusted Ray before, but Ray had burned him. Steve said he could have handled the whole matter of the $7,000 Ray had taken for the Moody's arson very differently. His anger rising, Ray took the statement as a threat. Steve said it was not. Steve said that if he had wanted to "deal with" Ray he easily could have done so. Now Steve just wanted to give Ray a chance to even things out between them, especially since, having been a police officer, Steve reasoned, Ray should know some "scumbag" who would be willing to do a job on the Pearl Harbor and Bentley's.

Ray later said that he did not want to get involved but something about their relationship combined with Ray's background drew Ray into Steve's problems. It might have been that, after leaving Rocky's employ and losing his job as a police officer, Ray was looking for someone to give him orders to follow. Or maybe it was the fear, which Ray later expressed, that if Ray said no, the Chippendales owner would use his vast financial resources to hire someone to kill Ray and maybe even Ray's wife. Steve certainly would not want Ray walking around talking about Steve's attempted arsons. And, of course, there was the $7,000 that Ray had taken for a job he never completed. In an ironic twist, Ray had been raised to keep his word. Now he was being pushed to keep his word, but to do it, he had to break the law—albeit not something he had been overly concerned with when he worked for Rocky.

"This ain't never going to end, is it?" Ray later recalled asking.

Steve grinned. "Sure it will, after you take care of the Pearl Harbor."

On December 28, 1984 at 2:30 a.m. Ray was parked on Washington Boulevard in Marina del Rey overlooking a park. From where he sat, he could see between two hotel towers the Red Onion restaurant and its Pearl Harbor nightclub. The restaurant/club was on Admiralty Way, which snaked its way along the irregularly shaped marina. On the landward side, apartment and hotel towers lined the four-lane street. One the seaward side, single-story restaurants bordered the water, offering their patrons' unobstructed views of rows of sailboats, yachts and cabin cruisers. Admiralty Way was wide and each restaurant had a large parking lot around it with extensive landscaping, giving the area an impression of space and, with the marina views, great wealth.

Just as with the first arson attempt, Ray had considered using Leon Defina or another crew-member for the job, which would have guaranteed success, but would have created a monster. Steve was now worth a fortune and any member of Ray's crew, who were as greedy as Scrooge before his encounter with the ghosts, would not hesitate an instant to squeeze Steve of every penny he had, even if it meant taking out Ray. Ray kept the professionals out of it.

Therefore, in the car next to Ray sat Mike Alvarez, who had done some work for the Mexican Mafia. Quiet and tough, Alvarez was a stocky 5' 9". He was always grinning and always dressed in black. In the back seat, also dressed in black, was 32-year-old Gilberto Rivera Lopez, known to Ray as Louie, but also known as Louis Lopez, Andy Rivera, Louie Malacatta or Malakadda, and a dozen other aliases. He had so many aliases that his long list of names would later cause some confusion for the government and defense attorneys when they prosecuted him. A small, wiry ex-con with a shaved head and a black mustache, Louie owed his gaunt appearance to his $300-a-day heroin addiction. In the back seat, he twitched and fidgeted like a shy teenager on his first date.

Ray asked Louie if he had the bottles of gasoline ready. The gasoline was ready. Alvarez led the way as he and Louie scrambled out of the car and ran across the darkened park. They each carried a gasoline-filled bottle with a rag sticking out of it. They paused at Admiralty Way. Seeing no one at such a late hour, they sprinted across the deserted street toward the restaurant.

Ray squinted, trying to force his eyes to see farther in the darkness. Streetlights threw circles of light at regular intervals but left broad, gloomy gaps. A block from the ocean, it was cold, in the low fifties. Even Southern California could be chilly in December. Ray zipped up his black jacket. He could smell the odor of rot that drifted in from the Pacific.

Ray saw a flame flicker in the distance. Two dark figures sprinted toward the road as sparks erupted into the night behind them. Flames licked at the Red Onion. Alvarez and Louie ran across the park and raced up toward the car. Moments later, the two arsonists were inside, puffing and wheezing like a pair of geriatric marathoners.

"It's done," Ray remembers Louie reporting, his chest heaving. "Let's get out of here!"

Ray started the car and pulled out carefully. It was no time to draw a speeding ticket. With memories of Steve's rage over the Moody's fiasco, Ray asked if they were sure. Regaining his breath, Louie said they broke a window near the bar and threw in the Molotov cocktails. The club, he assured Ray, was burning.

Louie settled back in the seat, a broad smile revealing his joy at a successful job. Quickly his mind turned to business; when would they get paid? He needed a fix, soon. Ray told them that if the club was indeed burning down, they would get paid in the morning.

The next morning, Steve called Ray. He was furious. Steve said the club had not burned down. He told Ray that he would pick him up in 20 minutes. An hour later Steve and Ray pulled into the parking lot of the Red Onion. Ray gasped as he saw workers removing burned carpet and scorched and blackened furniture from the Pearl Harbor, while other workers cut new carpet for installation. The Red Onion was already preparing for the lunch crowd.

Steve was seething, his knuckles white on his Mercedes' leather-covered steering wheel. Ray stared at the scene, so different from what he had expected. Steve told Ray to go over and investigate. Ray thought he was nuts, but Steve insisted. With great reluctance, Ray walked over to the nightclub. The carpet installers told Ray that someone set fire to the hall leading into the club. The night janitor smelt the fire and put it out before it spread.

Steve blamed Ray for the debacle. They drove in silence through posh Marina del Rey, past the palm-lined boulevards and expensive condominiums with ocean views on streets with names such as Bali, Mindanao and Tahiti. As they left the Ma-

rina and headed east along Venice Boulevard toward Chippendales, Steve calmed down. He told Ray to forget about it because he had a bigger problem: Nick De Noia.

By 1985 Steve and De Noia spoke to each other only when
it was absolutely necessary to conduct business, and even then
they barely managed to control their intense hatred for each
other. Their relationship was about to get even worse: De Noia
had devised a way to capitalize on Steve's 1984 Napkin Deal,
which gave De Noia 50 percent of any tour profits.

The owners of a nightclub in Philadelphia, Pulsations, proposed that De Noia bring the New York Chippendales dancers to their club several nights a week. The owners of Magique
opposed the deal, since they feared that women in New Jersey were as likely to drive down the New Jersey Turnpike or
ride the train to Philadelphia as cross the Hudson River to New
York to gawk at the Chippendales dancers. Even so, since Magique was closed several nights a week, De Noia jumped at the
chance. In his mind, the shows would constitute a tour, even if
the trip was only 90 miles across New Jersey to Philly.

When Steve heard about the plan he went ballistic. He argued that the Philadelphia show was not a tour. De Noia ignored Steve and, after a successful run at Pulsations, took the
show to Atlantic City, where the dancers appeared at a casino.
Steve and his attorney, Bruce Nahin, argued against the casino arrangement. They believed that Chippendales made far
less money performing at a casino, since customers were more
likely to spend their money in the casino rather than on booze,
tips and merchandise at the Chippendales show. De Noia per-
severed. He took the show to other clubs throughout the northeast, across the country and, later, overseas. As the tours played
to packed clubs and arenas, Steve changed tactics from opposing the shows to complaining that De Noia was cheating him by
falsely inflating his expenses to reduce the profits De Noia was
supposed to split with Steve.

Hating to see someone else making money, Steve then started his own tour. He had no trouble finding dancers. Thousands
of men applied, with more than 5,000 applying for just six dancer positions during one recruitment drive. Steve's first tour was
across the United States and Canada, but quickly expanded to
Europe, South Africa, Hong Kong, Australia, Guam, the Philip-

pines, and Britain, where the troupe played at London's vener-
able Strand Theatre. Shows sold out from Copenhagen to San
Francisco, Canberra to Berlin. At times there were three Chippendales groups touring Europe at the same time, each with
17 performers (dancers, singers, stripper lead, and emcee) and
about 13 crew, including security for the phenomenally popular dancers.

New dancers received $750 a week plus tips, which could
add up to $1,200 a night. Audience members who wanted a pic-
ture after the show with one of the leads paid $20 for the photo-
graph, paper frame included. One lead made $700 in one night
just off such photographs. Many of the dancers were sent flowers, stuffed animals and candy by admirers, as well as propos-
als of marriage and all manner of sexually creative and explicit
invitations. The most popular dancers were making $100,000
a year at a time when gas was a buck a gallon, movie tickets
were $2.75 and the median price of a single family home in Los
Angeles was $180,000.

Steve made sure his dancers stayed in shape, emphasizing
lifting weights and even hiring a chef for tours to keep them in
lustful shape. Steve also had his lighter side. He sent two garbage bags full of condoms to the dancers before one tour. Even
though some dancers were gay, most were not and were more
than willing to avail themselves of the many females throwing
themselves at the dancers after every show. The Chippendales
dancers were world famous. Four dancers even appeared on
Oprah, performing a toned-down striptease number.

With new clubs in Dallas and Denver, Steve wanted to ex-
pand even more. A group of wealthy investors proposed opening at least five new Chippendales clubs in various cities on
the east coast. Called the Ruderman-Cohen deal after the lead
businessman and the attorney who were arranging the deal, it
would be extremely lucrative for Chippendales, Steve and De
Noia. The investors would supply the capital and take the financial risk, while Chippendales would supply the talent, primarily De Noia and the dancers, and the Chippendales name,
which was now worth a dance troupe's weight in gold. Half-
way through a meeting in a posh Midtown Manhattan hotel
suite, open warfare erupted once again between De Noia and
Steve. De Noia pushed for a share of the licensing rights to

Chippendales' products. Steve was appalled at even the suggestion that anyone else had any right to a share of the profits from his Chippendales creation. He said De Noia was lucky to have 50 percent of the touring rights; the choreographer was an employee, nothing more. De Noia vehemently disagreed, arguing that not only was he a partner in the tours, but that Steve and Chippendales would be nowhere near as successful without him. Steve had just come up with a gimmick. De Noia's development of the show into a professional extravaganza had transformed the gimmick into a gold mine. De Noia's attorney, sensing the profitable deal going south, tried to defend his client. He said that De Noia deserved some financial compensation for his contribution to Chippendales' success. Livid, Steve argued that De Noia was more than justly compensated for his contribution. Then it was Steve's attorney's turn to try to save the situation by explaining that the meeting represented an excellent opportunity for all concerned. The potential profits from five new clubs should, the attorney argued, surely bring reasonable men to a viable agreement that would satisfy everyone.

Steve, however, had reached the end of his patience. His voice dripping with hatred, he said that De Noia was nothing but a rip-off artist. De Noia had, Steve claimed, been ripping him off on the road shows and had even tried to do shows without informing Steve. He told the potential investors that De Noia was a thief who would do anything to put more money in his pocket. The Chippendales owner finished his tirade by warning the potential investors that De Noia would rip them off just as the choreographer had ripped him off. De Noia shot to his feet to deny the accusations. He countered that Steve was the one who was so money hungry that he had a safe in his house full of cash he was hiding from the IRS. If anyone shouldn't be trusted, De Noia shouted, it was Steve.

One of the potential investors gathered his courage enough to intervene in the argument and said, with the greatest understatement, that the meeting appeared to be at an impasse. He suggested they all take a few days before making a final decision. The other businessmen quickly agreed and filed out of the room, promising to contact Steve and De Noia later after they made a decision. Everyone in the room knew the decision had already been made: there would be no further meetings, no investment and no five new Chippendales clubs with their potential profits in the millions. The Banerjee-De Noia War had reached a crisis point.

Chapter 7
The Ultimate

By the mid-1980s Steve was a wealthy man with the finest clothes, two Mercedes, a house overlooking the Pacific in Playa del Rey, and a daughter born August 27, 1985. Even so, it was far from enough and, worse, it was all in jeopardy. In 1986, De Noia's company, Unicorn Tales, sued Steve's company, Easebe, which owned Chippendales. De Noia argued that Steve's creation of a rival touring group violated the 1984 Napkin Deal. De Noia sought a temporary restraining order and a preliminary injunction against Steve from infringing on De Noia's touring rights. The Los Angeles Superior Court issued both, which prevented Steve from operating his tour in any form with even a scent of the Chippendales' style, name or essence.

Steve was livid, acting as if someone had just ruled that he was not the father of his own daughter. The court ruling came at a time of a series of setbacks for Steve. AIDS was big news in the late 1980s and the sexual focus of the show meant that concerns about the disease damaged Chippendales' business. Chippendales also faced several personal injury lawsuits that arose from the inability of the firm's previous insurance company, which had filed for bankruptcy, to pay claims by several Chippendales employees and patrons. Then the 1987 Chippendales calendar was composed by someone who had forgotten the rhyme, "Thirty days hath September, April, June and November." Every month in the calendar was printed with 31 days. As a result of the misprint, Steve had to recall almost a million defective calendars and print new ones. The cost of the fiasco: $700,000. Then the IRS found that Steve had failed to properly report corporate income. On top of fines for overcrowding and legal fees for gender and racial discrimination cases, one of which was filed by famous Los Angeles attorney Gloria Allred on behalf of a male patron denied entrance during the strip show, the disasters forced Steve's company, Easebe, Inc., to file for Chapter 11 bankruptcy protection on January 23, 1987.

Publicly Steve remained optimistic; "As long as women look at beautiful men and have fun, we will do well." Privately, he was desperate. In early 1987 soon after the bankruptcy ruling, he called Ray. Once again Steve convinced his reluctant old friend to meet him, this time at a Marie Callender's on National Boulevard in West Los Angeles. The restaurant was across the street from a supermarket and a block from the busy 405 freeway. The high wood-backed booths provided privacy and Steve had arranged the meeting for mid-afternoon, well after most people had eaten lunch. Steve picked a table in the back away from the other patrons. He did not want to be overheard.

Ray arrived to find Steve's eyes bloodshot, his shoulders sagging and his fingers fidgeting with the silverware. As Ray approached the table, Steve's eyes nervously scanned the restaurant as if he expected some new disaster to befall him at any moment. Bankruptcy, misprinted calendars and his battles with De Noia were producing enough stress on Steve to buckle steel. After Ray sat down, Steve moaned that his life was falling apart. Everything he had worked for was being destroyed.

Ray was skeptical. Chippendales was still a popular club and at least from the outside, even with its current problems, Steve's company looked like a cash cow. Steve explained that he had hired De Noia to revamp the show and that things had been going well until, Steve said, De Noia started cheating him. Ray advised Steve to fire De Noia. Steve said he couldn't fire

De Noia because of the Napkin Deal. The courts had ruled that De Noia owned the rights to the Chippendales tours. De Noia was no longer an employee; he was now Steve's partner. Steve had attempted to buy De Noia out for $1 million. De Noia refused. Steve said hiring De Noia was the stupidest thing he'd ever done.

Wishing Steve would get to the point, Ray asked what Steve wanted. Steve mentioned their old friendship and emphasized his desperate need for Ray's help. Steve said De Noia was eating him alive. Something had to be done. Ray asked what Steve meant.

Steve sighed, checked that no one was within earshot, and said, "I want the ultimate done."

Ray stared at Steve. He asked in a whisper if Steve was saying that he wanted De Noia killed. Steve slowly nodded.

Ray told Steve he was out of his mind. Doing such a thing, Ray later said, would be "a hell of a thing." He later claimed that he wondered, "What does he think I am, a hood?" It seemed an accurate description of what he had been for Rocky, yet, as Robbie Burns pointed out, only God can give us the gift to see ourselves as others see us—and He rarely obliges.

Ray later said he rose to leave, but Steve grabbed his arm. Steve implored Ray to hear him out. He explained that he did not expect Ray to do it himself. Ray just needed to find an outsider, someone no one would ever suspect, to commit the murder. Steve pleaded that Ray was the only person he could ask for help.

Ray asked Steve if he was serious. The club owner said he had thought about it for a long time. There was, he said, no other way. De Noia was bleeding him and he wouldn't stop until Steve was sucked dry. Revealing his twisted view of humanity, Steve even said that De Noia might, even then, be sitting at some other restaurant talking to someone about having Steve killed.

Steve said Ray must know someone from his days as a police officer who would be willing to kill their own mother if the price was right. He said that if Ray found someone to do the job, then Steve would never bother Ray again and would give him anything he wanted. Steve even offered to buy Ray a house. Ray said, "I already have a house."

Steve reached into his vest pocket and took out an envelope, which he tossed to Ray. The envelope contained $3,000
and De Noia's home and business addresses. Steve asked Ray
to go to New York to see if Ray thought it could be done. Ray
tried to decline, but Steve played on their friendship and when
that seemed to be failing, showed Ray a notice from the government, which said that Steve's name had appeared on a wiretap
related to organized crime. Ray was uncertain what the notice
meant, but Steve implied that he had the underworld connections to have Ray killed if Ray didn't do what Steve wanted.

About the time Steve was ordering a hit on Nick De Noia, Nick
and his older brother Val met in New York between two Chippendales tours. Val had a business in Philadelphia and the
brothers often met at Penn Station to talk about family, friends
and business. Val knew how stressful Chippendales had become for Nick and urged his younger brother to cut his ties
with the company. Val argued that Chippendales and male
strippers were not Nick's world; his world was Broadway and
Emmys. Nick countered that if it wasn't for him, Chippendales
would be nothing.

Val agreed, but he knew that Nick had been threatened by
some of Steve's associates, including by Dan Berg. Nick dis-
missed Berg as a "blow-hard." His threats meant nothing. A
worried Val asked Nick what good it was being such a success
if his life had been threatened?

Nick mentioned his refusal of Steve's offer of a million dollars to buy him out of Chippendales. Nick said he doubted Steve
could even raise that much money. Val saw a chance to get his
brother out of what he thought was a dangerous relationship
with Steve. He offered to raise the million dollars himself to
buy Nick out of his contract with Steve and the Rogers brothers,
who owned Magique.

Val told Nick, "I just want you out of there."

Nick refused to abandon what he considered to be his creation, even for a million dollars.

A few weeks later Ray stood beside a Burger King in Manhattan
looking down West 40th Street at the building that housed Nick
De Noia's office. Ray had told Barbara it was a business trip

related to producing a record. He even took Barbara and his mother along. They stayed at his sister's house in Selden, Long Island. During their visit Ray, alone, checked out De Noia's office and his apartment building. The office was south of Central Park and just southwest of Times Square. De Noia's three-bedroom apartment was in Midtown Manhattan, above a restaurant and across the street from the exclusive La Triumph, an upscale apartment building. Unbeknownst to Steve and Ray, the apartment address was out-of-date. By the spring of 1987, De Noia had moved across the Hudson River to New Jersey, where he lived at 611 Gregory Avenue in Weehawken. His home was just off the end of the Lincoln Tunnel on a tree-lined street of two-story red brick townhomes and houses. Unfortunately for Nick De Noia, the office address was still correct.

Even though Steve had asked Ray to arrange the murder, it did not mean that Steve trusted his old friend to actually do it. To prove that he was at least starting down the road toward murder, Ray called Steve from a pay phone near De Noia's apartment and described the building and the street to prove he was checking it out. Having convinced Steve that he had cased De Noia's apartment and office, Ray stayed at his sister's house for ten lazy days and then he, Barbara and his mother flew back to Los Angeles having enjoyed a nice vacation.

The next day Steve and Ray met for a late lunch at Izzy's in Santa Monica. The restaurant was almost empty, ensuring their privacy, since the lunch crowd had already departed. While Ray, confident that he had done enough to appease Steve at least for the moment, ate a ham and cheese sandwich, Steve poured out his troubles to his old friend. Steve had hired people to watch De Noia's shows. He was furious that De Noia had put on a Chippendales show in Ohio, which Steve's people reported had sold out, yet when it came time to divide the profits, De Noia reported had only drawn a miniscule crowd.

Having heard enough of Steve's complaining, Ray pressed Steve to determine how serious he was about "the ultimate." Steve again claimed that De Noia would bleed him dry and that murder was the only way out. Taking another tack, Ray later said he tried to raise the price to dissuade Steve. Ray said he might have to return to New York, which would cost more money. Steve said he would pay "whatever it took."

Steve then warned Ray to do it right and not to call him or visit his office. The fewer people who saw them together, the better. Ray asked how they were going to stay in contact. Steve said to call him and use the code name "Babe," the name of one of his former bar managers. Babe sometimes did call, so no one at Chippendales would think the call was suspicious.

During the next several months Steve and Ray met several times on quiet residential streets in Santa Monica. As they strolled past the expensive homes beneath the eucalyptus trees and palms, Steve ranted and raged about his business problems, the competition and especially about Nick De Noia. Ray stalled and later said he put every obstacle he could think of in the path of the murder plan, but Steve bulled ahead. Nothing would stop him. He was desperate. Ray went to New York several more times on Steve's dime to arrange the hit, but really to visit his sister. Ray hoped the rising cost of the job would dissuade Steve—or so he later claimed. Ray told Barbara the trips were related to the possible record-producing job. Through it all, Ray later told authorities that he hoped time would wash the murder plot out of Steve's mind. It didn't.

By late February 1987 at the Marie Callender's in West Los Angeles where Steve had originally raised the subject of murder almost two months before, Steve angrily told Ray that he was tired of waiting for the job to be done. If it was not done soon, Steve said he would hire someone to "whack" Ray. Ray countered that if Steve knew someone who would kill him, why not use that guy to whack De Noia? Steve replied that the guy he knew was in the Mob. Steve knew that if he involved the Mafia, it would only be a question of time before they owned Steve and Chippendales. It was ironic that the very reason Steve did not use his contact was the reason Ray had not used his own crew to commit the arsons or the murder.

Steve said that either Ray should find someone to do the job or their friendship would be over. Steve was not going to let Ray scam him again, as he had for the $7,000 Steve had given Ray to burn down the rival clubs. Steve had had enough.

Even after the heated exchange at Marie Callender's, Ray still managed to milk another few weeks' delay. It had a price though. Steve constantly called Ray's house at all hours of the day and night. Ray stopped answering the phone and when

Barbara did, Steve would just hang up. Unfortunately for Ray, Barbara thought he was having an affair. Ray figured he could sort that misunderstanding out later, but sometimes he made a mistake and answered the telephone. Steve breathed heavily into the phone like an asthmatic Darth Vader and then the club owner cursed Ray until he ran out of breath.

Ray knew time was running out. Steve might decide to have him killed. But who, Ray wondered, could he find to murder De Noia? Most of his friends were cops or guys like Leon Defina, with Mafia connections. The cops would never do such a thing and his crew would not hesitate to do the job and then muscle in on Steve to milk Chippendales of every last penny. Ray thought he might be able to trust Defina, but he was far from certain, and murder was not something on which he wanted to take the slightest risk.

After thinking about it for days, Ray finally thought of someone who might do the job. When he managed the Overland Palms apartments Ray had rented an apartment to a good ole Southern boy, Errol Lynn Bressler, who had reddish-blond hair that gave him his nickname, Strawberry. Bressler was a drifter and had spent a few years in Texas working on oil rigs. He had left a job as a mechanic at a lonely truck stop in the desert just outside Las Vegas to move to Los Angeles. Ray had known right away that Strawberry had a past. Something about him did not jibe. Strawberry drove a dust-covered Camaro, was obsessed with guns and spent hours listening to police scanners. After he rented the apartment Ray avoided him, but Leon Defina, who was staying with Ray at the time, befriended the redneck. They became friends, Strawberry even telling Defina that he had worked with the DEA and FBI as a drug informant and asking if Defina or Ray would be interested in such work. Both declined. When Strawberry announced he was heading back to Texas, Defina decided to go with him.

Even though Ray did not trust Strawberry, he could not think of anyone else for the job. He found Strawberry's phone number and called him. Strawberry was happy to hear from Ray. He had always liked Ray. Ray learned that after Strawberry and Defina reached Texas, Defina, as usual, had taken off with a girl. Defina had left his previous girlfriend with Strawberry and they soon had a baby together.

Ray asked Strawberry to call him back from a pay phone. Used to such tactics to obscure criminal activity, Strawberry quickly called Ray back. Ray explained that he might have a job for Strawberry. He said there was a guy in New York who was making trouble for some friends of Ray's and the problem was beyond the point of negotiation. His friends, Ray said, wanted "the ultimate performed" on the guy.

Strawberry asked who the guy was and who had ordered the hit. Ray said Strawberry would never be told either piece of information. He would be told where and when to do the job, get paid and that would be that. Strawberry was interested, but would only participate with his running partner.

It all came down to trust. In a world where nothing could be written down, your word was your bond and trust was the coin of the underworld realm. The friends you made as a kid, with whom you pulled small jobs from stealing hubcaps to extorting lunch money, became the men you trusted as an adult. There was something about the openness of children, of the young, that allowed trust to develop quickly. Friendships were formed before the defensive walls everyone builds around themselves as adults were built. Childhood friends know us better, often, than our spouses; for they knew us when we were young, full of dreams and with all our personality flaws exposed. The ability to hide flaws is not developed until years later when, as adults, we hide behind the guise of conformity and appear to follow the rules of society, whichever society we end up in. Even criminals have unwritten rules of conduct and behavior. Criminals, however, can never really be sure who will keep their word when the stakes are piles of money or years in prison. Time together could develop the depth of trust that boyhood friends already had, but it took years, numerous criminal acts together, and evidence of loyalty and trust on small things that slowly evolved into trust on bigger things. Strawberry had such trust with the guy he ran with and Ray had almost attained that level of trust with Defina, but not quite. Having migrated from New York to Los Angeles, Ray had lost touch with his boyhood friends. He now he faced the prospect of being unable to use his most trusted friend, Defina, because he did not trust him quite enough, and having to use someone who he did not know whether he could trust at all.

Strawberry said he would check with his partner. Ray hoped he had found someone to do the job, which would get Steve off his back once and for all. Days later, Strawberry called. His running mate was busy. Strawberry was not going to do the job alone, so he passed and Ray was right back where he started, including being on the receiving end of Steve's endless curse-laden telephone calls at all hours.

Ray almost gave up and had decided to offer the job to Rocky's crew, when he devised a way to stall Steve a little longer. The next time Steve called, Ray told Steve he needed $500. He had found someone to do the job.

A few days later, in March 1987, Steve drove Ray through Monterey Park along Atlantic Avenue. Monterey Park was a pre-dominantly Chinese section of Los Angeles, east of downtown. Ray had told Steve he was going to buy a gun for a hit man in the Chinese Mafia. Ray tried to dissuade Steve from coming, telling him the man he was meeting had said to come alone, but Steve was adamant. The club owner did not believe anything Ray told him anymore. Steve wanted to see the gun dealer in person. Steve asked Ray why he hadn't used the Chinese hit man months ago. Ray smoothly lied that the man had been out of town and he had been unsure whether the LA-based hit man would even want to do a hit in New York. Ray explained that hit men rarely leave their own surroundings. Apparently home field advantage was everything where murder was concerned, something Ray should have later remembered.

Steve pulled into the parking lot of a strip mall with a mul-titude of oversized signs in Cantonese and Mandarin advertis-ing everything from haircuts and trips to Shanghai to dim sum and cell phone deals. A movie theatre marquee advertised *The Lost Boys, Moonstruck, Masters of the Universe,* and *The Untouch-ables.* As Steve parked, Ray spotted his man standing beside a black Mercedes 450SL. Asian, with short, black hair, he stood straight-backed, yet at ease, as if he was a warlord without a care—or a fear—in the world.

Ray warned Steve to stay out of sight and then got out and walked over to the gun dealer. They shook hands as Steve watched from his car. Ray and the dealer walked to the rear of the Mercedes and opened the trunk. Steve could see the man hand Ray a shoebox, but then the pair moved behind the trunk, blocking Steve's view. A moment later, Ray came striding back toward Steve's car, the shoebox under his arm. The black Mercedes pulled out and was gone before Ray reached Steve's car. Steve got out and opened the trunk of his car so Ray could put the shoebox inside.

Ray asked if Steve wanted to see the gun, but Steve declined. Guns made him nervous. As they pulled out of the parking lot Steve said he hadn't actually seen the transaction. Ray snapped that he had paid the dealer for the gun. Steve countered that he hadn't seen any money change hands. His lack of trust in Ray after months of stalling was showing. Ray asked again if he wanted to see the gun. Luckily for Ray, Steve again declined— the box was empty. The alleged gun dealer was a friend Ray had met at an acting class. Since he had an interest in movies, Ray had been taking acting lessons and writing scripts. (He later gave his attorney, Jim Henderson, a story about a fictional Arab attack on New York, years before the September 11, 2001 attacks.) Ray had, in fact, already purchased a gun from an old friend who could procure anything up to a surface-to-air missile if the price was right.

The play-acting with his Asian friend bought Ray a little more time but only a little. Within a few days, Steve was back to calling Ray's house twenty times a day at all hours. Ray even moved out to Newhall, northeast of Los Angeles and left no forwarding information. Even so, the club owner quickly found Ray on a cul-de-sac at 26522 Hillsfall Court. Ray had to find someone to carry out the hit and fast, but whom?

After wracking his memory, Ray finally settled on Gilberto Rivera "Louie" Lopez, the heroin addict who had been involved in the disastrous attempted arson of the Pearl Harbor club. He seemed like the sort who would commit murder for cash to feed his habit. The problem was to find him. Ray had dropped the addict off at his mother's duplex several times while they were planning the Pearl Harbor attack, but Ray could not remember where the duplex was exactly. He did remember the neighborhood. He started driving along every street in the East Los Angeles barrio hoping to spot Louie or the duplex. Finally, late on the evening of April 5, 1987, Ray spotted Louie walking down Vermont Avenue. Ray pulled over and honked. Louie stopped and peered into the car. Recognizing Ray, he smiled and slid into the car. They drove to a hole-in-the-wall Mexican restaurant and talked while Louie wolfed down tacos. Ray pushed his refried beans and flank steak from one side of his chipped plate to the other.

Louie was still upset about not getting paid for the arson, even if it had failed. Even so, he was interested when Ray said Louie would definitely get paid for this job. Ray explained that certain people wanted "the ultimate done" to a guy in New York. As with Strawberry, Louie thought the hit was for the Mob, but wondered why a Mafia hit man was not being used. Ray asked if it would scare Louie if the Mafia was involved. The drug addict said, "Of course." The Mafia scared him, especially since Louie was afraid they might kill him after he made the hit. Ray assured Louie that only one person would know he had made the hit: Ray.

If Louie was willing, Ray planned to fly to New York the next day. Even though Ray didn't name the man behind the contract, he did tell Louie the order was from someone who was "going crazy" — the hit had to be done as soon as possible. Such a tight time frame also allowed less time for anything to go wrong, especially for Louie to talk to the wrong people. Ray would provide the tickets and the gun. Ray asked Louie for an alias to use on a plane ticket. Louie chose Louie Malakadda. Ray made the flight reservations with his credit card. He had no choice. After his numerous flights to New York, Steve had refused to advance him another penny until the contract was completed.

The would-be hit man asked how much he would be paid. Ray said it was up to Louie to set the price for his services. Louie thought about it, rubbed his nose and asked for $25,000, just above the 1987 average US annual income of $24,350. Ray later told the FBI that he had hoped the high price would deter Steve. It didn't. The Chippendales magnate agreed to the price without a moment's hesitation. Ray had found Steve his hit man.

Chapter 8
The Crime

On Monday, April 6, 1987, Ray packed a 9 mm handgun into a suitcase at his home in Santa Clarita. He drove south on I-5 to East Los Angeles and picked up Gilberto Rivera "Louie" Lopez. Louie announced that he needed enough heroin to last at least three days or his drug-addicted body would never survive the trip to New York. Seeing no alternative, but hating the sudden change in plans, Ray carefully drove through the narrow streets of the barrio looking for Louie's drug dealer. Ray constantly checked the mirrors and the road ahead for police cars or undercover officers, fully expecting the police to pull them over, find the gun and arrest them both. Finally, Louie spotted his supplier standing on a corner surrounded by a covey of junkies, like chicks clustered around a mother hen. Ray pulled over and handed Louie a couple of hundred-dollar bills. Louie darted out of the car and quickly returned with his drugs to find Ray looking around as he nervously scanned for cops. Louie told Ray to relax. Now he could do the job.

Oblivious to the risk and with a supply of his drug of choice, Louie was calm. As Ray drove to LAX, the addict asked if he could get something to eat at the airport before their 8 p.m. flight. It was only then that Ray realized Louie had never been on an airplane and did not know they would feed him on the flight. Louie was far from a frequent-flyer hit man.

As Ray and Louie drove to the airport, attorney Bruce Nahin was at home in Los Angeles. On an almost weekly basis Nahin flew east to manage the New York Chippendales operation. He had planned to go that day, but his baby son was ill and his wife, a new mother, wanted him to stay home. His wife may have saved his life; he cancelled his plans.

For Ray and Louie, the red-eye was uneventful. The gun avoided detection since checked domestic baggage was rarely X-rayed, let alone searched in the days before the attacks of September 11, 2001. While Ray stayed awake the entire flight, Louie, after devouring his dinner, slept soundly. They landed at Long Island-MacArthur Airport on the morning of Tuesday, April 7. Ray and Louie disembarked separately and stayed apart as Ray retrieved the suitcase from the baggage claim and rented a car. It was a clear, crisp morning. Louie smoked a cigarette as Ray picked him up. Then Ray navigated the busy Long Island Expressway as they drove the 50 miles west toward the jagged skyline of Manhattan. As they approached the Midtown Tunnel, Ray told Louie to look the other way so the toll booth clerk would not see his face. Ray paid the toll and entered the tunnel that led from Queens into Manhattan.

Once in Manhattan, they crept through heavy, mid-day traffic. Louie grinned like a child in a new, magical land as he watched people rushing here and there intent on their daily destinations of importance only to themselves, stared up at the tall buildings, and eyed the thousands of stores and restaurants. It was all new to him and so unlike the barrio of East Los Angeles where the buildings tended to be two or three stories, the people almost all Hispanic and only peons walked. Still blocks from De Noia's office, Ray got pinned behind a garbage truck emptying a dumpster on a narrow street, which felt even narrower with the skyscrapers looming on either side like canyon walls.

Louie said he wanted to jump out and buy some wine at a store he had spotted. Ray couldn't believe it. Louie said he would be back before Ray had even moved. Ray thought he was nuts but, exasperated, took out a five and handed it to Louie. The addict grabbed it, scrambled out of the car and ran into the liquor store. Ray glanced from the liquor store to the garbage truck and back to the store, praying Louie would get back before the truck pulled out. All he needed was to lose Louie in Manhattan.

The garbage truck began to move. Ray frantically watched the liquor store's door; no Louie. The cars behind Ray honked. He couldn't move. Not now. Not without Louie. Then, finally, as Ray gestured at the cars behind him to be patient, Louie, brown bag in hand, sprinted out of the store and piled into the car. Ray drove on.

Louie twisted the cap off his jug of red wine and took a long swig. He held his hand out in front of Ray; it did not shake. Louie said now he was rock steady. He offered a drink to Ray, who declined and warned him against flashing the bottle around. The last thing they needed was for a cop to see the wine and stop them with the gun in the suitcase on the backseat.

Louie then wanted something to eat. After an argument over whether they should stop, Ray gave in and parked in front of a Burger King on the corner of 8th Avenue and West 40th Street. De Noia's office was less than a block away. Across the street from the Burger King on 8th Avenue and stretching two blocks loomed the enormous Port Authority Bus Station. The busiest bus terminal in the world, buses churned along elevated ramps in and out of the mammoth structure as rivers of people streamed in all directions. More than 200,000 bus passenger trips a day originated or ended in the multi-story station.

Ray and Louie walked into the Burger King. His brain addled by drugs, Louie would later remember it as a McDonalds. While Louie ate a large order of fries and a double hamburger, Ray sat and waited, staring outside. Trucks, half parked on the sidewalk, belched exhaust as men unloaded boxes and crates. Rows of yellow cabs waited for customers along 8th Avenue in front of the bus station. Scaffolding masked the front of an adjacent building. A narrow subway entrance crowded passersby into what was left of the sidewalk.

Louie finished eating and, soda in hand, strode to the bathroom to shoot up. Ray picked up Louie's tray, dumped the remains of the addict's lunch in the garbage and stepped outside. A few minutes later Louie, frenetic, antsy and high on heroin, stood beside Ray, still clutching his soda. Louie looked as if he felt he could take on the world.

They crossed the street to a pay phone. The phone book was in tatters, but Ray, who had not even brought the phone number, managed to find the number for Chippendales. He punched in the number, trying to avoid looking at any of the hundreds of people rushing past. A man answered. Ray said he was a dancer who wanted to audition for the Chippendales troupe. The man on the line agreed to an interview at 4:30 that afternoon. Ray asked to whom he was speaking.

"Nick De Noia."

Ray had just spoken to a dead man.

Ray hung up. He turned to Louie and told him De Noia was in his office. They walked across 40th Street and down one building to 264 West 40th; De Noia's building. The top floors of the 1920s office building were stepped back with crenellations along each story's roof line. The building was topped by a square clock tower. Louie told Ray he was going to check out the inside of the building. (Louie later told police that Ray took him into the building and showed him De Noia's office. Louie's story is unlikely; none of the witnesses in the building ever recognized Ray or mentioned a second suspect, yet several described a man who looked like Louie.)

Feeling conspicuous alone in front of the building even as hordes of pedestrians hurried past in both directions, Ray meandered back down the street to the car. He paced aimlessly, glancing every few seconds at De Noia's building as squadrons of yellow cabs and a few cars and trucks crawled past on busy 8th Avenue. He glanced at his watch as the seconds turned into minutes: 2 minutes, 5 minutes, 10 minutes, 15 minutes, 20 minutes. Where the hell was Louie?

Finally, with a flood of relief Ray saw the heroin addict approaching, craning his neck like a tourist to take in the tall buildings. Ray demanded to know where Louie had been. The addict laughed. He had been up on one of the top floors watching Ray pace back and forth far below. The stairwell for the building, he said, was on the outside, so Louie could see Ray from up on high. The would-be hit man laughed at Ray's nervousness.

Ten minutes later Ray was behind the wheel of the rental car parked near the front of De Noia's office building. Ray reached for the suitcase on the back seat, unlocked it and took out the 9 mm automatic handgun. He handed it to Louie, who tucked the gun under his waistband and pulled his shirt over it. Louie got out, Burger King soda cup still in hand, walked across the street to 264 West 40th Street, and took the elevator to the 15th floor. Louie walked down the hall to the left into an office where a blond man, William Mott, worked in an outer office.

"Are you Nick?" Louie asked, his hand already reaching for the gun. He turned his head to the side, approaching the man "rather sidelong," as Mott later recalled.

"No," Mott said, having risen and stepped out from behind his desk to meet the visitor. "He's in the other office." He pointed at a door to an inner office with the name, Nicholas De Noia, stenciled on it. Mott shared office space with De Noia and had known him for 24 years. Mott later said that Louie was well groomed and casually but neatly dressed. He thought Louie was a delivery man, since he said Louie carried an inter-office delivery envelope. Mott invited Louie to knock on Nick's door.

"Thanks," Louie said. "I'll be back. I have to talk to Nick."

Louie left the office and walked down the hall to the men's room.

A few minutes later Mott stuck his head into Nick's office to let him know that someone had asked for him and would return later. Nick asked Mott if the man was Asian. Mott said no. Mott later said he thought Nick asked because it related to some danger Nick was in. The question about a possible Asian involvement was never explained. Mott told Nick he had to use the restroom and closed Nick's door.

The single-stall restroom was at the end of the hall, shared by all the offices on the floor. Mott found the restroom door ajar and heard water running into a sink. He returned to his office to wait for the restroom to become available. He made two phone calls and about 10 minutes passed before Mott returned to the restroom.

The door was still ajar, but Mott's need was urgent. He pushed open the door and was surprised to find the "delivery man" bent over the sink, splashing water on his face as if he was ill. This behavior, once again, prevented Mott from really seeing Louie's face. Mott stepped into the stall.

Figuring he now would have the office and De Noia to himself, Louie returned to De Noia's office. He had left his Burger King soda cup in the bathroom.

Less than a minute later, it was done.

Too pumped full of adrenaline to wait for an elevator, Louie darted down the hall, flung open the stairwell door and bounded down the stairs.

After having been in the stall 20 or 30 seconds, Mott heard a door close, then a loud crack, as if a pistol had been fired, followed by the slam of the stairwell door. Thinking rapidly through the recent events of the man, the envelope, his loitering, the crack, and the slam, a worried Mott rushed back to the office. He found Nick seated at his desk, listing to his left. His body was rigid and, Mott later vividly recalled, the look on Nick's face was like that of a child who has been slapped and doesn't know why. Mott called out to Nick and told him everything was going to be all right. He ran out to his desk and called 911.

After the call it occurred to Mott that the shooter might return. He locked the outer office door and returned to Nick. The tension had left Nick's body and he was slumped heavily to his left, wedged in his white, rattan chair against his desk. Blood, pouring from his head, dripped onto the carpet. Mott wanted it to stop. He pulled Nick from his chair and eased him to the floor. The face of Nick's black Casio watch was later found to be cracked, which may have happened when he was shot or when Mott eased him to the floor. Mott tried to comfort his old friend. He found no pulse. Nick was not breathing. Nicholas "Nick" De Noia was dead.

Having just murdered De Noia, Louie, sweating profusely, took the steps two and three at a time as he bolted downstairs. He later said he heard footsteps descending rapidly behind him, although Mott did not follow Louie. Pulling the gun out, Louie stopped, aiming at the stairway above him.

After waiting a minute and hearing nothing more—was the noise some unknown person or only a figment of his drugged imagination?—Louie continued down the stairs. He later told

Ray, "I didn't want to look suspicious. I didn't want to be out of breath or nothing. So right before, about half ways down to the main floor, before I hit the main floor that's when I slowed down and I took a second wind, Holmes, buttoned up. Act real cool, calm and collected. Walked out. And then I mingled with all the rest of the crowd."

Ray waited for Louie, watching for any sign that something had gone wrong. After what seemed an eternity, he spotted Louie running up the street, his chest heaving as the heroin addict fought for breath. The hit man jumped into the car.

"Let's go," Louie said, gasping. "It's done."

"What do you mean, it's done?" Ray remembered asking.

"It's done, Homes. He's dead. Let's go," Louie urged.

Ray wanted the gun back first. If the police stopped them, Ray would surrender. He did not want to be caught in the middle of a gun battle if Louie, hopped up on heroin, started shooting.

Louie glared at Ray, but handed him the gun. Ray put the weapon back in the suitcase, locked it, and handed Louie a baseball cap from the suitcase to partially hide his face. Ray started the car and pulled out. Louie told Ray that he had been seen by some "dude" in the "shitter." The incident did not appear to concern Louie, but Ray prayed the "dude" would not be able to give the police an accurate description of Louie.

As he drove, Ray realized that the streets of Manhattan all looked alike. Worse, every street was one way in the wrong direction. The map made no sense. Everything was vaguely familiar from movies and TV shows, yet none of it helped Ray figure out where they needed to go. It had all changed so much since he had lived in New York so many years before. He was lost.

Ray took a wrong turn and drove back past De Noia's building. Louie pulled the baseball cap low over his eyes as Ray desperately tried to escape the area. After a few minutes, Ray heard gentle snoring; Louie was asleep.

Ray drove and drove. Then he realized he was back on 40th Street for the second time. As he fought through traffic past De Noia's building yet again, the police had already arrived and were cordoning off the street. Ray just made it past the building before the street was blocked off. Thirty seconds later and Ray and Louie would have been stuck at a roadblock right at the crime scene in front of dozens of New York City police officers.

Moments later, with a flood of relief, Ray spotted a sign for the Queens-Midtown Tunnel. Somehow he had managed to cross Manhattan to the 34th Street tunnel entrance. Minutes later, they were speeding through the tunnel toward Queens, putting a river between them and the murder. Ray drove to a hotel just past Long Island-MacArthur Airport, north of the Long Island Expressway near Selden. He booked Louie a room. Once inside, Louie wanted to make certain they would return to Los Angeles the next day, since he had already used almost all the heroin he had brought. Lacking a supplier in New York, he needed to get home to get a fix or he would be in a miserable state. Ray assured him they would fly home the next day. He told Louie not to leave the room or call anyone from the hotel. The less evidence that Louie had been in New York, the better.

Louie planned to shoot up using the last of his drugs, but said he was hungry. Ray bought him a deli sandwich and a large Coke, and left him a few dollars if he needed something from the hotel's vending machines. Then Ray drove to his sister's house in Selden, where he received a warm reception at his unexpected arrival.

Ray and Louie both saw the news about what they had done that day on the news. Even though it was only one of 2,016 murders that year in New York, every evening newscast led with the story of the murder that afternoon in the Garment District of the Emmy Award-winning choreographer of the famous Chippendales exotic male dance troupe: Nicolas "Nick" De Noia.

Chapter 9
The Cost, the Price and the Investigation

Nick's niece and goddaughter, Marie De Noia worked in the newsroom of a television station in New Jersey. Part of her job was to take stories off the wire and distribute them to the appropriate desks. Just 15 minutes after she left for home on April 7, the report of Nick's murder came over the wire. If she had left 15 minutes later, she would have learned of her uncle's murder via a wire story.

Marie De Noia lived with her parents. When she arrived home, her Uncle Val called to talk to her father, who was out. Val sounded "furious," but when she asked what was wrong, he said it was "too disgusting to tell her." She waited while Val called her father. She was scared. She knew something terrible had happened. She called her dad 15 minutes later. Although he "sounded casual," when she asked if something had happened, he replied in a straightforward manner with no apparent emotion, "Uncle Nick was shot dead in New York. He's dead."

Marie collapsed, devastated by the news. After she recovered enough to talk, her father, who was probably in shock, asked her to call her five brothers and sisters with the horrible news.

Marie later said Nick's death "had an incredible impact on my family." From early in her life, Marie had dreamed of entering the television field and had an especially close relationship with her entertaining uncle. Nick supported, even lovingly pushed, Marie to pursue her dream. She later said that it was his belief in her that helped her become a television reporter. When she landed her first position in television production with a public station, the family wanted to go out for dinner and celebrate with champagne. The always supportive and confident Nick said, "No, we'll have the champagne when she's *on* television." He was right. She later was on television as a reporter and then an anchor.

"I wanted to be like him," Marie later said. He had an "exciting life; television, dancing and movies." At family gatherings, Nick was always the "special guest star." Marie remembered Nick saying once that he and Steve Banerjee had attended a wedding together. Nick had complained how boring it had been, then added, "I started dancing, and then it was wonderful." His murder, Marie later said, "broke the entire fabric of our family."

The instant they heard about Nick's murder, the De Noia family knew that the murder was tied to Chippendales and that Steve Banerjee was probably behind it. Nick had mentioned to several family members the animosity and greed at the top of the Chippendales organization. In one of his last conversations with Marie, Nick had said he was "done" with Chippendales. He mentioned another project he had going; not US Male, but something else. "I've had it with dancing guys." He said there were "terrible" people involved with Chippendales. When she heard that he had been murdered, Marie later said, "In my gut, I knew exactly who and the reason."

The day after the murder Ray arrived at the hotel to discover that Louie had not only left his room the night before to procure more food and drinks, but had bought several newspapers with headlines about the murder to take home as mementos. Having read the stories, Louie said he should have asked for

$200,000 given De Noia's prominence. Ray tore the newspapers into shreds.

To add to Ray's anger, when he paid for the room he spotted a charge for a telephone call to Los Angeles. Under Ray's questioning, Louie admitted he had called his mother. The hit man argued that Ray had seen his sister the night before, why shouldn't he call his mother? It was one more piece of evidence that Louie had been in New York.

Ray stopped at a pay phone on the way to the airport to call Steve. Not trusting his accomplice, Ray never took his eyes off Louie as the hit man sat in the car. Steve had already heard about the murder. They arranged to meet.

Ray and Louie landed in Los Angeles at 9:30 p.m. and then drove the 15 minutes north to the A-framed International House of Pancakes on Sepulveda near National in West Los Angeles to meet Steve at 10:45 p.m. Wedged between three- and four-story apartment buildings, the blue-roofed restaurant seemed secluded off busy four-lane Sepulveda, a main north-south surface street. Ray spotted Steve's Mercedes parked at the rear of the expansive parking lot by a dumpster. The back of the restaurant was windowless, so no one inside would see them. Ray did not want Louie to know who had hired him, so he told the addict to wait in the car and walked over to Steve's car alone.

Steve was nervous. He stuttered as he said he was afraid the hit man would know who had hired him. Ray felt disdain for his old friend's cowardice, but reassured him that the hit man thought the Mafia had hired him, which would deter him from ever even trying to find out who had really paid for the contract. Steve was reassured, but still said he had been scared shitless when he heard De Noia was dead.

Steve handed a brown paper bag to Ray, but said he had been caught off guard. Ray frowned, not wanting any hitches. There was a gigantic hitch: of the promised $25,000, Steve only had $10,000. Steve had been unable to get all of the money at such short notice.

Ray seethed. The hit man had just killed someone. He was going to want all of his money. Steve said not to worry. He would get all the money. It would just take a little time, a few days at the most. Ray had no choice, but he made sure Steve understood that he needed the money fast.

As Steve drove away, Ray walked back to his car with the $10,000. Ray told Louie he had done well. Glad that he had relieved the hit man of the gun, Ray explained that since his people had not known when the hit was going to go down, they had not been ready with all of the cash. He gave Louie the $10,000 and assured him he would have the rest in a few days. Louie said he trusted Ray. He would wait.

Two days later on April 10, Ray disposed of the gun. He contacted either his brother-in-law, William Nelson "Billy" Barnes, Jr., or Mike Alvarez, one of the would-be arsonist from the night of infamy at the Pearl Harbor club. Court records mention Barnes and Alvarez in different documents in relation to disposing of the gun. Although Ray said it was Alvarez, he consistently sought to keep his brother-in-law out of prison. One of them worked at a hardware store and told Ray that the store had a machine that melted metal. Ray later said he gave Alvarez the 9 mm handgun to destroy. Whether it was Alvarez or Barnes, Ray said he had no idea whether the gun was destroyed but, even if Alvarez or Barnes sold it in the East Los Angeles barrio, without divine intervention the police would never be able to trace the weapon back to Ray or Louie, let alone to Steve.

Over the following weeks, Ray tried to get the rest of the money from Steve. The club owner avoided Ray and when they did talk, Steve stalled. Ray had been back three weeks when Louie, wanting his money and not knowing Ray's phone number, tracked down the number for Ray's sister in New York. The addict called her repeatedly trying to find Ray.

Fed up with Steve's stalling and concerned for his sister's safety, Ray drove to the Chippendale's office one morning and strode past the startled secretary right into Steve's office. Ray demanded they talk. Steve waved off the secretary who had followed Ray in to apologize for not stopping the gatecrasher. Steve calmly asked the secretary to close the door on her way out and motioned Ray to sit down. He said he had thought Ray would appear at some point to beg for the rest of the money.

Ray went livid at the idea that he was begging. Even in the face of Ray's fury, however, Steve said he still did not have the money. He said he would have it in a few weeks, but business was tight at the moment. Unbeknownst to Ray, Steve's financial empire was in decline. Not in the least interested in the reasons for the cash-flow problem, Ray demanded the money right away. If he didn't get it, he threatened to tell the hit man, "a stone-cold-hearted killer," Steve's name and address. Then the hit man could come demand the money from Steve in person.

Visibly shaken, Steve went into an inner office as Ray yelled that he wanted an extra $6,000 to cover the plane tickets, hotel and other bills he had run up on his credit card to complete the contract.

Steve returned and gave Ray the $15,000 in a brown paper bag—10 days late and with nothing extra to cover Ray's expenses, let alone to pay him for his part in the murder. The lack of payment would always be a sore point with Ray—or a point to be made in showing authorities and friends that he was not such a bad guy, since he had not murdered for money, merely for a friend.

At least partially appeased, Ray drove straight to East Los Angeles. The last thing he wanted was for Louie to wait for his money a minute longer than was absolutely necessary. Ray arrived at Louie's apartment building to find the hit man and his wife washing a new van. Louie sent his wife inside and Ray gave Louie the paper bag from Steve containing the $15,000. The addict tucked the bag into his pants and gave Ray a high five.

Ray glanced at the new van and thought that Louie stood a much greater chance of running afoul of the law than he did. As nicely as he could, Ray told Louie that he never wanted to see him again. It was nothing personal, it would just be best for both of them. Louie understood and wished Ray well.

In reality, Ray and Louie had little to worry about because there was little chance they would be arrested any time soon. Veteran Detective Michael Geddes led the investigation of the De Noia murder for the New York Police Department (NYPD). Born in New York, Geddes joined the NYPD in 1973 and made detective in 1985. He spent a little more than year in Brooklyn working narcotics before transferring to Manhattan in 1987. He laughed when fellow Manhattan detectives complained that they were too busy; Brooklyn had been far busier than Manhattan. Busy or not, the De Noia case provided several witnesses but little to go on to identify a suspect, let alone the murderer.

At about 3:30 p.m. on the day of the murder, a freight elevator operator in De Noia's building, Ali Akram, reported seeing a 5' 5", 145-pound, 30-year-old Hispanic male rush past him after walking out of a stairwell. Akram said the man had short black hair, olive skin and no facial hair, although he needed a shave. The man carried a shoulder bag and wore a blue windbreaker with an emblem on the left front breast, dark pants and sneakers. When Akram asked what floor the man was coming from, the man replied, "Fifteenth, Chippendales." Such a reply seems highly unlikely from someone who had just murdered the Chippendales choreographer on the 15th floor, and Louie never mentioned this alleged conversation to Ray or the police.

William Mott, who worked in De Noia's outer office and discovered De Noia after he was shot, reported a similar description of the murderer: a 5' 7" Hispanic male, between 140 and 150 pounds, wearing a light brown jacket. Hearing Mott's description of the events of that afternoon, Geddes had the doors checked on the 15th floor where the murder occurred. With only a few offices on that floor, by slamming the doors and listening from the bathroom the police were able to confirm the sequence of events after the killer left the bathroom. Someone opened and closed De Noia's office door, Mott heard the shot, and then he heard the heavy stairwell door slam. Mott heard no other doors open or close. Therefore, it seemed likely that the man who had left the bathroom just after Mott entered had been the killer.

Cecile Platovsky, who said she shared an elevator with a Hispanic male just before the murder, provided a similar description, although she added a Fedora hat. Another witness, Jack Lafcourt told police he saw a man roughly fitting the shooter's description but, like Platovsky, said the man was wearing a hat.

Even with four somewhat conflicting reports, the police had a fairly accurate description of Louie, if they focused on the points where the reports matched: a Hispanic male, about 5' 6" and 145 pounds with no facial hair and black or salt-and-pepper hair. The police thought he was between 35 and 40 years old, and that he had worn a dark-tan, waist-length jacket and blue jeans. Unfortunately, the description fit thousands of New Yorkers, not to mention tens of thousands of Americans.

In an attempt to narrow down the number of suspects, Geddes focused on motive. He ruled out robbery, in part because after the murder De Noia's Emmy awards were still prominently displayed on a shelf in his office. De Noia also still had credit cards, cash and keys in his pockets, as well as a silver ring on one of his fingers. Although there was no sign of a struggle, the police were uncertain whether the killer had argued with De Noia, which would help determine whether it was a crime of passion or a pre-meditated murder, as well as whether the murderer knew De Noia.

Detective Geddes later said, "The first thing you do is look at the friends." At an interview with a close female friend of De Noia's, she mentioned that "things got a little heated" between Nick and another close friend of Nick's from the show, David Arad. The police interviewed Arad. He said he was just good friends with Nick and was involved with another man, David Schrem. Arad admitted having had business arguments with Nick, but said the arguments were behind them. Even so, the police thought Schrem might have been involved in some sort of love triangle with Arad and De Noia. A week after the murder, on April 14, the NYPD showed a photo-array with Schrem in it to two witnesses: Akram and Mott. Akram was "pretty sure" the shooter was Schrem, while Mott said it was "very probably" Schrem. On May 21, 1987, another witness, Lafcourt could make no identification from a photo-array, while Cecil Platovsky said, "I cannot recognize anyone," but "if I had to pick a person....I would pick Schrem."

Six months after the murder, on October 6, 1987, the NYPD put Schrem in a lineup. Viewing the lineup, Mott said Schrem "looks very much like" the person he saw in the bathroom at the time of the murder. Akram said, "That's the guy I saw coming out of the building that day. That's him 100 percent." Case closed? Far from it. Contrary to crime dramas on television, eye-witness identification without any supporting evidence is not enough for the police to arrest someone. The police found absolutely no evidence beyond the witness identification linking Schrem to the crime. They released him without charge.

Having checked friends, the police considered Nick's family, since in many cases a relative of the victim is the murderer. The police learned that an $80,000 life insurance policy had been taken out for Nick De Noia. Police suspicions were raised because the policy took effect just one week before the murder. The beneficiary: Nick De Noia's older brother, Valentine "Val" De Noia. This tantalizing possibility led nowhere. The police found absolutely no evidence that Val had anything to do with his brother's murder. The timing of the insurance policy turned out to be just a coincidence and not a plot straight out of *Double Indemnity*.

Once the friend and relative angles dried up, Detective Geddes turned to Nick's business, which is where he had felt from the beginning would be found the motivation for the murder. His belief was based on his hypothesis that if the murder had been personal, the shooter would have known who De Noia was by sight and would not have had to ask Mott if he was De Noia.

Geddes learned that Nick and Steve Banerjee often argued over the touring show profits. Bruce Nahin, Steve's attorney and partner, called Geddes several times to report heated arguments that had occurred between Steve and De Noia. Nahin told Geddes that he had been in the middle of one such exchange only a few days before the murder. Geddes suspected Steve, especially since the motive appeared clear, but as the investigation progressed there were no leads tying Steve to the murder. With no leads, there was little Geddes could do but wait. He later said he told the De Noia family, "If it was a crime, person-to-person, we'd probably solve it quick. If it was a hit type of thing, it wouldn't come until someone got arrested. Then they'd want to save their soul and they'd give it up." Detective Geddes knew criminals very well.

Chapter 10
Murder as a Business Practice

Soon after the murder, Steve called Ray using their agreed code name, 'Babe.' Even though Ray did not want any contact with the club owner, Steve insisted that they had to talk and, not knowing whether it had to do with "the De Noia thing," as Ray called it, Ray agreed to meet. One fine summer day on a residential street in Santa Monica, they talked as they strolled past the manicured lawns of the upper-middle class homes.

Steve told Ray that he had been out of the office when a detective from New York called about the De Noia murder. Steve almost fainted when he saw the phone message, but he steeled himself, called the detective back and left a message. The detective never called back, which in many ways was worse than if he had returned the call. Steve, and now Ray, was left to wonder what the police had on Steve, and why they wanted to talk to him. Ray did not think the police were investigating Steve as a suspect, since such an investigation would not stop after a single telephone message. Ray thought the NYPD probably believed that the killing was either a renegade hit or that the shooter, possibly an angry gay lover, had had a run-in with De Noia. In any case, Ray said, the police had apparently decided it was not worth the effort to talk to the Chippendales owner.

Steve worried that it just meant the police did not have enough evidence against him yet. He was afraid that everyone knew he had been involved, including his wife, Irene. To confuse the police, Steve explained that he had devised a diversionary plan. He had become acquainted with an old mobster and kept in touch with him so that if the police ever investigated him, the mob link might throw them off Steve's trail. Even given his fears, Steve said he liked the new respect that people now showed him.

"It's not respect they're showing you, Steve," Ray later recalled saying. "It's fear."

As the weeks passed and the police investigation appeared to be going nowhere, Steve grew cocky. Bruce Nahin established a reward fund for information leading to the arrest of Nick De Noia's killer. Even though he initially believed that Steve was behind the murder, when the police didn't arrest Steve, Nahin concluded that his suspicion must have been wrong, so he asked Steve for a contribution to the reward fund. Steve replied, referring to whoever murdered De Noia, "The guy did me a favor. Why should I make a donation?"

Steve called the De Noia family to ask about attending the funeral. The De Noia family strongly suspected that Steve was behind the murder, so Nick's nephew, Tom, told Steve to go to hell. Bruce Nahin did fly to New York for Nick's funeral, where he planned to offer his services to manage the tours. The De Noia family, uncertain about who else besides Steve was behind the murder, refused his help.

In what the De Noia family's lawyers would later call "a hardball fashion" in a "distressed situation," Steve at first tried to have his Napkin Deal with Nick De Noia voided. Steve argued that the deal had been a personal one with Nick; Nick was dead, so the deal was dead. The De Noia family rejected Steve's argument wholeheartedly.

At first Val De Noia, Nick's brother, wanted nothing to do with Chippendales or the tours, but a friend told him that such an outcome was exactly what Nick's killer wanted. So Val, Nick's senior by 11 years, and Nick's nephew, Tom De Noia, an attorney, took over the New York-based Chippendales troupe. At first no one in his family wanted Val to do it and, when he planned his first Chippendales tour to Indianapolis, a concerned Detective Geddes told Val to travel under an assumed name.

Not only did he not use an assumed name, Val let it be known that he would continue to operate the tour, even going so far as to tell Steve. Geddes warned Val that he was putting his life at risk. If Steve had murdered Nick over the tours, then he might do the same thing to Val. Geddes later said, "Val put himself out there as a target."

After a while, Val began to do what he later said were "stupid things," such as traveling alone at night after shows. Eventually, he asked himself, "What the hell am I doing?" Was Chippendales worth his life?

Certain Steve was behind the murder, Val arranged to meet the club owner in New York. Val called Geddes, told the detective that Steve would be in New York and said they should arrest him. Geddes told Val to back off. Steve was a flight risk and might flee back to India if the case was not handled carefully.

Resigned to letting justice take its slow course and not willing to risk his life for Chippendales, no matter how profitable, Val and the De Noia estate sold the rights to the touring show and all other assets pertaining to Chippendales, including Nick De Noia's company, Unicorn Tales, which operated the tours, to Steve for $1.3 million. Steve had finally regained complete control of his Chippendales creation.

Even so, Steve had not found paradise. After years of legal jousting, on July 28, 1988, the city finally confiscated the Los Angeles club's liquor license over a discrimination charge: specifically, not allowing male patrons into the club during the male revue. The club remained open but, without a liquor license, business was as slow as it had been at the Round Robin when Steve bought the club. The Los Angeles Fire Department finally succeeded in closing Chippendales for overcrowding for good on August 22, 1988. The once thriving Chippendales on Overland became a preschool and day-care center.

Even though Steve had lost a battle, he had far from lost the war. Chippendales dancers performed on the road across the United States, Asia and Europe, selling everything from jackets and calendars—with the correct number of days for each month—to videos, mugs and T-shirts. Without a partner anymore, Steve made millions.

In Los Angeles, Steve made a deal to stage a show at Carlos and Charlie's on the Sunset Strip, an area of trendy restaurants, clubs and bars. Carlos and Charlie's is now the House of Blues. For a brief time the Chippendales dancers performed in a room upstairs before moving to a club at 5517 Wilshire Boulevard in the Mid-Wilshire district. Called Wall Street, the club was in the historic El Rey Theatre. Built in 1936, the art deco theater was in the heart of LA's Miracle Mile and seated 500, more than double the size of the old venue on Overland. The move instantly ran into trouble. City officials said the strip show violated a zoning ban on certain amusement enterprises.

Far from deterred, Steve kept looking for a new venue. In late 1987 Steve had met Dr. Jagjit Singh Sehdeva. Like Steve, an Indian immigrant, Sehdeva lived in Banerjee's neighborhood of Playa del Rey. Known as "Dr. Joe" to his American friends, Sehdeva was a vascular and thoracic surgeon who shared an office with his wife, Parkash Sehdeva, an obstetrician/gynecologist. Sehdeva supported an orphanage in Mexico through his involvement with the Rotary Club, but he also had a keen eye for a profitable business opportunity. Pursuing Steve's dream of becoming as successful as Walt Disney, they planned to create an "adult Disneyland" with a Chippendales club and other forms of adult entertainment. They formed a new company, the 929 Club Corporation, and purchased the multi-story Variety Arts Center, an ex-Vaudeville theatre at 940 S. Figueroa Street in downtown Los Angeles.

Yet again Steve soon ran into difficulties. The deal called for him to contribute $100,000 to the purchase of the building, but he was unable to raise the money. Instead, he brought in Moise Hendeles, a real estate investor, as another partner. The three partners agreed to split the $200,000 down payment on the $2.5 million building three ways, but when Steve's check bounced, his grandiose plans outrunning even the prodigious income from the Chippendales touring shows, Sehdeva and Hendeles bought the building by themselves. Not wanting to be cut out of the deal entirely, Steve negotiated to lease the building from his former partners for $30,000 a month with an option to purchase an ownership interest at a later date. Even before the new Chippendales opened, Steve stopped paying the rent and Sehdeva and Hendeles evicted him. Incensed, Steve once again turned to Ray.

Even though he did not want to see Steve, the club owner insisted and Ray, not knowing if it had something to do with "the De Noia thing," agreed to meet at Izzy's restaurant in Santa Monica. Stressed about the murder, Ray was smoking and drinking more. On December 12, 1988 he was stopped for DUI in Newhall near his home in Santa Clarita, which resulted in a $1,078 fine and the loss of his job as a traffic school instructor.

Even before they sat down at Izzy's, Steve launched into a tirade against his newest partner, Dr. Sehdeva. Steve said he had spent far more than he had planned renovating the building and had demanded a reduction in the rent, but his partners had held firm to their agreement. Ray said it was simple, just pay the back rent and Steve would be back in business. Steve, however, had already burned his bridges with his arrogant style. His partners, especially Dr. Sehdeva, refused to even discuss a deal. They wanted Steve out.

Now viewing murder as a routine business practice, Steve said he wanted Sehdeva dead. Ray said he was not Steve's personal hit man, but Steve said, given what they had been through together, if Steve went down, Ray would, too. Ray still declined to get involved. Steve countered that if Ray stopped helping him, he could not afford to have Ray around. He could hire some junkie for the price of "a bottle of cheap wine" to kill Ray. Fed up with Steve's threats, Ray threatened that he might just have Steve whacked. Steve said he didn't think Ray had the guts.

Even with the threats, like characters in a film noir, Steve and Ray were stuck with each other. The De Noia murder bound them together more intimately than lovers.

Steve handed Ray an envelope containing $3,000 and Sehdeva's home and office addresses. Steve repeated that he wanted Sehdeva dead. Ray later said he fought the urge to walk out. If he did walk, he feared what Steve might do to him and his family. Ray took the envelope.

In the parking lot as Ray pulled out, Steve waved him down and leaned in the car window. Steve said he might teach Sehdeva a real lesson by having Ray arrange the murder of Sehdeva's teenage son. Ray had had enough. He threw the envelope at Steve and called Steve a "sick bastard," especially since Steve now had not only a daughter, but also a son, born August 4, 1990, of his own. Ray would not arrange the murder of children. Val De Noia would later say, "Even that pig Colon refused to do that."

Steve backed down, saying he was just kidding. He asked Ray to take the money and arrange the contract on Dr. Sehdeva. Steve held the envelope out and Ray gunned the engine, debated for a moment, grabbed the money, and peeled out.

Ray later said he had no intention of having anyone else murdered, but he knew he could not just do nothing. He rented a hotel room in Van Nuys and then asked Steve if he wanted to meet the hit man he had brought out from New York for the Sehdeva hit. Steve declined but wanted proof that Ray had indeed brought a hit man out from the East Coast. The next day Ray showed Steve the hotel room receipt, but the Chippendales owner said he no longer wanted the doctor killed. Ray had no idea why Steve changed his mind, but whatever the reason Ray was eternally grateful for the change in plans.

Sehdeva would go on to serve as the president of the Los Angeles City Human Relations Commission in 1990 and the Westchester Rotary Club in 1991. By 1995 Sehdeva and a group of investors had turned the Variety Arts Center into a popular dance club and theater. Following in Chippendales' footsteps, their club had more than 400 complaints for excessive noise filed against it within a few years, but as with Steve's other partner, Nick De Noia, Dr. Jagjit Singh Sehdeva was murdered— but not by Steve. On Tuesday, November 30, 1999, at 9:20 p.m., Dr. Sehdeva was found shot to death in his sprawling Playa del Rey home in the 7300 block of Rindge Avenue. Burglary may have been the motive for the still unsolved crime. The murderers stole a heavy floor safe, dragging it out the front door and leaving deep gouges in the flooring. Sehdeva was 60 years old.

Chapter 11
Chippendales vs. Adonis

The reason for Steve's change of plans about murdering Dr. Sehdeva may have been the advent of new competition for Chippendales. In 1990 Class Promotions formed a rival touring male dance revue called Adonis: Men of Hollywood. The new group included several former Chippendales employees, including choreographer Mike Fullington, emcees Reed Scott (also known as Scot or Schrotel) and Stephen "Steve" White, and dancer Phil Barone. Steve took their change of employment personally and threatened the men who left, especially Barone.

His threats having failed, Steve sought to prevent Adonis from touring Britain, the new troupe's initial focus. He demanded that venues that hosted the Chippendales dancers sign contracts barring other similar groups from performing at the same venue for one year. Such contracts would have severely limited where Adonis could perform. Adonis brought charges of unfair competition against Chippendales to the British Office of Fair Trading, which ruled against Steve and Chippendales.

Steve then scrambled to form several new Chippendales groups in an attempt to tour Europe before the 16-member Adonis troupe set out on its first European tour. Even as he formed the groups in April 1991, Steve demanded that Ray meet him. Yet again Ray did not know if Steve's demand to meet had anything to do with "the De Noia thing," so he agreed to meet on a residential street in Santa Monica.

When Ray arrived he found Steve livid at the effrontery of the Adonis group to have the gall to compete against Chippendales. Steve threatened to kill everyone involved with Adonis. Ray said he wanted no part of any such conspiracy, but Steve threatened that if Ray did not have the choreographer, Mike Fullington, killed he would have Ray murdered.

Used to Steve's threats, Ray told the Chippendales owner that there must be other choreographers Adonis could hire even if Steve had Fullington murdered. Steve said finding a new choreographer would take time and by then his Chippendales shows would have already toured Europe and raked in the lion's share of the profits.

Steve said Fullington was in rehearsal, since Adonis was flying to Canada for a show the following week before starting their European tour. Steve said he would pay whatever it cost to ensure that Fullington never made it to the Great White North. Steve handed Ray an envelope containing cash and Fullington's address in West Hollywood. Ray said it was $2,000, but he habitually claimed he received less money than the FBI later determined he had; the FBI later concluded it was between $7,000 and $8,000.

When Ray pleaded that he didn't even know what Fullington looked like, Steve said Fullington "looked like some faggot dancer" and drove a blue Jeep with zebra-pattern seat covers.

Fearing for his life and worried that Steve might rat him out about the De Noia murder, Ray decided he would have to arrange to murder Fullington. The thought of going to the police never entered his mind. He immediately considered who he could use. The only person Ray knew who could do a murder on such short notice was Louie, so Ray returned to the Lopez duplex in East Los Angeles. To Ray's surprise, he learned that Louie was in Mexico courtesy of the Immigration and Naturalization Service. Ray hadn't known that Louie was an illegal immigrant. The information made the De Noia murder appear even more foolish and risky than Ray had thought at the time.

Louie's older brother, Rubin* was at home. He was taller and thinner than Louie, but looked like his brother and just like Louie, was addicted to heroin. Rubin casually mentioned that his brother had told him all about Ray, his Mafia "connection," and the "little thing" Ray and Louie had pulled off in New York. Ray was shocked. If Louie had done the De Noia job for Rocky, he and Ray would be dead now. The Mafia frowned on hit men talking about contracts, even to their brothers. Ray asked Rubin where that left him, fearing blackmail. Rubin was not thinking extortion. He was thinking about employment. He said whatever Ray wanted done, he could handle it, maybe even better than his little brother.

Ray said Rubin looked like he had been slamming pretty hard. His eyes were red and his hands shook. Ray later remembered saying, "As they say, 'When you're right, you're tight, but when you're dusted, you're busted.'"

Rubin said that being an addict hadn't stopped Ray from using Louie and for a few balloons he would be in better control than Ray. Fearing working with another addict, Ray passed on using Rubin to murder Fullington.

The days passed and Steve again started calling Ray every hour of the day and night. At a loss as to who else to use, several nights later Ray and Rubin Lopez stood between a bush and a reeking garbage dumpster in the back of a parking lot behind a 1930s apartment building in West Hollywood. Known for its gay-friendly, celebrity studded nightlife in the bars, clubs and restaurants lining Melrose Avenue and Sunset Boulevard, West Hollywood was a busy place at night. The alley, however, was quiet. Ray and Rubin intently watched a blue Jeep with zebra-pattern seat covers parked under a carport.

After a long wait, Mike Fullington, carrying a shoulder bag, walked out of the apartment's back door. Ray and Rubin looked around; no one else was in sight. The windows above the parking area were either dark or lit through drawn blinds. Rubin started toward Fullington. Ray followed as Rubin reached into his pocket and started to pull out a .32 automatic Ray had given him. Fullington opened the Jeep's door and tossed his bag onto the back seat. Rubin walked faster as he approached the choreographer. Just as Rubin was about to raise the .32, Ray grabbed his gun hand and whispered, "Not now."

Rubin said it was the perfect time. While they struggled over the .32 and argued in whispers, Fullington started his Jeep, backed out and sped away, unknowingly having just missed dying that warm spring night.

Rubin was furious, but Ray paid him off with $200 and dropped the would-be assassin off at his mother's duplex in East LA.

(Even for all Ray's details, there may have never been such a narrow escape for Mike Fullington. The story of the attempt on Fullington's life in Hollywood is based on interviews with Ray. No other support could be found for it. Ray may have made up the entire incident to enhance his image as Steve's reluctant button man.)

The next day, Ray later said, Steve called to demand to know why Fullington was on his way to Canada. Ray did his best to sound surprised. He explained that he must have missed the choreographer. He swore that he had never seen Fullington or even his Jeep in the apartment parking lot. Ray prepared himself for an argument, but Steve surprised Ray by saying that it was just as well. Ray saw a glimmer of hope that Steve might, as he had with the plan to murder Dr. Sehdeva, cancel the murder contract. Steve, however, did not have cancellation in mind. In order to make the connection to him would be even more difficult to make, Steve wanted Ray's hit man to murder Fullington in Canada.

Steve ordered Ray to meet him at the Hamburger Hamlet in posh Brentwood at six that night so he could give Ray information for the hit. Ray said there was no way he was going to Canada. Steve said he didn't want Ray to pull the trigger, but he definitely wanted Ray to be there to make certain it happened. They met at the restaurant on trendy San Vicente Avenue. Steve gave Ray traveling money and the locations where Adonis would be performing in and around Halifax, Nova Scotia. He offered Ray $25,000 to hire someone to kill Mike Fullington and another $25,000 for the murder of Adonis' creative director, Read Scott.

Ray planned to go to Canada for Steve, but later claimed that he had no intention of killing Fullington or anyone else, so he never called Rubin Lopez. Since he disliked driving, Ray invited his brother-in-law, Billy Barnes, along to do the driving.

William Nelson "Billy" Barnes was born in Summers Point, New Jersey on September 26, 1959, and was one of four children. One of his sisters, Donna Murula, was a waitress in Arizona, while another, Joanna Barnes, lived with their mother in Palms in West Los Angeles and worked as a supervisor at Security Pacific Bank. His third sister, Barbara, was married to Ray.

At the age of seven, Billy's parents separated. In 1977 or 1978 his father committed suicide with a shotgun. Before the suicide, but after the separation, Billy and his mother moved to Palms. His mother was a nurse and provided well for the family, he later recalled. Billy attended three different high schools in West Los Angeles and claimed to have earned his GED while attending night school at Culver City High School. Records show that he received his GED on January 6, 1982, at the age of 22. Billy later said he earned six college credits at the University of California, Los Angeles, six credits at Santa Monica Community College, and nine credits at the University of Maryland, well short of graduating from any of them.

When he was 13, Billy started work at a 7-Eleven at 3450 Overland as a bottle boy. It was the same 7-Eleven that was just a couple of blocks from where Chippendales would later open its doors, and was where Ray found Paul and Jerry, his first would-be arsonists. Billy rose to be a cashier before quitting to clerk at a Vons supermarket in nearby, wealthier Cheviot Hills.

Billy joined the army on March 2, 1982 after having served in the reserves for two years with the 950th Maintenance Company in Van Nuys, California.

Just before he joined the army, on February 19, 1982, Billy married 27-year-old Audrey Carmen Duncan. The marriage ended in divorce in February 1990. They had a son and a daughter who lived with their mother in Cache, Oklahoma. Billy later said he was on good terms with his ex-wife and tried to see his children as often as he could.

Billy was discharged as an administrative specialist from the Army on November 9, 1990. While in and out of the army over a period of eight years, he had received three honorable discharges and one general discharge under honorable conditions. By 1990 he had attained the rank of E5 sergeant, but was discharged as an E3 private, probably due to drug and alcohol problems. He later said he had received numerous decorations and awards, including the Army Achievement Medal, Army Commendation Medal, Overseas Medal, Leadership/Development Medal, and a Service Medal. When he was discharged he was on 10 percent disability due to a bad back, which was caused by a motorcycle accident that happened when he was 17.

By April 1991, the 5′ 9″ Billy was living with Ray and Barbara Colon. In his early thirties and just out of the army, Billy had no job, almost no assets and owed $8,600. He received $83 a month in VA compensation and owed $300 a month in child support.

With nothing to do and no money, Billy agreed to accompany Ray to Canada. Ray told Billy the trip was to look into a potential music job. Even though Steve told Ray that the Adonis show would be in the Halifax area for no more than a week, Ray waited five days before he and Billy flew to MacArthur Airport on Long Island. They rented a car and then drove—not north to Canada—but east to visit Ray's sister in Selden, Long Island. Adonis would have probably already left Halifax by then, but Ray and Billy then spent two weeks at Ray's sister's house, drinking beer and swimming in her pool in the late May sunshine before they finally headed north. Ray's plan was to drive to Halifax and call Steve to tell the club owner that he couldn't find Adonis. Ray knew Steve would make him provide a telephone number Steve could call back to make sure Ray was actually in Halifax. Ray would be in Halifax, just a couple of weeks late. Ray's plan seemed foolproof, but he had not counted on the Canadian border.

When Ray and Billy arrived at the border in the middle of the night, Ray answered all the Canadian border guard's questions, but the guard wanted to inspect their vehicle. Since it was almost 3:30 a.m. and there were only three officers on duty, they could not search the car until 7 a.m., unless Ray paid $100 to have another officer come on duty to conduct the search. Ray declined to pay to have his own car searched. He and Billy checked into a motel in nearby Houlton, Maine, just off I-95. Ray planned to try the border again at 7 a.m., but he and Billy slept in until 10:30. By then Ray had had enough of Canada and headed south.

On April 12, 1991, Ray and Billy stopped at a truck stop in West Enfield, Maine on the Penobscot River, just north of Bangor. Ray called Steve from a pay phone. He told Steve that he had just returned from Canada, but had been unable to find Adonis after a week-long search. Just as Ray had thought, Steve asked for the number Ray was calling from. He gave Steve the number. Then Ray waited and waited for Steve to call back. Nothing. What had happened? Finally Ray realized the telephone did not accept incoming calls.

Ray and Billy drove on and stopped at a gas station with a restaurant. Once again Ray called Steve. This time the phone took incoming calls. The Chippendales founder was enraged. What the hell had Ray been doing? Adonis had already left for England. Steve ordered Ray to return to Los Angeles immediately. Relieved that Fullington was now an ocean away, Ray flew home with Billy.

Back in Los Angeles, Ray met Steve for lunch. Steve said Adonis had been in England for two weeks, but he had already scheduled shows in Britain, so he was a step ahead of them. He also had an Adonis schedule for April 15 to December 21 from a spy he had in the Adonis organization. Ray would know exactly where Adonis was performing from their April 15 date in Newmarket through shows in Brighton, Sheffield, Dorset, Portsmouth, and Wolverhampton, with a dozen other cities in between.

Steve surprised Ray when he said to forget about Fullington. "The prick's got AIDS," Ray remembers Steve saying without a trace of sympathy. Steve didn't think Fullington would live more than a couple of months. Fullington died later in 1991 from complications of HIV/AIDS. Even so, Steve was far from done with murder. He wanted Ray to go to England to find Steve White, who had quit Chippendales about six months before to join Adonis, and Read Scott, Adonis' creative director. Ray asked if Steve wanted two men killed now.

"What's the difference?" Steve asked. "Your man kills one, two; the crime's the same."

Steve said he was not going to allow anyone to "fuck him." Ray said it would be hard to convince his man to kill two people. Steve offered $25,000 a head and, if the hit man killed another ex-Chippendales dancer who now worked for Adonis, Steve would pay $100,000 for all three.

Ray later said that to buy time until he figured out what to do, he sent Billy across the Atlantic to gather information about Adonis. Billy wanted Ray's help to become a police officer, so Ray later said he told Billy that he had been hired to do some low-level industrial espionage about the Adonis group. The trip, Ray told Billy, would be a good test of Billy's investigative skills. On June 12, 1991, Billy landed at Heathrow airport just southwest of London. He spent five days in England, but failed to find Adonis. The itinerary Steve had given Ray was incorrect, although Billy did manage to get an itinerary that showed that Adonis would be performing in Blackpool in a few weeks.

After Billy's return, Ray met Steve again. Ray later said he complained about the inaccurate itinerary to mask his stalling. Steve said his spy had called soon after he thought Ray had left for Britain and told Steve that Adonis had changed some of their performance dates and locations. If Ray had called him, as Steve had told Ray to do, Steve could have given Ray the updated schedule. Ray countered that at least they knew Adonis would be in Blackpool. Steve said to keep the hit man available, but Ray said that keeping the hit man on retainer, so to speak, would cost money. Steve said he had given Ray all the money he was going to get and told him to use his own money, promising to reimburse him after the job was done.

Driving home, Ray later said that he reached a decision. He was not going to do anything more for Steve. He decided to let Steve try and kill him. Steve might be bluffing and, even if he was serious, once he realized Ray was through with him, Steve would probably find someone else to do his dirty work. Steve certainly had enough money to find someone else to do his jobs. Yet again, no thought of going to the police even appeared on the fringes of Ray's mind.

Ray's decision—if indeed he ever made it, and his later behavior seemed to go against such a decision—was not easy to stick with. Within a few days Steve knew Ray was doing nothing to arrange the murder. Just like before, Steve started calling Ray's house 40 times a day. He hung up whenever Barbara or

Billy answered. If Ray answered, Steve cursed and yelled until Ray slammed down the phone.

Ray was out and Billy and Barbara were watching television in the den one evening a few days later when Ray's dogs began to bark. Barbara muted the television and thought she heard a noise upstairs. She asked her brother to go take a look, but he declined, saying it was nothing. Glaring at her brother, Barbara got up and cautiously walked upstairs to the master bedroom. She froze when she saw two men dressed in black and wearing ski masks outside trying to pry the balcony door open. She screamed and dashed back downstairs. She flung open the back door.

"Brut! Buffy! Danger! Danger!" Barbara shouted as her dogs raced into the house and dashed upstairs straight for the balcony doors. The German shepherd mix and Rottweiler barked viciously as they slammed into the glass doors in their attempt to attack the would-be intruders. Billy led the way back upstairs with Barbara close behind. She rushed over to the headboard cabinet to get Ray's .38. Now armed, she ran to the sliding doors in time to see the two men running down the street in full retreat.

Ray had just turned onto his street when a dark utility van careened past, almost sideswiping his car. He arrived home to find Barbara and Billy in a panic. Barbara rushed over and threw her arms around Ray, shaking like a leaf in a gale. He gently took his gun from her and put the safety back on as she stammered out the story of the black-clad men. She wanted to call the police, but Ray already knew who was probably behind the attempted break-in. The last thing Ray wanted was the police digging into his relationship with Steve, so he assured her that he would take care of it. Barbara and Billy were far from convinced.

"They won't dare come back now that they know we have two trained dogs and a gun-toting wife," Ray said.

Barbara managed a smile at his weak joke. Ray persuaded her and Billy not to call the police, although Barbara insisted they install stronger locks and an alarm system. Just as Ray had calmed them down, the phone rang and everyone froze. Ray walked into the kitchen and answered the telephone.

"You're a fucking dead man!" Ray recognized Steve's voice.

Ray yelled that Steve was going to be the dead man if he ever came near his family again. Steve countered that the job had to be done. If it wasn't, their friendship was over and they would be enemies. Steve said there would be no more warnings.

That night Ray lay in bed with his gun on the night stand beside him. He had no way of knowing for certain whether the two men had anything to do with Steve. It might have just been two random burglars. If Steve had hired them to take Ray and his family out, why didn't he just hire them to murder the Adonis leaders?

Whoever the would-be burglars had been, Ray had to get Steve off his back. Gilbert Rivera "Louie" Lopez was in Mexico and even if he was around, Ray was not about to send a heroin-addicted illegal alien to England to commit murder. The authorities would detain him as soon as his sneakers touched Heathrow's tarmac. Ray could have asked one of his crew, but they would be pissed off that Ray hadn't used them from the beginning. Their trust in him would evaporate and they would wonder what else Ray was keeping from them. Worse, they would take charge of the whole operation and God only knew what would happen to Ray and Steve. The way Ray saw it, he was in serious trouble unless he could find someone to do the job, and fast. Ray wracked his mind and finally thought of his old tenant at the Overland Palms, Errol Lynn "Strawberry" Bressler.

In early July 1991, Ray called Strawberry. Ray asked him if he remembered the job they had talked about a few years before, which Strawberry had declined because his running mate had been unavailable. Strawberry remembered. Ray asked if Strawberry was interested in doing another similar job. This time, Ray said, it would be two, not one. Strawberry said he had been laid off for a month, so he needed the money, but he would have to know a lot more before he would commit to anything. He asked where it was supposed to take place. Ray said England, which surprised Strawberry, although he was still interested. He wanted to check with his wife. Ray had no idea what Strawberry told his wife, but Strawberry arrived two days later in Los Angeles from Texas in his black Ford sedan. Since they last met, Strawberry had lost a front tooth, which only increased his redneck appearance.

That night, Ray, Strawberry and Billy ate TV dinners around the kitchen table while Barbara was at work. They discussed the information Billy had gathered in England. It did not amount to much. He had a copy of the Adonis itinerary, a map of London showing the bus stations, and a business card of the hotel at which he had stayed. Adonis was supposed to appear at the Winter Gardens in the seaside resort of Blackpool on the northwest coast of England in late July. In many ways their preparation for the planned murders was laughably amateurish, but even amateurs can kill.

Billy still thought his trip had been related to corporate espionage, at least until Strawberry asked Ray what weapon he should use. Ray later said he ended the conversation and when he was alone with Strawberry warned him never to involve his brother-in-law in what they were about to do. Billy later said that Ray had told him that Ray and Strawberry would be talking about "something," and that Billy should just "go along with whatever he [Ray] was saying."

The next day Ray bought tickets for Strawberry to London and for himself to New York. Ray had decided to go to his sister's house on Long Island, so, he later said, when Strawberry called from England Barbara and Billy would not be involved.

Ray and Strawberry decided on a weapon. A gun was out of the question. It would be detected on the international flight. Poison seemed a good option; small and easy to conceal. The poison of choice: potassium cyanide.

Billy said Ray asked him to deliver $2,500 to an unknown individual, which Billy thought was payment for cyanide. The FBI later discovered that the cash was to repay a loan. Ray appears to have acquired the cyanide well before the conspiracy to use against gophers that were destroying his yard. However he acquired it, Ray had potassium cyanide in his garage.

On July 11, 1991, with Barbara at work and Billy out of the house on an errand, Ray and Strawberry donned rubber gloves. Strawberry insisted on mixing the poison himself, saying, according to Ray, "If I'm the one who's going to use it, then I want to make damn sure it's gonna work."

With Ray alongside, standing over the kitchen sink, Strawberry took a syringe and inserted a mixture of cyanide and water into a Clear Eyes® eye-dropper bottle.

The next day, July 12, with $1,200 from Steve, a map of England, the Adonis itinerary, and the cyanide, Strawberry was ready to go. Ray drove Strawberry, who had dyed his red hair black as a disguise, to LAX to board a Virgin Atlantic flight to London. On the way, they dropped off Strawberry's car at his daughter's house for safekeeping while he was away. Strawberry told Ray he had a friend in London, Jake Smith, with whom he might stay.

On July 13, Ray tried to call Steve to tell him about the plan but couldn't reach him. Ray wired $300 to Strawberry in London via Western Union and then flew to Selden, New York to stay with his sister.

When the job was done, Strawberry was supposed to call Ray and say, "I signed up that draft choice from the south." Ray waited anxiously at his sister's house for the call. The days passed slowly for Ray. He could not stop thinking of all the things that might go wrong. Even so, all he could do was wait.

Finally, on July 21 at about 2:35 p.m., Strawberry called Ray's home in Newhall, California and talked with Billy, who later said he just "went along" with the conversation about a "hit" because Ray had asked him to do so. Strawberry and Billy discussed whether the cyanide should have turned red. Billy said it should have. When Strawberry asked if the cyanide was still good, Billy said that it was. When asked, Billy assured Strawberry that he would have time to walk away before the cyanide took effect. From the conversation it sounded as if Billy was far more involved than he or Ray later claimed.

Minutes after calling Billy, Strawberry called Ray in New York.

"Hey, old buddy! How's it going?"

"You were supposed to call me over a week ago," Ray said. "What happened?"

"It took me a little longer to find them than I thought it would. I didn't want to bother you until I was sure, but I finally got lucky. I'm in Blackpool and I've already seen both guys. I'm just waiting for the right time. Last night I was walking right behind one of them on the pier. I'll probably try and do that guy tomorrow night after the show, but I don't know about this cyanide stuff. Are you sure it's going to work?"

Ray replied that the stuff was "real fermented." He and Strawberry agreed that the target would "probably die right away." Then they both laughed.

"Tomorrow night should be the perfect time to do at least one of the dogs, if you know what I mean," Strawberry said. "But suppose the stuff don't work. It turned red in the bottle after I got here. I'm just wondering if it's still good, that's all."

"You got me. It should be good."

Strawberry then complained about the difficulty of killing both targets at the same time. Ray insisted that both had to be killed.

Ray flew home the next day and later said he thought something wasn't right. Strawberry was far from the swiftest of hit men, but he wasn't stupid enough to discuss murder on an overseas telephone call. Ray tried to convince himself that he was just overreacting, but it was a hard sell, even to himself.

That night, July 22, Strawberry called Ray in Los Angeles. Barbara answered but as soon as she heard it was Strawberry, she handed the telephone to Ray and retreated upstairs with a grimace at her husband's choice of friends.

Strawberry again expressed concern that the cyanide would not work. "I hope you and Billy did your homework on the cyanide."

"You have to watch what you say," Ray warned. They had used code names, such as the Snowman for Steve White, in an attempt to foil any phone taps, but their painfully simple code would do little to fool anyone listening in, unless the listener was in kindergarten.

Strawberry asked if it made any difference if they got an innocent person.

Ray said, "It makes no difference."

Strawberry asked for $200 to be wired to his friend who lived in London. Strawberry said his friend, Dan West, was vacationing in Las Vegas. Ray said he would do his best to send the money.

Strawberry asked if he should "spike the booze" with the cyanide. Ray said no.

"Should I stick him in the neck? The emcee takes a walk near the beach."

"Talk in circles," Ray warned.

"I could stick a knife in the dude."

"Yeah."

Strawberry then asked whether the guy who hired Ray would "screw them" on the pay.

Ray said no, then urged, "Just get it done, will you?"

Strawberry asked if he should hit the targets in the head first, to which Ray agreed. Ray said, using the word 'dog' to refer to one of the targets, "You know, like say you take this, ah, dog that's always shitting on your lawn."

"Yeah."

"You know what I mean? The one that's always taking a stroll by the beach."

"Yeah, right. I gotcha."

"Shit, you can, you could whack him on the back of the head, man. That fuckin' dog gonna go down. Then you could stick him [with the cyanide in a syringe], you know?"

"I gotcha. I gotcha."

Ray said Strawberry could hit "the dog" and crack its skull open. The dog would pass out without any noise.

"I'm not worried about the dude on the beach," Strawberry said. "He's the easy one."

Ray then reminded Strawberry that he was talking about a dog.

The next day, July 23, Billy and Strawberry talked again. Billy suggested that Strawberry put the cyanide in a drink for the victims. Strawberry told Billy that Ray had suggested mixing the cyanide with Draino to make sure it was potent. Billy advised against such an undoubtedly lethal, but probably undrinkable mixture.

Strawberry asked what kind of cyanide they were using, to which Billy, who apparently had become an expert on poisons, replied, "The best."

When Strawberry asked if Billy was sure it would work, Billy replied, "It will work." Then in a whisper added, "Put it in his drink first."

On July 25, Strawberry reported to Ray, "Well, buddy, I did one, and now I'm going after the other."

"Are you serious?" Ray asked, lowering his voice as he stood in the kitchen of his house in Newhall.

"Dead serious. I caught the little dog in the bathroom right after the show. I stuck the you-know-what in his neck, hit him over the head with a brick, then shoved his head in the toilet. He's done, trust me."

"Are you sure?"

"Of course I'm sure. The stuff alone probably did him in."

"That's good. Certain people will be real happy to hear that."

"They'll be a lot more happy after I do the other one. That should happen sometime tonight if things work out like I plan."

"Are you sure you can do the other one? It would be great if you can, but maybe you'd better quit while you're ahead."

"I'll be as careful as hell, but I shouldn't have much of a problem."

"Great. As soon as you're finished get your ass home right away."

Strawberry said he planned to, but wanted to know if Ray had sent the money to his friend in Las Vegas since he didn't have enough money to fly home. Ray promised to send the money that afternoon.

After the call, Ray later said he became increasingly certain that Strawberry had rolled on him. Even Strawberry wasn't dumb enough to talk about murder not once, but twice on the telephone. The clincher was that Ray remembered that Strawberry had said his friend's name was Jake Smith, not Dan West. Ray later said he thought West was probably a cop.

Chapter 12
Arrest

Dan West was not a cop. He was an FBI Special Agent. The FBI would use the money Ray sent West as evidence of a murder conspiracy.

When he came to the conclusion that Strawberry had betrayed him, Ray later said that his first thought was to destroy any incriminating evidence, such as the cyanide in the garage and his digital address book, which contained the contact information for Steve and everyone else involved in the conspiracy. However, after some thought, he decided not to destroy anything. The FBI probably already had him on tape, so there was no point. Even if he told the Feds he had flushed the cyanide down the toilet, they would take his house apart stud by stud searching for it. Ray realized it was all over.

After Strawberry's call, Ray was watching the television show "COPs" on July 25, 1991, in his boxer shorts when he heard vehicles screech to a stop in front of his house. Although he had expected it, he was shocked when he heard pounding on his front door and Barbara let in the FBI agents. Ray rushed to the top of the stairs and looked down into the foyer at Agent Andrew "Andy" J. Stefanek, a 29-year FBI veteran who had been serving in Los Angeles since 1967. Stefanek had thinning brown hair and a short, compact frame. He yelled that they had a warrant to search the house. Agents streamed past Stefanek, securing every room.

Stefanek asked Ray to come downstairs. Ray asked if he could at least put his pants on. Before Stefanek could answer another agent ordered Ray downstairs immediately. Ray said he was going to put on his pants. If they wanted to shoot, so be it.

Barbara and Billy were near panic as the agents systematically searched the house. An agent started on each wall as they slowly and methodically checked everything, so unlike how searches are shown on television. Barbara demanded to know what they were doing in her house. A female agent explained that they had a warrant to search the premises and to please calm down.

Then Ray, fully clothed, came downstairs. An agent ordered Ray to sit beside his wife, but Ray said it was his house and he wanted to stand. He had not wanted to handle it this way, but the agents aroused deep emotions in him which he had not expected. It was his house and they were intruders. Stefanek tried to smooth things over by telling Ray quietly that he should tell them where the cyanide was since they would find it one way or another. Ray told Stefanek to find it himself. While Barbara alternated between crying and yelling at the agents to get out of her house, Ray seethed and the agents continued their search, quietly, efficiently and thoroughly.

Later Stefanek asked Ray if he had any weapons and Ray, somewhat cooled down, said he did. An agent went upstairs to retrieve Ray's guns: a Smith and Wesson Model 39 semi-automatic pistol with a blue-steel barrel and a 9 mm Taurus PT-92 semi-automatic pistol with a blue-steel barrel and a brown hand grip.

Stefanek asked Ray for his phone book. Ray lied and said he didn't keep one. He said he used Barbara's if he needed a number. As Stefanek asked for and took into evidence Barbara's phone book, Ray casually dropped his electronic phone book into a flowerpot near the stereo: a small victory in the defense of his home.

Upstairs, two agents searched Ray's office and found his passport, but nothing else of interest. Two other agents carefully searched the garage and found a jar emblazoned with a skull and crossbones: cyanide.

As Ray sat on the sofa and the agents searched, he smiled. The agents had failed to find the safe in the master bedroom closet that contained $60,000. Ray later claimed that none of the money was from Steve, but that would not have mattered to the FBI. They would have taken every dollar as evidence anyway.

Stefanek and another agent started to interrogate Ray. The other agent told Ray that he was facing at least 15 years in federal prison, if not more. Ray should cooperate to try and save at least a part of his ass, because either way, he was going to prison. Ray said he had been a cop, so he knew all of the scare tactics. The agent's threats didn't scare him. They could only put him in prison, Ray said, but certain people could have him killed. If the agents wanted him to cooperate, he wanted immunity and new identities for him and his family. The agent said he was not about to promise anything.

Stefanek took over and told Ray that they were not going to arrest him that night, but they would arrest him at some point. It might be in a week, a month or a few months, but it was going to happen. In the meantime, Stefanek wanted Ray to think about what they had said and make sure he understood that he was not going to walk away from this thing. Stefanek was a professional who, Ray sensed, did not say something unless he knew it was true. Stefanek scared Ray.

After four hours, as the agents prepared to leave, Ray noticed that although they had taken the serial numbers off his guns and inspected his passport, they had left the guns and passport on his dining room table. Why didn't they seize them as evidence? They couldn't know that the guns had not been used in the De Noia murder or that he would not flee the country the second the door closed behind the last agent.

As Ray followed the agents to the front door, Stefanek stepped aside and let the others file out. Once alone, Stefanek suggested that Ray think about what he had said. He also warned Ray not to let anyone else know that they had been there or try to warn anyone else.

After the agents left, Barbara demanded to know what was going on. Ray told her that he had got into some trouble, but that he could handle it. Barbara did not believe him, but Ray refused to explain. She did not need to know, for it would only put her in even more potential danger.

The next day, after reassuring Barbara once again, Ray drove to Woodland Hills in the San Fernando Valley to see two attorney friends from his days in the record business. Ray explained his situation. Although both were experienced attorneys, they were unfamiliar with federal criminal laws, since they practiced primarily business law in the state system. Even so, both agreed to help Ray until he was able to find a more suitable attorney. On Ray's behalf they would approach the Assistant US Attorney working the case and try to negotiate a deal. To familiarize themselves with the case, the attorneys had Ray make a tape of him telling everything that had happened, beginning with when he first met Steve and ending when the FBI left his house the day before. Lawyer-client privilege would see to it that the tape would never be heard by anyone except his two attorneys.

The US Attorney soon faxed Ray's attorneys an offer, although given the strength of the government's case, it was more of an ultimatum than an offer. For his complete cooperation the government would give Ray no guarantees, other than that his cooperation would be noted. Ray's attorneys thought the offer was laughable and advised Ray to tell the US Attorney nothing.

Even without Ray's cooperation, the FBI was rapidly building a case against him. Ray had been right when he once told Steve that they only had to worry if the FBI got involved. Unbeknownst to Ray, Lynn "Strawberry" Bressler had not even gone to Blackpool. He had stayed in his hotel room near Heathrow and had second thoughts. The second thoughts had led to third and fourth thoughts, none of which included murder. Strawberry dumped the cyanide in the Clear Eyes bottle down the drain and then called the Drug Enforcement Agency's office in Miami and tracked down Agent Nick Hicks,* with whom he had worked as a paid informant. At first Hicks seemed uninterested, but his interest level skyrocketed as soon as Strawberry mentioned a possible mob-funded hit. Strawberry told Hicks the whole story from Ray's first telephone call to his trip to London. Strawberry said he went to England thinking that it was all a joke. Strawberry wasn't stupid. He knew the FBI would doubt his story, especially his level of involvement. The would-be hit man knew he would need his old DEA contact, Hicks, to smooth things over with the FBI for him.

Hicks believed Strawberry's story enough to contact the FBI Field Office, for some reason, in Las Vegas. At first, the FBI was suspicious, believing "that said individual was destitute and in need for [sic] money." Even so, the FBI sent Strawberry a ticket from London to Las Vegas and, when he arrived, debriefed him at their office in the gambling Mecca. He told them everything he knew. When Strawberry called Ray as if he was calling from England, the FBI taped every damning word.

Convinced they were onto a Mafia hit, the FBI put Dale Mitchell* (probably Charlie Parsons), the special agent in charge of the LA Organized Crime Division, in command of the operation and placed Strawberry under witness protection for safe keeping. They had ample evidence against Ray, but Strawberry said Ray was not the paymaster behind the conspiracy. The FBI wanted the man behind the plot.

First, however, they made sure the targets of the conspiracy were safe. The day before the FBI searched Ray's house (July 24, 1991), Detective Superintendent Graham Gooch, Criminal Investigatory Department, Lancashire Constabulary, informed Adonis' Australian business manager, Steve White, whose family was with him in Blackpool, that Ray Colon had hired someone to travel to England to kill him and Read Scott, whose wife and newborn son were at home in Dallas. The murderer, Gooch said, would probably attempt to poison them. White said there was only one person who could be responsible: Steve Banerjee. White had formerly worked for Banerjee promoting the Chippendales dance troupe in Australia. The British police placed the Adonis members in protective custody.

After obtaining a warrant for Ray's phone records, the FBI discovered that Ray had called Steve Banerjee many times. Stefanek, who had worked the De Noia case, had a long-shot hunch that, besides the murder conspiracy in England, Ray might also be involved in the New York murder. On July 30 Stefanek called Ray to tell him they were on their way over with a search warrant for one of his guns. He reassured Ray that they were not coming to arrest him. Ray was grateful that Stefanek called.

At the door, Stefanek handed Ray a warrant for his Smith and Wesson Model 39 semi-automatic handgun. Stefanek also handed Ray an unpleasant surprise: a court order instructing Ray to open his safe. Ray had thought that the agents had missed the safe when they searched his house. He was wrong.

With new respect for the FBI, Ray led the way upstairs to his bedroom closet where he opened the floor safe, which was hidden under Barbara's shoes and the carpet. Stefanek emptied the safe of various folders, papers and a stack of money, marking it all as evidence.

Stefanek took Ray's 9 mm handgun and his passport. At the dining room table Stefanek wrote Ray a receipt for the gun, the passport and the money, which Stefanek carefully counted. Even though he was angry that the FBI was confiscating his money, Ray could not tell them that the money had nothing to do with the attempted murders in Blackpool. It was money from a drug dealer Ray and Leon Defina had ripped off. In poetic justice, Ray never saw the money again.

After attempting once more without success to convince Ray to cooperate, Stefanek prepared to leave. Ray told Stefanek, "If and when you decide to arrest me, do me a favor and give me a call. I'd rather turn myself in than go through the embarrassment of having my wife and neighbors see me getting arrested."

Stefanek promised he would try to do so.

The FBI tested Ray's 9 mm gun. It was not the weapon that had fired the bullet that killed Nicholas "Nick" De Noia.

As the days passed Ray tried to live a normal life, but he knew the FBI was watching him like a cat stalking a chickadee. The tension ate at him. He wished they would just arrest him and end it. One afternoon as he was leaving a shopping center in Santa Clarita, he saw a white minivan parked a few spaces from his Toyota. He recognized the van as one that he had seen twice before during his errands that day. Frustrated, Ray stopped at the driver's door as he walked past the minivan. Two men in work clothes sat inside. Ray reached into the van and grabbed a walkie-talkie from the seat between the men. He keyed it and had it up to his mouth before the men could react.

"In case you're wondering, I'm on my way home now," Ray said and tossed the walkie-talkie back into the van.

As Ray stalked back to his car, the startled driver leaned out and yelled, "What's your problem?"

Ray cursed the driver, got into his car and drove off having let off a little of his frustration at what he thought was an FBI surveillance team.

The walkie-talkie prank, however, did not alleviate Ray's main problem: he had no cash. His lawyers needed money and the only person he thought might be able to help him was Steve Banerjee. So, a few days later at a pay telephone on Ventura Boulevard at the corner of White Oak in Van Nuys, Ray called Steve, using the code name Babe.

Steve was shocked that Ray was still in Los Angeles. He was supposed to be in England. Ray explained that something had gone seriously wrong. They had to meet. Steve asked why, but Ray didn't want to say what had happened over the telephone. Steve was booked on a flight to Europe that evening, so he said he didn't have time to meet and, more importantly, he didn't even want to talk to Ray until the job was done. Ray was adamant. He threatened to burst into Steve's office again. Realizing Ray was serious, Steve relented and told Ray to come over, but to make it quick, since he had to leave by 4:30 for his flight.

Ray rushed to his car to get to the Chippendales' office before Steve left, but Ray could not find the office. Steve had moved his office since Ray last visited Steve's office. After a frantic call for directions, Ray finally arrived at the new office. Even though the delay had been his fault for not giving Ray the new address, Steve was seething, at least until Ray sat in a chair and said the crucial word, "Busted."

Steve stopped sorting the papers he had been organizing for his trip. Ray repeated that he had been busted and added that he needed money for an attorney. Steve asked who had busted him. Ray said the Feds had come to his house and then, realizing the office might be bugged, cryptically added that the Feds knew about Adonis.

Steve did not believe him. If it was true, he asked, why was Ray free? Steve said he was not about to be played for a sucker again. He was not going to give his old friend another dime.

Ray could not believe Steve wouldn't help him after all he had done, and tried to do, for the Chippendales owner. Ray said he was within spitting distance of being arrested. Steve seemed to think Ray was just trying to get out of finishing the Adonis job. The club owner said he would be back from his Europe in a week and if Ray was arrested in the meantime, Steve would help him then.

Announcing that he was going to be late for his plane, Steve picked up his briefcase and strode toward the door. Holding the door open, Steve waited as Ray debated what to do. He would have liked to have snapped Steve's neck, but that wouldn't have solved anything. Ray stalked past Steve and they walked out to Steve's car in silence.

Steve wanted to finish the conversation when he returned from Europe, but Ray said he would probably be in prison by then. Steve got into his Mercedes and drove away, leaving Ray standing in the parking lot alone and just as broke as before he met Steve.

Soon after, on August 1 or 2 (court documents disagree), 1991, Ray, Barbara and Billy were eating pizza and watching television when someone hammered on the front door. Billy opened it, only to be shoved back by FBI agents, guns drawn, who stormed into the house. Mitchell, the agent in charge, grabbed Billy and roughly pushed him back into the den. The FBI had warrants to arrest Raymond "Ray" Augustine "Angel" Colon and his brother-in-law, William "Billy" Nelson Barnes, Jr.

Four agents seized Ray and Billy. Barbara, hysterical, rose from the sofa to follow her husband as they led him away. An agent shoved her back onto the sofa. Ray cursed the agent and threatened to smash his face in. Mitchell told Ray to shut up. Ray swore at him too. A female agent stepped between Ray and Mitchell to defuse the situation. Barbara was sobbing. As he was led outside, Ray later said he looked back at Barbara and felt his heart break at the pain he had caused her. He yelled that everything would be alright and that he loved her.

On vacation, Stefanek was unaware of the plan to arrest Ray. When Stefanek returned, Mitchell said he had judged that Ray was a flight risk. Stefanek disagreed. If Ray was going to run, he would have fled the minute they left his house after the first search. Stefanek believed that Mitchell had ruined any chance of convincing Ray to cooperate. Mitchell argued that they didn't need Ray's cooperation. They had him cold. Stefanek knew that without Ray's help, they would have to spend a few hundred needless man-hours trying to discover the identity of the person who had hired Ray.

The FBI took Ray and Billy in separate cars to the Metropolitan Detention Center (MDC), where federal prisoners were held. In downtown Los Angeles, the MDC was right beside the 101 freeway. The sounds of the busy freeway barely seeped through the narrow slits that passed for windows in the blockish, multi-story concrete structure. The gray, ominous building looked like a mammoth bunker from World War II. Barbed wire ran atop four protruding balcony areas that stretched between the building's two wings. Passersby on the street were told to move along if they stopped to sit on the low concrete wall that bordered the property. The building looked about as welcoming as a castle with its portcullis down and its drawbridge up.

Ray was housed on the 6th floor of the detention center in 6 Block South. Billy was held in another cell block. Getting caught had never entered Ray's mind and only now that he had been caught did he finally think that he should never have done anything illegal. In an extreme case of self-deception or an attempt to paint himself in a better light, Ray later said he thought of himself as "100% honest." He even claimed that the Palm Springs Police Department wanted him back as a reservist because he was "the best that the police department had." Ray later told a probation officer he was embarrassed because he had counseled kids, and given anti-drug and anti-crime lectures at local schools. He said, "I feel horrible and devastated. I really feel like a coward. I don't know what to say....I became everything I hated....I was an officer for voting, an Elks member....It's horrible. I can't believe it. I just can't believe it. My wife, too—I just don't know what to do."

Ray later explained to whoever would listen that during all his years as Steve's button man, he did not go to the police because he believed that Steve had organized crime connections. "Even if I had gone to the cops, I would have [had] to be protected. There is no way that the individual [Steve] would let me go, knowing the information that I do." Ray said he did not think the authorities could protect him. He explained that when he had agreed to commit the crimes, he had been "thinking of the lives of his family and his wife." He said that even though the individual who had ordered the murders never mentioned killing his wife, he was concerned because he knew that the individual had wanted to kill other people who were younger than Ray's wife. Speaking about the conspiracy to murder the Adonis members, Ray said, "I think about what if it had happened. In the true sense of the word, Strawberry did me a favor. It's a relief, I can breathe....I let my family and myself down." In his interviews with the authorities, he never said anything about the victims of his crimes or their families.

Chapter 13
Court

On August 4, 1991 in Los Angeles, Ray was arraigned in Federal Court. Ray told the judge that he did not have an attorney and requested that the court appoint one for him, at least until he could retain one himself. US Attorney Barbara E. Gilliland, tall with brown hair, argued that Ray was more than financially able to retain counsel and should not be allowed to further burden the People by making them pay for his defense.

"Better me than some damn illegal alien!" Ray blurted out.

A marshal ordered Ray to shut up.

Gilliland argued that Ray should not be allowed to claim "pauper" status since he lived in a $250,000 house, owned several vehicles, and Ray and Barbara, an RN, earned a comfortable living. Although substantial amounts of money had been found in his home, Ray argued that he was broke. If there had been any cash in his house, he argued, the government had seized it, while the bank held the mortgage on his house and the pink slips on his cars. The judge agreed with Ray, although he warned Ray that if it was later discovered that Ray had the assets to retain counsel, he would lose the services of the court-appointed attorney and would have to reimburse the state for the cost of the attorney up to that point. The bailiff then read the charges: conspiracy to commit murder and use of interstate commerce facilities in the commission of a murder-for-hire. Ray pled not guilty.

Ray was assigned Gail Stevenson,* a tough, smart and experienced attorney. Ray's only regret was that she only worked bail hearings, since she spent most of her time with her family, especially her two young children. Ray believed that if she had been his attorney throughout his case, there would have been a good chance that the outcome would have been very different.

At his bail hearing the next day, Stevenson stood with Ray, while three US Attorney's, including Gilliland and Sally L. Meloch, a brunette with shoulder-length hair that framed her bespectacled, pretty face, stood at the prosecution table. Stevenson asked that the courtroom be cleared, except for Ray's wife, mother and several FBI agents. Stevenson anticipated that during the hearing it would be disclosed that Ray had once been a police officer. She did not want other inmates at MDC learning that fact, since his life would then be in jeopardy. Furthermore, any discussion about Ray's cooperation might also touch on matters that would be best kept secret from Ray's co-conspirators. The judge agreed.

With the courtroom cleared, Gilliland presented the government's case. She established that the FBI had found 46 grams of potassium cyanide in Ray's garage. Only 200 milligrams would kill one person. Therefore, Ray had enough cyanide to kill 2,300 people. Ray wondered how many gophers 46 grams would kill, since he had never defeated the voracious beasts no matter how much poison he had used.

Stevenson countered that the FBI had been unable to find any of the cyanide that had been taken to England because, they said, Strawberry had poured it down the sink at St. Bernard's Guest House in Hounslow, Middlesex, just east of Heathrow Airport. Therefore, there was no evidence that the cyanide in Ray's garage had ever been taken to London by anyone, let alone by Strawberry to murder the Adonis members. Lynn "Strawberry" Bressler then testified that Ray and Billy Barnes had mixed the poison, even though Ray, probably trying to protect his brother-in-law, had said that Billy had not been involved with the cyanide. The key to the government's case were the FBI tapes of Strawberry's calls to Ray, which showed that on the orders of a third party, Ray had given instructions to Strawberry to murder two people. Stevenson countered that Ray's passport contained no evidence that he had ever been to England.

Stevenson then argued for bail. The FBI agents had told Ray during the initial search of his house that they had a strong case against him, that he would be arrested and that he would serve a long sentence, yet he had not fled. They had left Ray his passport. He had even requested that if they wanted to arrest him, he would prefer to surrender to the authorities. Therefore, she argued, he was not a flight risk. On the issue of Ray being a threat to the community, the FBI had left Ray in possession of firearms after their initial search of his house. If he was such a threat, she asked rhetorically, why had the FBI left guns in his possession?

Opposing bail, Gilliland argued that Ray was a danger to the community in general and to certain individuals specifically. Ray was responsible for planning an attempted double homicide. Ray hired Strawberry, gave him $1,500, dispatched him to London, provided the names of the individuals to kill, and instructed Strawberry on the manner in which he was to commit the murder. Ray also gave Strawberry the cyanide, which was found in Ray's garage where the informant, Strawberry, told the FBI it would be found. Ray owned firearms that were, in and of themselves, dangerous. The government did not know if the contract was still out on the targets and if Ray was still involved in the conspiracy. Therefore, Ray was a danger to the intended victims in the case who were still alive. Gilliland argued that the judge should not let a person with such a lack of moral standards and respect for human life back out onto the streets.

The judge asked the key question, "If the government was, and is, so concerned and has such a belief that this gentleman may be a danger to the community, how do you reconcile that with the fact that from July 25, after the initial search of his house, until his arrest on August 1, he was allowed to remain free?"

Gilliland said the government had been continuing its investigation, confirming their informant's story, and negotiating with Ray's attorney. It was only after the government decided that Ray was not going to cooperate that they arrested him.

The judge asked, "Whether he intended to cooperate or not, wouldn't he still be a danger?"

Gilliland said that no matter what transpired in those few days, the fact remained that Ray was a danger to the community and especially to certain individuals who had been the target of the murder conspiracy.

"The government," Stevenson argued, "if it truly believed that the victims identified in the complaint were in imminent danger of being murdered, had probable cause to swear out a complaint and have Mr. Colon arrested at once. They chose not to do that." She argued that Ray was a long-term resident of Southern California, had a long, stable marriage, and a significant asset in his home, which had more than sufficient equity to secure a bond set by the court.

The judge granted bail. Ray would post an appearance bond of $100,000 with a cash deposit of 10 percent. Gilliland requested that Ray be ordered to remain at home and wear an electronic monitoring device to ensure he did so, and not be allowed to speak with his co-defendant, Billy Barnes. The judge granted all of Gilliland's requests. Relieved, Ray looked forward to going home. His bail victory, however, was short-lived. Within a few days, Gilliland appealed the decision and bail was denied.

After the second bail hearing, Barbara came to see Ray in the first-floor visiting room at MDC. Ray put up a brave front, saying that it would all work out, but Barbara said she knew he would be going to prison for a long time. The government lawyers had warned her not to put their house up for bail because, they said, Ray would run if he was released on bail. Barbara said she knew he wouldn't run, but she had been shaken by all the awful things the prosecution had said about Ray in court. She could not believe they were talking about her husband. Ray knew that most of what had been said was true, but he could not explain it to Barbara because he did not understand why he had done such evil acts. Barbara was also upset because Ray's arrest had scuttled their plan to adopt Ray's 14-month-old nephew, who had been living with them.

After Barbara left, Ray met with his court-appointed lawyers, David S. McLane and Lupe Martinez, in one of the soundproof attorney rooms beside the MDC visiting area. McLane was in his early thirties and had been admitted to the bar in 1986 after earning his law degree from UCLA. He was well dressed and articulate. Martinez, about forty, wore glasses and had thinning hair. Martinez had been admitted to the bar in 1971 after graduating, like McLane, from UCLA. Ray wondered why he had been assigned two lawyers. Martinez explained that at the moment the case was one of the most important in the Federal Court.

McLane advised Ray not to discuss his case with anyone, including his wife, and especially not with any other inmates. Judge William J. Rea would hear the case. McLane believed Rea was pro-government but was not the worst judge Ray could have drawn. Martinez said they would request bail again, but it was unlikely Rea would reverse the already appealed bail decision. The new lawyers needed all the facts, so Ray once again told his story from the day he first met Steve.

In court, Ray found that Judge Rea was an older, large-framed man with gray hair. No one, including Ray, was surprised when Rea sustained the bail ruling. Ray would remain in the MDC.

As they prepared for trial, Ray's attorneys fought hard for him. Arguing that certain information would put their confidential informant, Strawberry, at risk, the Feds refused to give McLane and Martinez discovery information in a timely manner or refused to provide it at all. Even so, McLane and Martinez did win some small victories. Strawberry's wife, Tammy, complained that Barbara had been calling and harassing her. An FBI agent called Barbara and threatened her with jail on an obstruction of justice charge. Ray's lawyers used telephone records to prove that Barbara had never called Tammy. The judge ordered the FBI agent to apologize to Barbara. It was one of Ray's few legal victories.

The court schedule was grueling. Every few days guards woke Ray and any other prisoners due to appear in court that day at 2:30 a.m. The guards searched the inmates, gave them civilian clothes, and then took them across the street to court. The long, emotional days wore Ray down mentally and physically, which made it hard to follow the court proceedings, let alone fully participate in his own defense.

Barbara was facing her own problems at home. Their neighbors had read about Ray's arrest and his crimes in the newspaper and made it clear that Barbara was unwelcome. One night local boys toilet papered their house. Worse, some of the neighborhood boys threw lawn darts into their yard. Luckily, none hit the Colon's dogs. A few of Ray's so-called friends called Barbara or came by the house, but not to offer support; they asked her out. Ray couldn't believe it. One friend even told Barbara that Ray had pursued numerous affairs. The friend said that he felt it was his duty to tell her. Barbara slapped his face, threw him out and told him she would tell Ray what had happened. Just like Steve, who had garnered an aura of fear, Ray was also now seen as someone to fear; the "friend" promptly moved to Mississippi.

Chapter 14
Rocky

Ray was in the common area of 6 South watching a game of checkers when the buzzer rang. A guard opened the door and Mafia boss Rocky Delamo strode in carrying his bedding. Ray's heart dropped through the concrete floor. Had Rocky been sent to kill him? Panicked, Ray started toward a guard for protection. Then he stopped, not wanting to believe his own worst fears.

Rocky had not yet seen Ray. A guard checked the Mafiosi in and assigned him a cell. Ray knew he could not hide from his former boss for long in the limited confines of 6 South. He just had to wait for Rocky to make his move. Ray prayed he was wrong about why his former mentor was in the MDC. Rocky finally spotted Ray. Rocky smiled and walked over to embrace Ray, kissing him on each cheek even as Ray trembled from fear. Ray blurted out that he couldn't believe Rocky was in the MDC. The Mafia boss was equally surprised to see Ray. He hadn't heard that Ray had been arrested. Rocky said he would find his cell and then they could catch up over coffee. Ray begged off, saying he had a few things to do before lock down at 9 p.m. He promised to see Rocky in the morning. Disappointed, Rocky asked if Ray was alright. Ray said he was fine, just tired after a long day in court.

The next morning Rocky sat on an inverted trashcan smoking a cigarette on the rec deck. Other inmates sat around him, talking and smoking, glad for a chance to see the sky. When Ray, carrying a cup of coffee, entered the rec deck, Rocky waved him over. Ray hesitated but, realizing it was unavoidable, walked over and sat on an overturned can beside his former boss.

They commiserated over the hard bunks, which did Rocky's bad back no good and only made Ray's polycystic kidneys more painful. As they made small talk, Ray tried to figure out if Steve had paid Rocky to take him out in exchange for a piece of the Chippendales action. Rocky was a friend, but friendship only went so far when money was involved.

Ray stretched and, sipping his coffee, said he had to go. Rocky blew up, asking why Ray couldn't sit and visit with an old friend for more than five minutes? Ray, his heart thumping in his chest like a kettledrum, said he just had a few phone calls to make and walked away.

A few days later, as Ray read a paperback on his bunk alone in his cell, Rocky strode in. Ray managed a weak smile, but his voice faltered as he greeted his old boss. Rocky ordered Ray to come and have a cigarette so they could talk. Ray didn't move. Rocky grabbed Ray's book, tossed it aside and took his former soldier's arm, dragging Ray off his bunk and out the door. Ray debated whether to break free and run to a guard for protection, but Rocky's hand was like a vice on his arm. Ray looked for a guard. A few guards stood around the area, but they seemed far too far away. Rocky could stab him in an instant.

Rocky wanted to know why Ray had been avoiding him. At first Ray was hesitant. He wanted to know why Rocky was in the MDC. A guy could not just walk into a federal prison whenever he wanted, but there were ways to guarantee that you would be housed in a certain block if you knew the system, and the Mafia knew the system. Rocky said that about a year before he and an East Coast wiseguy were having lunch at a restaurant in Woodland Hills. Unbeknownst to them, the FBI was watching the wiseguy and thought that he and Rocky were setting up a score. The Feds waited almost a year before they decided the pair were only having lunch, but they popped Rocky anyway for associating with a felon, a violation of his parole. He was given six months for his lunch lapse.

Ray told Rocky about being a police officer. Rocky surprised Ray by embracing him. Rocky said he had known that Ray had been a cop, but that it didn't matter, since Ray had never rolled on Rocky or any of his crew.

Their conversation turned to Chippendales. After hearing about Ray's various crimes for Steve, Rocky was in a rage. He said the first thing Steve should have made certain was that Ray's wife and family were taken care of, and made damn sure "they didn't need for nothing." Then Steve should have arranged for Ray to have the best lawyer in town. Instead, Steve let Ray rot in jail.

Ray thought that since Steve hadn't helped him, he would probably try and have him whacked. Rocky was sure that if Steve could find someone to kill Ray, he would do it. Rocky, however, didn't think Steve had the juice to have anyone whacked by the Mafia. Even so, with Steve's money, Ray was sure the club owner could find someone to do it, with or without his connected friend.

Rocky said he would find out the identity of Steve's connected friend and whether he was even a Mafiosi. Rocky would pass a note to his wife, who was visiting that day, and she would pass it on to his crew. A few days later Rocky had his answer. Rocky said the Mafiosi Steve knew was an old wiseguy. For lack of a better word, he was retired. Rocky doubted if the retiree was involved in anything, let alone having Ray whacked. The load on Ray's shoulders lightened considerably, but not entirely; Steve could hire someone else to take Ray out. Rocky disagreed. He believed Steve was waiting to see what Ray did first.

Rocky wanted Ray to reach out to Steve. "Eventually," Rocky said, "Steve's going to have to deal with you."

His dejection clouding his judgment, Ray couldn't see why Steve would ever talk to him.

Rocky said that if Steve didn't talk to Ray, then Ray would roll on him. Rocky broke into a broad, malevolent grin and said Ray was going to roll on Steve anyway, but Steve wasn't going to know that until it was too late.

Ray looked up at Rocky, dumbfounded. He asked why Rocky, of all people, was telling him to roll on somebody.

"What are you talking about!" Rocky roared, shocked by Ray's attitude. "The guy's some schmuck from fucking India, who's out there right now enjoying the free world while you're in here rotting for him and he could care less. Listen to me. You'd be fucking crazy to do time for that piece of shit after he turned his back on you. Besides, he's not Italian, so fuck him."

"Neither am I."

Rocky took hold of Ray's cheeks and kissed Ray on the forehead. "Ah, but you're my boy! Besides, there's a little Italian rolling around in you somewhere."

Ray still did not understand why Rocky was advising him to roll on Steve. There had to be something in it for Rocky. Smiling an evil grin, Rocky admitted that he planned to bleed some cash from Steve.

Rocky ordered Ray to start making some noise. Ray started calling Steve's office every day, but it wasn't easy. Inmates could only make collect calls, so Ray had to pay an inmate who had a three-way line at his home via which he connected Ray to the Chippendale's office. When Ray got through, the secretary would either say Steve was out or was unavailable. Ray also started writing letters to Steve. Ray wrote that he was not going to roll on Steve, but needed money to pay his attorneys. Afraid that his mail would be opened and read by the authorities, Ray paid other inmates to have their visiting relatives deliver sealed envelopes to Steve.

Ray's frustration increased as Steve continued to avoid answering the phone and never wrote back. The hope Ray had gained by Rocky taking control of things evaporated. He was in the same place he had been before Rocky arrived at the MDC. Worse, Ray's kidneys were deteriorating. The prison doctors, Ray said, were "a joke" and just told him to take it easy. The pain increased.

After weeks of futile attempts to contact Steve, Rocky decided he would have one of his crew pay Steve a little visit after Ray had filled him in on all the details of the arsons, the De Noia hit and the attempted Adonis murders. The crew member would tell Steve that Ray was one of Rocky's crew and that they had made the "De Noia thing" happen. The crew member would say that Steve was going to pay big time for letting Ray rot in jail. Rocky's plan was to squeeze at least $500,000 out of the Chippendales mogul. Before Rocky could dispatch his crew member, however, his attorney told Rocky that he had arranged for Rocky to serve the last four months of his sentence at a camp. Rocky decided to see Steve himself, to make sure it was done right. He told Ray to wait until he got out.

Rocky was not going to let Ray languish while the Mafia engineered the draining of a few hundred grand from Steve's bank account. Rocky came to Ray's cell just before his transfer with the resume of James "Jim" D. Henderson. Henderson had graduated from Arizona State's law school in 1972 and until 1987 had been a Special Attorney in the Organized Crime and Racketeering Section of the US Department of Justice. He had worked as a Prosecutor on the Chicago Organized Crime Strike Force and prosecuted top Mafiosi, including Tony "The Ant" Spilotro, an enforcer for the Chicago outfit, and "Mad Sam" DeStefano, one of Chicago's most notorious loan sharks and killers, who murdered his brother. Henderson then headed the Los Angeles Organized Crime Strike Force. He flipped acting boss Jimmy Frattiano and Mafia Enforcer Tony "The Animal" Fiato, which led to the conviction of the Don, Rocky and half the LA family.

Ray was shocked that Rocky wanted a government lawyer to represent him, let alone one who had helped put Rocky away. Rocky said Henderson was the best there was and now worked as a defense attorney. In a twist, after he left government service, Henderson helped LA Family Capo Louie "Little Man" Caruso escape a long prison term.

Ray disliked the idea of changing attorneys midstream, but he trusted Rocky. Ray contacted Henderson. A few days later Ray met his new lawyer in one of the MDC's client-attorney rooms. Henderson was a muscular, well–dressed Irishman who looked more like a linebacker than a bookish attorney. He was intimidating and Ray hesitated to even enter the same room with him. Henderson asked who had recommended him.

"I'd rather not say since it was you who put him in jail," Ray remembered saying. "But he said you were a damn fine attorney."

Henderson grinned. "Coming from someone I put away, I'd say that's a damn fine compliment."

Years later, Henderson remembered Ray as "Sort of a low-key, friendly kind of guy. You'd never guess he was involved in any of that kind of [criminal] stuff. Not a big, tough hoodlum type." When asked if he thought Ray may have been involved with the Mafia, Henderson said, if true, such a thing would "surprise" him.

Once again Ray told the story of his relationship with Steve from their first, chance meeting at Destiny II up until his arrest. Henderson paid close attention and took notes, asking clarifying questions and making sure he understood every event. It took three hours, but by the end Henderson agreed to take the case, but with no guarantees. Henderson said that unless Ray was willing to give the government something worth more than himself, such as the owner of Chippendales and the solution to an unsolved murder, he had better plan for a long courtroom fight, which might very well end in prison time. Ray remembers Henderson's fee as $100,000. Henderson remembers $40,000 or $50,000, but he worked for a large law firm and was only tangentially involved with billing.

Whatever the true amount, the fee staggered Ray. He had a few dollars stashed away, but nowhere near $50,000, let alone $100,000. Henderson suggested getting the money from Steve, stressing that it was not a crime for Steve to help Ray financially. Steve would just be helping a friend.

Ray returned to making his daily telephone calls and writing letters to Steve. A few days after Rocky was shipped out, Steve finally took one of Ray's calls. Carefully choosing his words so as not to blow what might be his only chance, Ray told Steve not to worry. Ray wanted Steve to be secure in the belief that he would not incriminate the Chippendales owner. Ray explained that he needed a good lawyer to help him avoid prison. He explained it was not illegal for someone to loan money to a friend to pay legal fees. Then Ray asked for the money. Ray suggested that Steve take the money to Barbara, hoping such a delivery route would assuage the businessman's fear about giving Ray money directly. Steve said he would think about it.

A few days later, as Barbara talked to Ray on the telephone, she began to cry. She hoped he wasn't mad, she said, but she hadn't meant to do it. Ray didn't know what she was talking about, but he finally got the story out of her. Steve appeared at St. John's Hospital, where Barbara worked, and wanted to give her $70,000 in a brown paper bag. Steve said he was giving it to Ray to defend him on a drug charge. Barbara knew Steve was lying about the charge, so she refused to take the money. Ray told her it was alright. He wasn't mad at her. Although it wouldn't have been illegal for her to accept the money, he told her he would have Steve deliver it to someone else.

Ray hung up and screamed in frustration, attracting the attention of every inmate and guard in 6 South. He rushed back to his cell to write Steve a letter before the Chippendales owner panicked and Ray lost any hope of ever getting enough money to pay Henderson. Ray told Steve to send the money to Martin "Marty" Bress, who owned a nightclub in West Los Angeles called D.B. Coopers. Steve knew Marty so the Chippendales owner would be more likely to believe that Marty wasn't an FBI informant. Ray then called Marty, an old friend, and told him the situation. They had often held cash for each other. Marty agreed to help.

Ray needed the money now worse than ever. To support Barbara, he had called in all the money he had loaned out on the street. There was no more. Steve was his last hope. Ray feared that if he got 15 years in prison he would lose Barbara, his house, his cars, everything. He had to get the money to pay Henderson to avoid a long prison sentence.

A few days later, Steve drove up Motor Avenue, turned left on Woodbine, and parked near D.B. Coopers. The single-story bar was dark. It was named after the man responsible for the only unsolved airplane hijacking in US history. In 1971, a hijacker, whose name on his ticket was D.B. Cooper, took $200,000 in ransom for a hijacked airliner before parachuting into the dense forests of Oregon, never to be seen again.

After watching the bar for several hours, Steve was satisfied it was not a setup. He had a courier deliver $70,000 to D.B. Cooper's on November 20, 1991. Ray almost fainted when Marty told him he had the money. Ray told Marty to take $40,000 to Henderson's office immediately. Ray's defense was about to go into high gear. Steve sent another $20,000 in January 1992 and a further $74,700 on March 26, 1992.

The cash arrived at Henderson's office in brown paper bags. Henderson later said, "Ultimately we figured out it did come from Steve. Hush money, which Ray used to pay for his lawyer, who then advised him to roll on Steve. It's the way of the world."

Chapter 15
Insurance Mafia Style

Ray was always worried that another MDC inmate would recognize him as an ex-police officer. Luckily only one inmate ever did and he kept his mouth shut. As it turned out, Ray had more to fear from his Mafia past than from his police background.

Ray was sitting in the common area watching a Dodgers game when the guards escorted in a new inmate. Frank Caponi was 6' 3" and a portly 275 pounds. The minute Ray saw Caponi, Ray knew he was a wise guy.

The next day, while Ray walked around the rec deck, Caponi stepped in front of him. Ray looked up at the man who had seven inches and at least a hundred pounds on him. Caponi offered Ray a cigarette. They walked around the deck, verbally sparring as they tested each other's underworld credentials.

Ray had been right. Caponi was a wise guy. He was connected to Vinnie "the Chin" Gigante, head of the New York Genovisi family. Caponi said he had been arrested for a parole violation. The pair spent some time together, talking about mutual acquaintances and telling old stories, although never with enough information to convict any of the participants. Trust had not yet been established.

Finally one day Caponi got serious. He leaned toward Ray and, lowering his voice, said he knew Ray was in on a murder-for-hire case. He didn't know if Ray had arranged the murder "as a solo pilot by some schmuck who just wanted his partner dead" or if he had been connected with "bigger players"–the Mafia.

Ray said he didn't know what Caponi was talking about. Ray was not about to talk about his case to anyone, let alone a connected wise guy.

Caponi said he knew Ray and Rocky were close. Caponi said he thought Ray might have told Rocky he had been working solo and got himself "into a pickle." Rocky, Caponi guessed, probably promised to take care of the situation and smooth things over with certain people. When Caponi asked if he was getting warm, Ray replied, "You're not even moving the mercury." But Ray's mind raced as he tried to figure out how Caponi could know so much, even by guessing.

If he was wrong, Caponi said, then Ray had nothing to worry about. But if he was right, then Ray had gone to the wrong guy for help.

Caponi said Rocky was nothing, "a zero." Worse, Rocky was not even a made guy: not a Mafia member. The portly wise guy said Rocky couldn't do shit for Ray. Caponi, however, could make sure no one would bother Ray either in or out of the joint. He knew Ray was involved with the Chippendales situation and that the club owner, no matter what Rocky had told Ray, had friends who were more than willing to help him by taking Ray out. Caponi said he could stop that from happening.

"What's in it for you?"

"We'll figure that out later," Ray remembered Caponi saying with a smile. Caponi would let certain people know Ray was a friend of his and arrange for Ray to show them "a little respect."

What was the best way to show respect? Cash, of course, and lots of it. Caponi wanted $20,000, but would settle for $10,000 to start, just to see how receptive the appropriate people were to Ray's overtures. Caponi would give his uncle, Vinnie "the Chin" Gigante, the $10,000 along with his sanction and, if all went well, Vinnie would see things Caponi's way. Once that happened, Caponi promised, no one could touch Ray. It was life insurance, the Mafia way. It was the same as normal life insurance, except if you didn't pay, you didn't live out your natural life.

Ray didn't know what to believe. He had known Rocky for years. Rocky had always been a straight-up guy. There was no doubt, however, that Caponi was connected. He knew too much about various wise guys and all the New York families. Ray tried to get word to Rocky through his boss's wife, but she could not reach him. All Ray could do was wait and worry as he stalled Caponi. Finally, unable to sleep from the stress and with his polycystic kidneys feeling like a pair of open wounds, Ray decided he couldn't risk foregoing Caponi's offer. If the wise guy was telling the truth, Caponi's connections would trump any connections Steve had. In any case, ten grand wasn't worth risking his life over. Ray called Marty Bress and told him to give Caponi $10,000. Caponi's son soon arrived at D.B. Cooper's for the money.

Still debating whether Caponi's line on Rocky was true, Ray called Rocky's home in Thousand Oaks. To his surprise, Rocky was at home. Rocky had never heard of a Frank Caponi but, he said, if it felt right to Ray, then he was right to have given him the protection money. Even so, he warned Ray to be careful.

A few days later Ray's questions about Caponi's background were answered. Guards rushed the big wise guy out of his cell and, keeping the other inmates at a distance, whisked him out of the MDC. All the inmates knew within minutes that Caponi was a rat. He was being taken into protective custody.

Ray later heard that Caponi had been one of the biggest horse race fixers for the Mob on the East Coast. Once Caponi was arrested for race fixing among other things, he rolled and became an FBI informant, testifying against his former Mafia partners. The FBI put Caponi in the witness protection program. A changed name, however, was not enough to protect him. He had an argument with his girlfriend and pulled a shotgun on her. He was arrested and brought to the MDC, where Ray ran into him. An FBI agent had it in for Frank and during an interview mentioned Caponi's real name, which then appeared in the *Los Angeles Times*. Caponi was probably Tony Schuller, aka Callabrese, which was the same last name as a major Chicago

Mafia family. Callabrese was a client of Henderson's and was at the MDC when Ray was incarcerated there. No doubt Frank (or Tony) was shocked reading about himself in the paper and screamed for protective custody. He knew that once the Mob knew where he was they could kill him as easily inside as outside prison. Much later, Ray heard that Caponi's son had been dating Henderson's secretary, which was probably how Caponi found out about Ray's case, although Ray could never be certain. In any case, Ray was out $10,000. He figured that with as many people who would be trying to get their hands on Frank Caponi, he needed the money far more than Ray. Run, Frank, run!

Chapter 16
Severing the Cord

"It's time to sever the cord and get yourself out of this mess," Rocky told Ray in late January 1992. "Tell 'em whatever they want to know, capiche? Fuck this Steve guy and do the right thing."

Ray realized that Rocky must have bled Steve his six-figure "fine" for not helping Ray. Now Rocky could let Ray roll on Steve. Ray gave the go ahead and Henderson made a deal.

As Ray was being taken to a meeting with the US Attorney to sign the deal, he met Agent Stefanek, who had searched his house, and Agent Scott F. Garriola. In his mid-thirties, Garriola was 6' 2" with short, wavy, brown hair and pale eyes. Garriola had been an FBI agent for four years. Polite and professional, Ray took an instant liking to Garriola. When they met in the courthouse corridor, Garriola removed Ray's handcuffs and they shook hands. A marshal told Garriola that all prisoners had to remain handcuffed while they were in the building. Garriola apologized and re-cuffed Ray, at least until they got into an elevator out of sight of the marshal, when Garriola again removed the cuffs. Ray thanked the agent. Garriola said he didn't want to make it any harder on Ray than it had to be.

They got off on the seventh floor and entered US Attorney Sally L. Meloch's office, where Jean E. Gilliland, the other US Attorney on the case, waited with Jim Henderson. Meloch handed Ray a copy of the agreement to sign. Ray would plead guilty to two charges. He would provide all information about his criminal activities related to Steve Banerjee and Chippendales in return for immunity to charges on all crimes unrelated to Chippendales.

Bewildered by the legal language, not to mention the gravity of the situation, Ray stared at the document and then looked at Henderson, who nodded. Henderson later said, "They had him [Ray] dead. Banerjee wanted him to kill someone else. It's not too hard to make a deal when you can say, this is what I want and this is what you get: a hit list that would save people's lives. I would have given it to them anyway. We weren't going to let someone else get killed, but I used it to the benefit of my client."

Ray signed. Then, while the lawyers took notes, Ray once again told his story from the time he met Steve up to his arrest.

On February 10 or 11, 1992 (court documents disagree) in the Los Angeles Federal Courthouse before Judge William J. Rea, Ray pled guilty to one count of violating Title 18, US Code, section 1958, Murder for Hire and one count of Title 18, US Code, section 371, Conspiracy in relation to the murder of Nicholas De Noia and the attempted murders of the members of the Adonis troupe. At the last minute Gilliland asked that the government have the power to void the agreement if they thought Ray was denying them any information. It would have meant that the government could have milked Ray of all the information he had, then voided the agreement and charged him again. The judge denied the government's request.

Gilliland asked that the case be sealed, since she expected Ray to provide evidence about co-conspirators whom she did not want warned by news that Ray had made a plea bargain. The judge agreed and case CR-91-721(C)-WR, The United States vs. Augustine Ralph Angel Colon and William Nelson Barnes, Jr. was sealed.

The deal was struck. Ray would cooperate and serve time for conspiracy and murder-for-hire instead of facing two charges of attempted arson, one of murder for hire, and two counts of conspiracy to commit murder for hire. Henderson had earned his fee. Sentencing was set for April 6, 1992.

The next day, February 11, William "Billy" Nelson Barnes, who had no criminal record, pled guilty to conspiracy and causing another to travel interstate to murder Stephen White and Read Schrotel (or Scott). The government conceded that Billy unknowingly became involved in the conspiracy when Ray sent him to England. However, when Billy became aware of the murder conspiracy, he remained involved for months. Billy spoke to Strawberry several times on the phone about the planned murders and, the FBI believed at that time, may have made a delivery of cash to pay for the cyanide.

Billy later told an interviewer at the MDC on March 9, 1992 that much of the case agent's reports contained "exaggerations because he was actually just going along with the plan because co-defendant Ray Colon requested that he just agree and go along with it so that he would be able to convince the confidential source [Errol Lynne "Strawberry" Bressler] to travel to England to complete the contract killing." Billy said he felt "terrible about the whole situation and is extremely glad that the hit never took place because his conscience could not take it." The interviewer noted, "The defendant stated that he knows the offense was extremely wrong and that no one should have the right to say who lives and who dies." When asked why he could let such a thing happen, "he explained that he was scared, and was afraid that if he went to the authorities his brother-in-law, Ray Colon, would be hurt or possibly killed as a result of police investigation."

After his arrest, a probation officer interviewed Billy's wife, Tammy, who noted that she had married Billy because "He is one of the nicest men she has ever met" and that she had "made a commitment to endure the good times as well as the bad times. As such, she had no plans to divorce him." True to the cliché, Billy's mother was also supportive, visiting him at the MDC several times a week. She said her son did not know what was going on and that he was afraid of Ray.

Billy Barnes was scheduled to be sentenced on December 7, 1992.

Over the remainder of February 1992, Garriola and Stefanek took Ray to the US Attorney's office every few days. Gilliland and Meloch took notes as they grilled Ray on every detail related to building a case against Steve Banerjee and the triggerman, Gilberto Rivera "Louie" Lopez.

The case soon progressed to a point where Ray had to be released so that Stefanek and Garriola could gather more evidence against Ray's co-conspirators. But where would the FBI keep Ray while he worked the case? Gilliland, Meloch and Stefanek wanted to hold Ray in a local jail at night. If that was the government's plan, Ray said they could return him to the MDC and he would just serve his time because they could forget about ever getting Louie, let alone Steve.

Meloch suggested Ray could tell Steve and Louie that Barbara had left him, so he was staying in a hotel. Ray said that "sounded suspicious as hell." Steve knew Barbara and that she wouldn't abandon her husband so easily. Ray said, since he was supposed to be out on bail because of his kidney problems, he had better be in the hospital or at home, because Steve could call his house or the hospital at any hour of the day or night to make sure he was there. Ray asked what Barbara was supposed to say if Steve called, "Hold on while I call the FBI so they can bring Ray over here from the hotel to talk to you?"

While the government decided what to do with Ray, Garriola and Stefanek were already working with Ray in the MDC. The agents had Ray, using the code name Babe, call Steve. As usual, Steve refused to answer. They had similarly bad luck trying to contact Louie. According to his mother and brother, Louie was out of state. It did not look like the cases against Steve or Louie were going to be built in a day.

Garriola gave Ray a beeper. Flabbergasted, Ray asked how he was supposed to return calls from jail. Stefanek explained that the beeper was for contacting Louie. Ray would call Louie's house and if they said he was still out of state, he would give them the beeper number so Louie could call him back from wherever he was. Garriola called Louie on his cell phone and Ray left the message.

The US Attorney's quickly secured court approval to have Ray released into FBI custody so he could assist with the case. Ray would leave the MDC often from February through July

1992. The US Attorney's and the FBI finally decided that he would work with Garriola and Stefanek during the day and remain at his house with a monitor on his leg at night. The monitor would transmit an alarm to an FBI monitoring station if Ray went more than 300 feet from his house. Ray didn't mind wearing the monitor. He was going home.

On the way from the MDC, Stefanek made the trip even sweater for Ray by removing his handcuffs. Then, Ray later recalled, Garriola pulled out his gun, slid a round into the chamber and tossed the gun to a shocked Ray in the back seat.

Ray remembered Garriola saying, "There it is, pal. Take it, 'cause if you're thinking of running, just shoot us now and get it over with. If you run, my career is over anyway, since Andy and I went way out on a limb getting you out of the MDC."

"I can still hear the Justice Department screaming at us," Stefanek said, rubbing one of his ears as he drove.

Ray picked up the gun, looked at it a moment and tossed it back onto the front seat. "Why the fuck would I run? Even if I did, where would I go? Living your life on the run has got to be ten times worse than doing time. Forget about it. I ain't going nowhere, except home."

"If you ever do decide to run," Garriola said, putting his gun back in his holster, "just let me know so I can enjoy a nice, thick steak before I let you shoot me."

The agents took Ray to the monitoring office in Carson, where he was fitted with a 3" by 3" monitoring device on his ankle. The FBI had already installed a small box attached to the telephone in Ray's house, which would transmit a signal if Ray and his ankle monitor strayed too far from home.

Next stop was Ray's house in Santa Clarita, at the foot of the Santa Susana Mountains north of Los Angeles. Ray was shocked at the state of his property. The yard was overgrown with weeds, the paint was peeling on the house, and the roof tiles were chipped and several were missing. Ray immediately understood, at least partly, why the neighbors had been treating Barbara so poorly. The house looked like it belonged in a slum amidst the middle-class homes around it.

At the front door Stefanek and Garriola hung back as Barbara opened the door and, crying, hugged and kissed her long absent husband. Ray's first stop was the refrigerator for three beers. The agents stayed to drink their beers with Ray, then called the control center and tested the monitor before they left. That night Ray and Barbara made up for lost time. Ray could not believe he was finally home. If not free, at least he was outside the MDC's ugly, gray walls. Barbara kept squeezing him as they cuddled in bed to make sure he was not just a waking dream.

Ray apologized repeatedly for putting Barbara through hell. Worse, it was far from over and Ray knew he would have to serve some prison time before it was over. Barbara cried at the thought of losing Ray all over again, but there was nothing he could do to change his fate.

Although Ray was at home, he was not about to live a quiet, peaceful life. A few nights after he arrived home Barbara was watching television in the den when someone pounded on the front door. She ran to the door and saw Stefanek through the peephole. The agent was not in his usual suit; he wore shorts and a T-shirt. She opened the door. The agent demanded to know where Ray was as he rushed inside. Barbara said Ray was upstairs, asleep. Stefanek bolted up the stairs three at a time and into the master bedroom.

"Ray!" Stefanek yelled, stooping down beside the bed to pull up the sheets and reveal the monitor on Ray's ankle. As Ray rolled over, groggy and pulling the covers up to his chin, Stefanek stalked back downstairs. The ankle monitor had malfunctioned and sent a signal to the FBI that Ray had left his house. To make sure neither of them had to make another nocturnal dash to Ray's house, Garriola and Stefanek took turns for a few nights sleeping on Ray's sofa until they were sure the monitor was functioning properly again.

Ray could now see his doctor about his kidneys, but his doctor refused to see him. The physician had heard about Ray's arrest and wanted nothing to do with a man involved with a murder-for-hire. The doctor asked Ray's insurance company if his patient could be assigned to another physician, but the company refused. Bowing to the all-powerful insurance company, the doctor agreed to an appointment.

Ray was apprehensive on his first visit, since he knew the doctor envisioned him as a stone-cold hit man. Once they got talking about Ray's condition, however, they became friendly.

The doctor later apologized for how he had acted and later even wrote the government that Ray should be put on probation rather than given jail time so he could receive proper medical care for his polycystic kidneys.

Ray continued to call and write Louie Lopez, but still had not heard from him. Finally, Louie's brother, Rubin, told Ray that Louie was in prison on a charge unrelated to the De Noia murder. Ray gave Rubin a message asking Louie to write him because Ray had something important to ask him.

Most of Ray's time was spent with Garriola and Stefanek. The agents took Ray to various locations to gather evidence for the case. They went to Moody's, the club where Paul and Jerry almost blew up a city block by igniting a gas line, and to the Red Onion, where the agents interviewed the janitor who had extinguished the fire the night Mike Alvarez and Louie Lopez had attempted to set the Pearl Harbor on fire. The agents collected the number of every pay phone Ray thought he had ever used to call Steve from Santa Clarita. They went to the motel in Van Nuys where Ray had once stayed when he told Steve he was meeting a hit man. To substantiate Ray's story, the FBI pulled the phone records to find calls from those phones to Steve. Ray was glad to show the agents the office of Dr. Sehdeva, Steve's partner in the adult Disneyland project; someone Steve had asked Ray to have killed, yet was still alive.

Garriola and Stefanek took Ray to D.B. Cooper's. Entering the club alone, Ray asked the surprised owner for his money. It appeared that Marty Bress had thought that Ray would remain in jail and never appear on his doorstep asking for his money. Recovering quickly, Marty said he only had $8,000. The rest was hidden elsewhere or loaned out. Ray didn't like the sound of 'loaned out,' but Marty told him not to worry, he would get Ray's money back. Ray said he hoped so, since they had been friends a long time and he hoped Marty wouldn't violate their friendship.

Ray took the money and gave it to Stefanek, who started counting it as Garriola drove them back along the 405 Freeway toward Santa Clarita. Stefanek counted the money and said there was only $8,000. Where was the rest?

Ray told the agents what Marty had said. Garriola asked whether Ray believed Marty. Ray said he thought the bar owner was ripping him off. Garriola said they had to get the money for the government's case. Ray said his attorney believed the money was his, since it was not illegal for someone to give money to a friend for their criminal defense. Since the cash was in all probability the result of illegal acts, Garriola vehemently disagreed and called the cash, "Blood money." In the end, Garriola's point of view won out; Ray never saw any of the money ever again.

The money from Marty was to be one link in the chain of evidence linking Steve to Ray, and Ray to the De Noia murder. The next step, Garriola and Stefanek decided, was to try to get Steve to talk to Ray, while he wore a wire. The right words on tape would seal Steve's fate.

The FBI had Ray continue to write Steve in an attempt to set up a meeting, as well as to ask for more money to establish a stronger link between them. In May 1992 the FBI helped Ray draft a letter to Steve, complete with grammatical errors so as to appear authentic. "Once again I find myself having to write another letter, since it's now been some time that you've made contact with me.....It is not my intention to have to continuously bother you, however,...my attorney's fees alone would run well over $100, and so that therefore $200 is more than reasonable considering the circumstances. It is my understanding that the amount received fell well short of what I believe is fair, and asked for...Frankly I find it completely shocking that even at this late date you have such contempt for me and the idea of giving me any assistance, that you would have not given me in full the amount asked for, instead of making me believe that the remainder would arrive within a reasonable time, which it obviously has not. Now forcing me to write yet another letter. The fact remains that I don't trust you, since in the past you have not, as we know, been a man of your word. I've kept my end of the deal, and now I want the balance I'm entitled to and nothing more."

On May 11, still with no response from Steve, Ray wrote again. His block lettering pleaded, "I hope that soon I will hear from friends....I go next week for another hearing to see if I could get medical bail so I could go to my own doctor and hospital. The government is putting up one hell of a fight, but my attorney says I have a fifty-fifty chance, which I seriously doubt, but we'll see. Anyway, take care, and come on will you just get it over with."

Ray then wrote in an undated letter, "To Friends! I've tried several times to reach you, and all times you refused to take my call. And for the life of me I don't understand why. Look! I'm out on a medical bail, so it's not like I'm going to be out forever and I have all the time in the world to be chasing you. What is your damn problem? There is nothing wrong with you talking to an old friend, it's stupid for you to act like you don't know me, when the whole damn world knows that I've known you and you me for over 15 years. The reason I've not stopped at your office or your home is because for you. I don't want to be seen walking in there. I'm almost sure at this point the Feds are not bothering with me, because believe me I'm always checking. Like I said over and over again, I'm going to ride this damn train alone, but I still want the balance of what I believe is fair, and there are a few things I'd like to have guaranteed before my bail runs out. Look! Don't make such a big deal over all this. I'll do my part like I said I would and it's time to do yours. Stop acting so damn suspicious with your behavior already and take my damn call or you leave me no choice but to walk right into your office and ask to see an old friend….There is nothing wrong with calling or visiting a friend, so take my damn call will you. P.S. The two times I went to the hospital for my treatments (I'm a lot sicker than you think) I drove by your office and your damn car was there, so I know you were there to. I didn't go in, for your sake not mine. Believe me, I'm not going to do or ask you to do anything that's going to put you on the spot. Now let's quit the games and talk."

By early June, the FBI had given up waiting for Steve to reply. Early on June 10, 1992, at the technical room of the FBI's office in the Federal Building in Westwood, a Tech Agent fitted Ray with a wire and transmitter. Ray drove an old Mustang, closely trailed by an FBI unit, to the Chippendale's office in Santa Monica. Ray parked across the street from Steve's building, while the FBI unit kept watch from up the street. Ray expected Steve to arrive by 9 a.m., but he didn't show. Ray kept waiting as the minutes ticked by and finally decided to give up if Steve didn't appear by 10. At 9:56 Ray spotted Steve's Mercedes pulling into the parking lot across the street.

Ray jumped out of his car and rushed toward Steve, calling for him to wait. Steve stood by his car, clutching his leather briefcase, looking as shocked as a nun coming upon an orgy. Ray, smiling, put his arm around Steve's shoulders.

"Relax," Ray said. "I only want to talk to you a minute."

"I don't have time to talk to you right now," Steve said in a low voice, made harder to understand by his heavy accent. He looked around nervously as if he expected to see a battalion of FBI agents closing in on him from all sides.

Ray said he appreciated what Steve had done for him, but he wanted to get a few things straight. Steve said he didn't want to talk because Ray was working for the government. Ray wasn't surprised that Steve had guessed the truth, but he denied it and explained that the only reason he was out on bail was because of his kidneys. Besides, he said, if he was working for the government, why was Steve still free?

While the businessman pondered that question, Ray guided him across the street to get a soda at a corner store. Steve could not take his eyes off Ray's body. Ray noticed his friend's wandering eyes and asked if he wanted to search him, raising his arms for Steve to frisk him. The club owner shook his head and said he didn't have to search Ray. He knew his old friend was working for the government since Steve's attorney had told him that Ray's case had been sealed.

As he grabbed two cold sodas and handed one to his old friend, Ray said Steve was wrong and changed the subject to his plan to flee the country. They walked toward the counter, where Ray paid for the drinks. The two men loitered by the door drinking their sodas. Steve asked why Ray had to leave the country. Ray said that if he went to trial they would "hang him." He wanted to leave the first chance he got, but needed a fake passport, which would cost lots of money.

Visibly nervous, his eyes flitting from customer to customer in ceaseless motion, Steve said he couldn't talk any more. He told Ray to call him in a few days and he would see what he could do. Then Steve was out the door, across the street and into his office faster than an Olympic sprinter.

The FBI was disappointed that Steve had said so little. It only served to reinforce Ray's belief that getting Steve to trust him enough to say anything incriminating was going to take a long time. Garriola, however, was surprised Steve talked to Ray at all, since Steve thought Ray was cooperating with the government. Ray said Steve had no choice. If Ray was cooperating, then Steve was screwed. Therefore, Steve wanted to believe Ray wasn't working for the government and was actually planning to jump bail.

Ray felt certain he could eventually get Steve to talk. Even Ray, however, did not dream that just one meeting would produce results. The next day, Marty Bress reported that a courier delivered $14,000 to D.B. Cooper's for Ray. The FBI later traced the courier pickup to a bakery next door to where the Chippendales troupe was rehearsing. Steve had decided to take a chance on Ray. If the money kept Ray from talking, it was cheap insurance for Steve. Garriola and Stefanek picked up the $14,000, although they had no better luck than Ray getting the rest of the money Steve had sent Marty Bress for Ray from the bar owner. Marty sang the same song and danced the same dance; the money was loaned out and it would take time to get it all back. The FBI agents believed he was lying, but there was little they could do about it.

In the summer of 1992, Garriola and Stefanek took Ray to New York to further build the case against Steve. Ray led the agents to public telephones he had used to call Steve. The FBI pulled the records to corroborate that Ray had called Steve from New York at the time of the De Noia murder. Ray also showed the agents all the sites related to the murders. Garriola photographed the various sites and both agents scribbled copious notes while Ray explained what had happened at each location.

While in New York they worked with FBI agent Tom Wacks, whom everyone called Wacko. (His brother, Michael Wacks, played a key role in nailing New Orleans crime boss Carlos Marcello in the BRILAB [Bribery and Labor Investigation] operation and later played a small role in the 1995 O.J. Simpson double-murder trial.) About fifty, Tom Wacks was slim, with thinning hair and a wispy mustache. His sense of humor was a welcome relief to the long, emotionally draining days that Ray said he experienced as he relived the events related to what he continued to call "the De Noia thing."

Although Chippendales no longer had an office in the building where the murder occurred, the agents photographed the building's lobby, stairs and hall, as well as the former Chippendales office. The agents also talked to all of the witnesses the NYPD had identified and spoke with anyone else who might have seen anything important. It was slow, tedious work but formed the bedrock for building a case against Steve and Louie.

After another long day, Stefanek, Garriola, Wacko, and Ray had dinner and then walked to Rockefeller Center to unwind. Garriola suggested they hit Sullivan's Grill. Wacko seconded the motion, but asked what they should do with Ray, since they were supposed to be guarding him. Stefanek said Ray might run, at least according to their boss, Mitchell, who wanted them to keep Ray handcuffed during the day and in a local jail at night.

"Fuck Mitchell," Ray remembered Wacko saying. "The only thing he knows how to do is sit at his desk and type memos in triplicate." Wacko turned to Ray. "Are you going to take off on us and make us all lose our jobs so we'll all have to go looking for you so we can shoot you?"

Ray said he wouldn't run, and that he could use a few drinks himself. Garriola said he had seen Ray's face as much as he wanted to for one day and certainly didn't want to go drinking with him. Garriola suggested putting Ray in a cab to Penn Station where he could take the Long Island Railroad to his sister's house in Selden. Ray hated that plan. A few months before a gunman had slaughtered commuters on the Long Island Railroad and there was no way he wanted to take that particular ride.

Wacko pulled out his gun. "No fucking problem. You can have my gun."

Stefanek and Garriola then pulled out their guns.

"Here," Stefanek said, "take mine; it's a much better weapon."

"The hell it is," Garriola said, shouldering Stefanek aside and offering his weapon. "This is real fire power."

Ray asked, "Are you guys fucking nuts?"

Wacko said, "Some people say I am."

"I ain't taking no gun on that train, forget about it. I'll get arrested."

"Then just take your chances like a real man," Garriola said.

"And you know what a real man is, huh?" Ray asked.

"I don't have to, I have a gun."

"Alright, I'll go."

The agents waved down a Yellow Cab and sent Ray on his way.

"I hope you all have a shitty time," Ray called through the cab's open window.

"Impossible," Garriola said. "You won't be there."

The next day they searched for the hotel where Ray had stashed Louie the night after the murder.

From the back seat of the FBI sedan Ray said, "Thanks for calling in the middle of the night to make sure I was at my sister's."

"The bars don't close until four," Stefanek said.

"You guys stayed out that long?"

"No," Wacko said, sitting beside Ray in the back seat. "We were good boys. We left the bar at three."

"I thought you'd be in Canada by the time we called," Stefanek said.

"I thought about it, but then I thought, why run, when I can hang around and bug the hell out of you assholes?"

Ray had trouble remembering the location of the hotel. Finally they found it. The search had been made more difficult because the hotel had been remodeled. Garriola and Stefanek talked with the manager and returned with a copy of Ray's MasterCard receipt for the room. Just as Ray had said, Louie had called Los Angeles from his room the night of the murder. They had arrived just in time; the manager found the receipt in a box he was about to throw out.

The government was happy with Ray's cooperation, since everything he had told them had been corroborated by physical evidence, witnesses, phone records, and by fire and police department reports. Steve's phone records, including his house, office and car phones, also linked Ray to Steve.

The FBI agents and Ray returned to Los Angeles. On the drive from LAX to Ray's house, Stefanek and Garriola debated what to do about the monitor. Ray's legs had swollen during the cross-country flight and the monitor would not fit around either of his ankles. Garriola decided not to bother with the device. The control room would not activate it until they told them to anyway. After warning Ray to stay close to home, the agents left Ray monitor-free.

Days later, US Attorney Gilliland asked if Ray was secured at his house. Stefanek and Garriola glanced at each other. They assumed that Ray was at home, although he had not worn the monitoring device for days.

"He ain't going anywhere," Garriola said, telling what he firmly believed was the truth, but not quite answering the question. Gilliland did not notice the distinction.

Chapter 17
Building a Case

On June 18, 1992, the FBI had Ray try writing Steve yet again: "I figured since I'm sitting here at St. John's waiting for some more kidney tests, I'd write. Sorry I had to come see you the other day, but really you left me no other choice. I don't know what it is about some of my friends that makes them think that their phones are all monitored, or that they can't even talk to me....I really doubt that they are tapping yours or any others phone....Believe me, if I thought for one moment my friend's or my phones were tapped do you think I'm that stupid to call them?...Stop acting like we're not friends. I don't ever want to meet you by your office again, but damn it, just act normal when I see you, and stop acting so damn nervous or suspicious. I really don't think you understand that not only would I not put you ever on the spot, but that nothing can happen to you, and I mean nothing!! I'm not going to do you wrong, I've already told you that at least 100 times before, but I have to know where I stand. I have to know that my future is secure, and damn it, I can't do that peeking out of cars and waiting to see if my friend is going to talk to me....We are friends, and friends call, talk and see each other at least once in a while, damn it.....There are a few things you need to know for your own benefit as well as mine, but how in the hell am I going to tell you unless I see you, and I damn sure am not going to put it down on paper.....It's not like I have all the time in the world since I'm only out on medical bail and may be my only chance to inform you on a few things.....I appreciate the package, but it's not just about money. I want to see you. I've never done anything to hurt you and have tried to respect your wishes, so now at least respect mine."

The next day, June 19, Ray wrote again: "It's for our mutual benefit for us to talk. So call me from a pay phone or a car phone (it can't be tapped) or I'll call you on a pay phone or your car phone." Ray then set out code names for them to use. If Steve did not like the phone, Ray suggested using a messenger to send a note via Marty at D.B. Cooper's.

In another undated letter Ray wrote Steve about where he might plan to flee: "Well, it's about that time. I'll be taking that long needed vacation we talked about in about two or three weeks max. I'm just waiting for something that can help me get around, which by the way is costing me a hard 10. But it's worth it, if it does the job. Before I go to the Indian part of town, I'm going to first check out little Italy or the Spanish section first. Anyway, I'd like to have a short (very short) meeting with you next week so I can tell you where I'm going to be and kind of where you're going to be so we can meet at that side of town. Call me like you did before and tell me where I could call you to hook up. And I hope you're not throwing these letters in your garbage."

With the letters failing to elicit a response, Garriola hooked up a tape recorder to a public phone in Brentwood and had Ray call Steve's office. Ray again used the code name Babe. Ray expected the secretary to say that Steve was unavailable, but she put Ray through to the club owner right away.

Steve demanded to know why Ray kept calling him. Ray said he was just calling an old friend. Steve said he didn't want to talk on the phone and he had already helped Ray as much as he could. Ray said he had to see Steve. The club owner asked why, but now it was Ray's turn to say he didn't want to talk on the phone. Steve said he was too busy to meet, but Ray insisted.

They went back and forth, but finally Steve agreed to meet at 2 p.m. on June 23 at the International House of Pancakes on Santa Monica Boulevard. The FBI had their meeting.

Garriola, Stefanek and Ray drove to the Federal Building on Wilshire Boulevard across from the rows of white headstones in the national cemetery. An FBI tech agent prepared a wire for Ray to wear to his lunch meeting. Ray was worried. First thing, Steve would check for a wire. If he found one, it would destroy any chance they had of ever getting the Chippendales creator to talk. The agents insisted Ray wear a wire. However, if Steve came to the meeting armed and he found a wire, it would be Ray's life on the line. The agents were adamant. Realizing he had no choice, Ray said that if he had to wear a wire, then he would be the one to rig it. Garriola and Stefanek glanced at each other and nodded. The tech agent handed Ray the wire and transmitter.

At home, Ray spent an hour carefully aligning the wire in the inner seam of a pair of undershorts with the utmost care. He shoved the wire in from the back of the shorts through the crotch. He worked it through the seam until the tiny microphone was in the front. The miniaturized transmitter was just in front of where his testicles would be. Using the same color thread, he sewed the seam back into place with as much care as a neurosurgeon operating on his only child. When he was done, it was impossible to see the wire. Even feeling the seam would not necessarily reveal the wire, since the seam itself was thick and somewhat rigid.

On June 23, Garriola, Stefanek and several other FBI agents kept the International House of Pancakes on the ground floor of a Best Western hotel on Santa Monica Boulevard under careful but hopefully unnoticed surveillance. Agents watched from across the street in an armed forces recruiting storefront and kitty-corner in an insurance agency's office. Several FBI-manned cars blanketed the area in case Steve decided to drive Ray somewhere else to talk. Two agents sat in an FBI van parked directly across the street from the hotel watching with binoculars through a tinted window. Another agent ate at the counter in the restaurant, while yet another masqueraded as a hotel clerk behind the front desk.

Just before 2 p.m., Ray walked into the lobby, sat in a stuffed armchair near the check-in desk and waited. Steve's Mercedes pulled into the parking lot. The Chippendales owner got out, scanned his surroundings and walked into the lobby carrying his briefcase. He motioned to Ray and led the way down a corridor to the rest rooms. Ray was wary, but figured Steve couldn't kill him before the cavalry arrived.

In the restroom, Steve motioned for Ray to follow him into a stall. Ray hesitated, but then followed Steve inside. Ray was about to say something when Steve put his index finger to his lips for silence. Steve motioned for Ray to pull his pants down and lift up his shirt. Ray undid and dropped his pants to his ankles, and then lifted his shirt, feeling completely ridiculous. Steve looked him over and then started rubbing his upper and lower body. Still not saying a word, Steve untied Ray's shoelaces and removed his shoes and socks. He tapped the monitor on Ray's ankle and looked up at his old friend with a suspicious look. Normally, Ray said, he couldn't leave the house or the monitor sent a signal to a station and the Feds came running like a pack of hounds after a fox. Today he told the Feds he had to see his doctor at St. Johns Hospital just up the street.

Steve looked unconvinced and continued searching Ray. He slid his hand up Ray's crotch and grabbed his testicles.

"C'mon, Steve," Ray said, pushing him away. With this level of intimacy, Steve just might find the wire. "You're going overboard! Somebody walks in and they're gonna think we're two faggots fucking around!"

Steve again motioned for him to be quiet and started kneading Ray's undershorts. Steve was getting much too close to the transmitter. Ray grabbed his pants and yanked them back up. He yelled at Steve that he wasn't wearing a wire and asked how he knew that Steve wasn't wearing one.

Steve stepped back in the cramped stall and began to undress. Ray said, "Forget it." He knew Steve wasn't wired, but he asked why Steve thought he was wired. Steve bent down, opened his briefcase and took out a yellow legal pad and a pen. He wrote a note and showed it to Ray; "I know for a fact that you are working for the government."

Ray threw up his hands in despair and asked who had told Steve that. Steve wrote another note; he had hired two attorneys who had gone to all of Ray's court appearances. Steve claimed to know everything.

Ray said the attorneys were wrong. The only reason he was out of jail was because of his kidneys. His case was sealed, not because he was working for the government, but because the Feds had got to his brother-in-law, Billy Barnes, and they were trying to use him to get to Ray. Steve flipped the page over and wrote another note, once again claiming that his attorneys kept him informed about everything.

"If that's true, how come they didn't tell you about my brother-in-law?" Ray asked. He asked Steve to at least listen to him. He had spent almost a year in jail and hadn't rolled on Steve. He deserved at least a hearing.

Steve considered for a long time. Finally he ripped the pages he had written on off the pad, tore them into little pieces and flushed them down the toilet. Then he led the way back to the lobby, where they sat in two over-stuffed chairs at a table. Steve took out his pad and pen again. Ray, exasperated, asked how they were going to talk if he had to wait while Steve wrote everything down.

Steve leaned over and whispered in Ray's ear, "You talk. I listen."

"Okay, fine. If you insist on being that paranoid, I'll do the talking. I'll start by telling you that I am not working for the fucking Feds!"

Steve wrote: 'I don't believe you.'

"I can see that! You keep writing shit down on that paper like you're a mute."

Steve scribbled another note: 'You talk. I listen.'

"What are you Merrill Lynch now? You're driving me crazy with all this shit!"

Steve jabbed his finger at the note; 'You talk. I listen.'

Ray gave up and said he would just explain what he planned to do and Steve could take it from there. Ray reiterated that he was not working for the government, but said that they had him on tape on the Adonis thing. There was no way he would walk. Steve nodded. Therefore, Ray said, his only chance was to get out of the country. To do that he needed money; enough for a passport and to live on for a long time.

Steve wrote: 'What happened to all the money I gave you?'

Ray explained that Marty was holding it for him along with some of his own money, but he dared not go near the bar owner. Ray didn't think the Feds were watching him and, if they were, not that closely, but he didn't want to take any chances. Steve nodded.

Ray said all he wanted to do was get out of the country before they "slammed the door" on him forever. It would be rough without his wife and family, but it was either that or he would not see them for the next 20 years anyway. He thought he might go to Italy or Spain. Again Steve nodded.

But, Ray continued, he needed a passport and money. He reassured Steve that he was not working for the Feds because, if he was, they would have arrested Steve already. Steve had taken several trips out of the country since Ray was arrested and if the Feds were after him, there was no way they would have let Steve leave the country.

Steve tossed the pad and pen into his briefcase and slammed it shut. He motioned for Ray to follow him back into the restroom. Once inside Steve tore up the pages he had written on and flushed them down the toilet.

Ray walked with the silent Steve out to the parking lot. Finally the club owner spoke, "The fucking Feds are probably watching me right now." He opened his car's trunk and tossed in his briefcase.

Ray reassured him that the Feds were not even close to knowing who Steve was and that he wouldn't tell them a damn thing. Steve looked around before he reached into his trunk, took out a sealed envelope and handed it to Ray. He leaned toward Ray and mumbled something about money and then added, "Don't call me again."

Steve slammed the trunk, climbed into his car and drove off. An FBI unit followed Steve's Mercedes to make sure he left, while Garriola picked up Ray as he walked up Santa Monica Boulevard toward St. John's Hospital. Garriola congratulated Ray as he got into the car and asked him what Steve had given him.

Ray thought Steve had said it was $4,000. Garriola said he noticed that Steve kept writing things down on a legal pad. Ray said that was all he did. The FBI later checked the toilet bowl for any stray fragments of Steve's writings. They found a few pieces that corroborated the tape of the meeting. Back at their office in the Federal building, Garriola and Stefanek counted the money Steve had given Ray. They used surgical gloves and tongs, hoping to find Steve's prints on the bills.

That night, Garriola called Ray at home to ask him how much he thought Steve had given him. Angry, because according to his attorney the money was his property, Ray snapped that he had already told them; $4,000. Were they accusing him of lying? Garriola said he didn't think Ray was lying, just that Ray was wrong. Steve had given his old friend not $4,000, but $40,000.

To help relieve the stress of working the case, Ray worked in his yard. He finished a flower bed near the front door, as well as adding lights and a brick path. He leveled the yard, seeded it and planted flowers, bushes and a tree. He also painted the house. With some cash hidden in his house and a small amount the FBI was paying him since he was not allowed to work, Ray bought the materials for his home improvement projects. Without the monitor, he could make quick trips to local stores for supplies. Yard work allowed him to take his mind off his troubles, his impending prison time, the deteriorating state of his marriage, and the stress of trying to get enough information to convict Steve and Louie.

Having made some progress with Steve, the FBI turned their attention to Louie Lopez. In Garriola's white Bronco, Stefanek and Garriola drove Ray to East Los Angeles, one of the Hispanic sections of the City of Angels. They parked on the corner of Vermont and 24th Street. Louie lived in his mother's duplex on 24th.

Garriola told Ray that he and Stefanek would get out and walk to a nearby corner he indicated. The agents slid out and Ray got behind the wheel. He drove to Louie's duplex. Rubin, Louie's older brother, answered the door.

Rubin said he had given Louie the message to contact Ray, but it was going to be a while before his brother hit the bricks. Rubin, however, said he could handle anything Ray wanted done. Not wanting to offend him, Ray said he was sure Rubin could handle any job, but his people trusted, and knew, Louie. Even so, he promised there would be other things coming along soon for which he could use Rubin. They shook hands and a discouraged Ray returned to the Bronco.

Ray drove to the corner where Stefanek and Garriola were supposed to be waiting; no FBI agents. Ray drove around; still no sign of the agents. He passed the burned out shells of buildings torched during the recent Rodney King riots. King was an African-American who was beaten by Los Angeles Police Department officers after a long chase in which King had been attempting to avoid arrest for drunk driving. The beating was videotaped and sparked riots in parts of Los Angeles. Ray was worried. East Los Angeles after the riots was not a good place for two white guys whose haircuts and dress screamed they were cops of some sort to take a stroll.

Ray took two 9 mm automatics from a compartment by the front seat. He tucked the guns in his belt. He wanted to be ready if he ran into trouble. Frantic, he drove past the appointed corner and up and down side streets for 5 minutes, 10 minutes, 15 minutes, 20 minutes. He was eyeing the radio in the Bronco to call for help when he spotted Stefanek and Garriola strolling out of a corner store carrying sodas. Ray pulled into a driveway, jumped out of the SUV and yelled at the agents, demanding to know where they had been and why they had scared him half to death.

Stefanek calmly asked what Ray was doing with the guns. Ray said he had been worried someone might have jumped the agents. Garriola, his voice dripping with sarcasm, asked if Ray had planned to come save their asses. Ray said he had been planning to rescue the agents and had been on the verge of calling headquarters for help. The agents were relieved he hadn't made such a call; they would have been taken off the case.

Once back in the Bronco, Garriola joked that Ray hadn't called because he had been afraid he would be assigned agents who wouldn't be as nice to Ray as they were. Ray said the agents were far from nice, making him worry so much. Garriola said he was nice; when he saw Ray with the guns, he hadn't shot Ray.

Chapter 18
Steve Without a Wire

Early in the summer of 1992, at the US Attorney's Office in the Los Angeles Federal Courthouse, Stefanek, Garriola, Sally L. Meloch (Gilliland was on leave), and the Agent in Charge of the Organized Crime Division, Dale Mitchell, met to discuss the next stage of the operation. Ray had to go to New York and Maine to verify the locations from which he had called Steve, as well as the hotel where he and Billy had stayed near the Canadian border.

Meloch wondered how they could keep Ray from running when he was so close to the border. Mitchell was adamant that when Ray was in Maine, Ray should be handcuffed at all times during the day and locked up at night. Garriola disagreed. He said that Ray had cooperated in every way possible, and Ray had already had plenty of opportunities to run and had not done so. There was always a chance Ray might run, but Stefanek seriously doubted it.

Mitchell asked if Stefanek was willing to stake his career on it.

"I am," Stefanek said.

"I stick with my partner," Garriola said, and then added, "for better or for worse."

Meloch decided they would not handcuff Ray. Mitchell, attempting to salvage at least part of his position, said he didn't want Ray anywhere near the Canadian border.

Ray, Stefanek and Garriola flew to New York and met Wacko. They spent two days in New York, checking telephones Ray had used to call Steve. Then they drove north on I-95 toward Houlton, Maine, where Ray and Billy had stayed the night they had tried to cross into Canada. Ray easily found the motel.

The owner almost had a seizure when the FBI agents identified themselves. Garriola thought the owner had been skimming money to avoid paying taxes and had destroyed receipts, because the hotelier could not find any records or receipts for the year they wanted, 1991, yet had every other year ready at hand. Discouraged that they had no receipts and that the owner could not remember Ray, Garriola photographed the room, which looked exactly as Ray had described it and, therefore, at least partially corroborated his story.

Next they tried to find the truck stop where Ray had called Steve after failing to enter Canada. Again they found it without much difficulty. Ray could not remember exactly which telephone he had used, so Garriola wrote down all the numbers from a row of grime-covered public telephones. With the records from the phones, the FBI would be able to link Steve to Ray's trip and his attempt to cross into Canada to arrange the murder of the Adonis troupe members. Unfortunately, the phones did not accept incoming calls, so the evidence would be weak. They needed to find the next telephone, on which Steve called Ray back.

Before they looked for that crucial next telephone, Garriola decided they had to do something else of paramount importance. They drove to the Canadian border and stopped at a large sign that proclaimed, "Welcome to Canada." Stefanek, Garriola and Wacko posed around the sign like the three monkeys who see no evil, speak no evil and hear no evil. Ray crouched beside the sign as if he was sprinting into the Great White North. With the aid of the camera's timer, they took a photograph with one particular person in mind.

Then it was back to business as they drove down I-95 through the natural beauty of Maine. The next stop was harder to find, since Ray and Billy had driven 20 or 30 miles before Ray called Steve back. Maine was dotted with small towns and there were numerous gas stations, restaurants and truck stops that all looked alike. Ray tried to spot familiar landmarks, but he kept drawing blanks as the miles flew past. Garriola feared they might have missed it and debated whether to turn back. Ray kept looking from one side of the highway to the other as they sped along as if he was watching a marathon tennis match.

They stopped at several possible exits, but without any luck. Ray was afraid he would not even recognize the place anymore. Then he spotted an off ramp that looked familiar. Garriola slowed and headed down the ramp. They entered the one-street town. Then Ray saw it. He pointed at a single-story, square building that housed a small restaurant. They did not see any pay phone out front, but Ray was certain it was the right place.

They went into the restaurant, which also housed a grocery store, and approached the clerk behind the Formica-topped counter in the grocery area. Eager to verify his story, Ray described the building as he remembered it. There had been a pay phone outside that wasn't working and two doors from the outside—one each for the restaurant and the grocery store—because there had been no door inside between the two businesses. The surprised clerk said Ray was right. The door connecting the two areas had been installed six months ago and the pay phone had been moved inside almost a year ago. Garriola took down the number of the telephone to check against Steve's phone records. If there was a match it would be another brick in Steve's prison walls.

Back in Los Angeles, Garriola pinned the photograph of the three FBI agent-monkeys and Ray's "sprint" into Canada on a bulletin board at the FBI offices. When Mitchell saw the photograph, he almost blew smoke out his ears. No good joke goes unpunished and this one was no different. Mitchell announced that he had convinced the Department of Justice and US Attorney Meloch that Ray was a grave flight risk. They now wanted Ray locked up when he was not working on the case. Garriola, however, learned that Meloch just wanted Ray to put up his

house for bail to give him an incentive not to run. Mitchell ordered that Ray should be in jail at night until his house was
secured. Garriola broke the bad news to Ray.

Ray resigned himself to returning to the MDC until his house
could be secured for bail, but Garriola said Ray wasn't going
anywhere. He told Ray to stay indoors and out of sight. Ray
asked if Stefanek knew about Garriola's impending insubordi-
nation. No, but Garriola said he would call his partner later that
night when Stefanek was sitting down having a beer listening
to his favorite country music. That way, if Stefanek passed out
he wouldn't bump his head. Ray thanked Garriola, but the big
FBI agent said the only reason he was doing it was to get back
at Mitchell. Ray had nothing to do with it.

After a week and a half, in July 1992, Ray was officially out
on bail secured by a $79,000 bond. Bail had the side benefit,
which Mitchell obviously had not intended, of allowing Ray
much greater freedom. On bail, he did not have to stay at home
when he wasn't working the case. Furthermore, since he was
still under FBI jurisdiction, unlike individuals on bail, he did
not have to report to a Federal Probation Officer once a week.

Soon after, Stefanek and Garriola, both grinning like drunk-
en sailors, knocked on Ray's door. They had caught a break:
Louie had finally written back. It turned out that Ray hadn't
known Louie's real name, Gilberto Rivera Lopez, which was
why the FBI had failed to find him in the National Crime Information Center (NCIC) database.

In his letter Louie said Rubin had told him Ray was looking
for him, which surprised Louie since the last time they saw each
other Ray had said to forget he even knew Ray. Even so, Louie
said Rubin had told him his old employer wanted to talk to him
about something important, which was "cool." If it was about
doing a job, that was also "cool." Louie said he would get out of
prison soon and he asked Ray to write him back.

Stefanek asked Ray what they should write back. Ray said
he would tell Louie what he wanted to hear; there was another
job waiting for him as soon as Louie got out and it would pay
very well. Stefanek said Ray couldn't just spell it out, since the
prison guards read all the inmates' mail. Ray said he would use
street language, the kind of words Louie would understand,
but the guards would not.

Ray's reply worked. Louie started writing Ray on a regular basis. Then Louie started calling Ray collect. At first Stefanek or Garriola taped the conversations, but soon they left Ray to run the tape recorder alone.

Ray also met Rubin several times. Louie's brother was eager for Ray to get him involved in something profitable. Whenever they met, such as at a McDonalds in East Los Angeles, Stefanek and Garriola were always close by, watching and listening through a wire on Ray. Each time they met Ray gave Rubin money in hopes of cementing his relationship with Louie. Eventually, when Ray was firmly in contact with Louie, he drifted away from Rubin, but not before Rubin took the government for almost a grand. After several months of letters and phone calls, Louie asked Ray to visit him in prison. Louie said he would send him an application and Ray, acting ignorant of the prison system, sounded surprised that you needed an application to visit someone in prison. "They don't let just anybody in," Louie said. They had to make sure you were clean but, he said, Ray shouldn't have any problem. Louie need not have worried. The FBI ensured Ray's application was quickly approved.

Even as the case progressed against Louie, the Feds had far from forgotten Steve. The FBI agents decided it was time for Ray once again to approach his former employer. The issue of wearing a wire arose again. As before, Ray was opposed, especially since Steve had almost found the last one. Garriola thought Ray might be right, but Stefanek could not believe Garriola was seriously considering letting Ray not wear a wire. Garriola argued that if Steve found a wire now, it would cripple the case. They already had evidence of Steve giving Ray money. The next objective was to get Steve to feel safe with Ray, so Steve would talk about the murder. Stefanek reluctantly agreed; Ray would not wear a wire.

On September 23, 1992, with Garriola and Stefanek alongside taping the call, Ray called Steve from a pay phone in Brentwood and used the code name Dave Davenport, a name Steve had suggested the last time they had met. Ray played the role of a businessman interested in having the Chippendales troupe perform at several clubs he owned in Europe. Ray asked if Steve would have time to meet for lunch that afternoon, since

Ray said he was due to leave for Europe very soon. Steve asked when he would be leaving. Ray said in a few weeks, although he was having a little difficulty with his passport. It was nothing serious, Ray said, wanting to reassure Steve that he would be leaving. Ray again asked if they could meet for lunch and waited anxiously for his old friend's reply.

Steve said he was busy but after a long pause asked Ray if he knew where the Vons supermarket was off 9th Street in Santa Monica. Steve said he would meet him there at 2 o'clock and they could go somewhere for lunch.

The FBI operation that afternoon was on a Napoleonic scale. Since Ray would not be wearing a wire, the FBI wanted Steve and their confidential informant (CI), Ray, under surveillance at all times. Although the possibility of Steve killing his co-conspirator was slight, the agents did not want to risk Ray without prudent precautions. If they lost him, the case against Steve would be gravely weakened. Ten agents and an FBI tech van met in a parking lot near Vons to review the operation. Garriola explained that the goal was to observe Ray and Steve at all times, while ensuring that Steve never saw them.

One agent asked what kind of car Steve would be driving; a gold 300SD Mercedes Benz. The agent then asked what car the CI, Ray, would be driving. Garriola said Ray would drive his own car, a yellow Mercedes 300SD.

"Hell, I should become one of the bad guys," the agent said, which sparked laughter from the other agents.

Ten minutes later Ray stood in the parking lot of the Vons waiting for Steve. Garriola and Stefanek sat in their car parked a half block up the street. Wacko sat in his car parked a half block away in the opposite direction. The tech van was parked in the Vons lot with a clear view of Ray. Another FBI unit was parked several blocks away on Wilshire Boulevard, another on Santa Monica Boulevard, and yet another on Ocean Avenue forming a box around the Vons. Whichever way Steve drove after picking up Ray, he would have more company than he planned.

Even though he was watching the street, Ray didn't see Steve's Mercedes pull up beside him. Steve rolled down the passenger window and shouted, "Get in!"

Ray jumped into the passenger seat and barely had time to buckle up before Steve roared off, almost hitting an oncoming car. Steve asked if anyone was following them as he craned his neck back and forth, scanning the lot behind them even as he accelerated into the street.

Ray braced himself against the door and dashboard as Steve began to pat Ray down for a wire. Ray did not mind being patted down since he wasn't wearing a wire, but as he patted Ray down, Steve drove with one hand like a drunken cocaine addict.

Steve suddenly made a left turn, cutting across traffic. A car almost slammed into Ray's door before Steve gunned the engine and they slipped between two cars into an alley. Leaving an accident behind them, Steve sped down the narrow alley.

Finally they reached Loew's Hotel in Santa Monica without causing any more traffic accidents. Steve led the way through the lobby straight into the restroom. Once again, Steve thoroughly searched Ray for a wire. Ray asked if Steve was going to have to search him every time they met. Steve replied that Ray could check him any time he wanted. Ray declined. After the search they went into the restaurant off the lobby. A waiter wearing a black vest and a colorful tie acceded to Steve's request to be seated in the back corner of the almost empty restaurant. The lunch crowd had left and dinner was a long time off. Steve and Ray ordered lunch and ate as they made small talk about the food, the weather and their families. Their conversation, however, soon turned to Steve's most serious problem: Ray.

Hoping to get Steve onto the subject of murder, Ray said Steve could always have him killed.

Steve said, "That isn't even funny." If he had wanted Ray killed, he would have had it done long ago. Between Ray and his Mafia friends, Steve said he didn't even want to think about how much Ray had already cost him. Steve thought Ray was probably worth more than he was now.

With all the Mafia people Ray knew, Steve wondered why Ray hadn't just hired one of them to do the job instead of some "stupid redneck?"

Ray said he had been trying to protect Steve. If the Mafia had got involved, Ray remembers saying, "God only knows what might have happened."

"What's the difference?" Steve asked. "They're involved anyway and I'm handing out money like some sort of Wall Street Santa Claus."

Ray admitted making some mistakes. Steve blew up, claiming Ray's mistakes had cost him a fortune. Steve said he would have been better off "dealing with De Noia and those other pricks!"

Ray wished he had worn a wire; the operation would have been over.

"Now who's being careless?" Ray asked, glancing around the empty restaurant. "Don't even mention that shit."

Steve scanned the room and asked Ray if he was really going to Europe. Ray assured him he was leaving as soon as he got a phony passport. Steve wondered what the odds were of the authorities catching Ray in Europe. Ray assured him that he had a better than average chance of never getting caught. As an ex-cop, he said, he knew how the system worked. The biggest mistake most people on the run make, he said, was to try and make contact with their family or friends. "You just can't do it."

Steve nodded and asked when Ray would be leaving. Ray didn't know for sure, but said, "Three weeks at the latest." He just wanted to make sure Steve wouldn't turn his back on him once he was in Europe. Steve said he would be crazy to leave Ray out in the cold, since if they caught Ray, he would be next. Ray promised that even if he was arrested, he would never roll on Steve. The Chippendales creator didn't believe him. He wondered if Ray should even go to Europe. As soon as the FBI knew Ray had run, Steve said, they would alert Interpol and Ray would be a wanted man all over the world. Ray said there had been people who had been on the run for 30 years. Steve suggested hiding in India or Cuba, where the authorities would never think of looking for Ray.

"India!" Ray said. "Are you nuts! I'll be damned if I'm going to live in some Third World country with a red dot on my head like some target waiting for my brains to be blown away."

Steve exploded that Ray was talking about his country. Ray apologized, but said that it was Steve's country, not his. Furthermore, Ray said he didn't want to go to a country where Steve could have "some poor slob kill me for the price of a quart of milk." Steve said India would be the perfect place for Ray. He could live like a king. Steve even offered to arrange for a kidney transplant. Ray grinned and said, "And arrange for me to never wake up from the operation."

Stung by the remark, Steve said Ray had always been like a brother to him. He could never think of doing something like that to his old friend.

Ray said he might go to Spain. He had been there before and, being of Puerto Rican descent, he would blend in well there.

Finally, Steve said he had heard enough of Ray's plans and said he wouldn't meet or talk to Ray again until Ray was out of the country. Steve offered Ray $50,000, but only after Ray had left the country.

Ray assured Steve that the next time they met, it would be on the "other side of the world," assuming, Ray added, he even made it there.

Steve grabbed the check and, throwing some bills on the table, said Ray shouldn't talk like that. Ray remembers Steve saying, "C'mon, let's get out of here before I get so depressed that I kill myself right here and now."

Ray thanked Steve for lunch, and then asked for a few dollars for gas.

"Walk," Steve said. "Until I know you're in Europe, I ain't giving you another dime."

Ray drove back to the FBI garage and complimented the agents on their shadowing. Even Ray hadn't spotted them. Stefanek angrily replied that they weren't seen because they had lost Ray and Steve. Garriola asked where they had gone and was shocked when Ray said the restaurant at Loew's Hotel. Garriola had checked it out. He hadn't seen Ray or Steve. Ray insisted they had been there and described the waiter. Garriola asked if Steve had given him any more money. Ray shook his head. "You sure?" Stefanek asked. Ray spread his arms to be searched, but the agents told him to forget it. While Wacko and Stefanek debriefed Ray, Garriola planned to return to Loew's Hotel to verify Ray's story. Ray was angered by Garriola's lack of trust in him, but the agent said it had nothing to do with trust. Unless they had corroboration that Ray and Steve had been at the restaurant, in court it would be just Ray's word against Steve's.

Garriola found his corroboration in the waiter and several other people at the restaurant who had seen the pair.

The agents were frustrated that Steve would not talk to Ray until he was in Europe. The Justice Department would never approve such a trip. The government did not let convicted felons leave the country. Ray had told Steve that he would not leave for several weeks, which at least gave the agents some time to try and convince their bosses and the Justice Department to allow the trip, even though the agents knew they had a better chance of building a ski resort in the Mojave than of winning approval for such a trip.

They were not surprised, therefore, when Mitchell roared that Garriola and Stefanek were not even sure what Steve had told Ray, since he hadn't been wearing a wire. For all they knew, Steve and Ray were planning to flee together. Going to Maine was one thing, Mitchell said, but taking Ray to Europe was out of the question. Stefanek and Garriola argued for the trip but knew that if Ray ran, their careers would be finished. Even as the agents tried to obtain permission for Ray to go to Europe, Steve traveled extensively to Europe, Canada and Asia overseeing the Chippendales tours.

While others debated whether to let Ray go to Europe, Stefanek and Garriola once more visited Marty Bress at D.B. Cooper's. The FBI already had $54,000 Steve had given Ray at three meetings, but the more money they could get the tighter their case. Marty was a better song and dance man than Fred Astaire, however, and they came up empty. Worse, every time they visited Marty, Ray sweated that Marty might tell the agents that he was also holding some money Ray had given the bar owner before his arrest. Short on money and tired of battling his nerves every time the Feds visited Marty, Ray drove to D.B. Cooper's one morning.

After patiently and carefully checking the area for any FBI surveillance and seeing none, Ray parked and walked over to the bar. Ray later said he found his old friend taking inventory in the liquor room. When Ray asked for the money from Steve and his own money, Marty told the same old story; he was having trouble pulling it together from the people to whom he had loaned it. He promised that Ray would get all of his money back. "Have I ever done you wrong before?" Ray remembers Bress asking.

"No, but you've never had this much money before," Ray said. Fearing he might not have the opportunity to deliver his message again, Ray added that he had known Marty for 15 years. They were supposed to be friends, so Marty better not think he could pull a fast one on him.

Marty shoved a box of mixer onto a shelf, rattling the bottles inside, and promised to do the best he could to get Ray's money together. Then he brushed by Ray, who shouted, "I know what you were thinking, Marty. You were thinking that Ray is never coming out. He's in for the run, but I surprised you, didn't I? Remember, Marty, I'm not always going to be under the gun! Remember that, Marty! Remember!"

Ray had delivered his message, but the next day Garriola delivered his own message. As Ray watered his front lawn, Garriola and Stefanek screeched up in their sedan and stalked up to him. In foul moods, they said they had to talk and led the way into Ray's den. Garriola yelled that they knew about Ray's meeting with Marty. If Ray ever went near the bar owner again they would charge him with obstruction of justice and put him right back into the MDC. Garriola didn't even want to see Marty's number on Ray's phone bill.

Ray yelled back that Marty was lying to them. Stefanek and Garriola said they knew that, but they needed the bar owner to testify against Steve and Marty knew it, which was why he could play games with them.

Stefanek asked, "Why else would he call us to say you were threatening him?"

The question had a withering effect on Ray.

"Maybe you should learn to pick better friends," Garriola suggested.

For the first time in a long time, Ray just wanted to laugh at the irony of it all. Marty was screwing Ray, just as Ray was trying to screw Steve, and there was not a thing Ray could do about it.

By then, Ray needed a good laugh. He was writing a motion picture script to try and take his mind off the case, his future in prison, and the state of his life. Depression was growing in him like a black cloud that seeped into his heart, soul and thoughts.

Things he once took pleasure in no longer even brought a smile. He felt weighed down by life and the worst of it was that he knew he had brought it all upon himself. Steve had been the catalyst, but Ray had stayed involved with the Chippendales magnate throughout their various crimes together. Worst of all, there was a growing gulf, widening by the day, between Ray and Barbara. They hugged less often, kissed less often and talked less often. They were two people acting like a couple; shadows of their former married selves. Ray was already beginning to pay, at least a little, for his crimes.

Chapter 19
Visiting Louie

By late 1992 Ray had become Louie's golden goose. Louie thought that once he was out, he would hit the jackpot with more work from his old employer. Ray was writing Louie regularly and the one-time hit man was asking for things, including cash for himself, $1,500 for his wife and children, a *Los Angeles Times* subscription, and a top-of-the-line radio for a female inmate at another prison, who was not his wife. The FBI arranged everything. They wanted Louie to keep talking to Ray in hopes the subject of murder would come up.

Finally it was time for Ray to pay Louie a visit. On October 1, 1992, at 3:00 p.m., Stefanek, Garriola and Ray waited in Garriola's Bronco outside the California Rehabilitation Center (CRC) in Norco. The center sat on the former site of the opulent 700-acre Lake Norconian Resort in Riverside County, southeast of Los Angeles, which had opened in 1929 and became a playground for the Hollywood elite. After suffering during the Great Depression and serving as a naval hospital during World War II, part of the land was sold to the state in the early 1960s to build a prison. The CRC at Norco, a contraction of North Corona, opened in 1963 as a male-only prison. On 98 acres, it had about 1,100 staff and an inmate population of about 2,500 in what was called Level II housing; open dormitories with secure perimeter fences and armed coverage. Its best known programs were six structured Substance Abuse Programs; at the time the world's largest in-custody substance abuse program, although the effectiveness of the programs was debated. After much study, they appeared to have little effect on recidivism. By the turn of the 21st Century, the prison was overcrowded, dilapidated and fights were common. One indication of the deterioration was that the power had to be turned off during rain storms to avoid electrocuting the prisoners.

Just outside the CRC, the assistant warden explained to Ray and the FBI agents that his guards would ensure Ray entered the prison without any problems. The last thing the FBI wanted was for Ray to be seen to be anything other than a guest of one of the inmates.

As Ray drove into the prison, the assistant warden led Garriola and Stefanek to a small, Spartan office with a one-way mirror facing the visitors' patio. Garriola set up a camera with a zoom lens on a tripod to photograph the meeting. They also had a receiver to listen to the conversation via a wire hidden on Ray.

After parking the Bronco, Ray followed the other visitors, some in their Sunday best, through the steel doors of the prison and up to a metal detector. As he approached the detector the guard hesitated. Ray feared the plan was about to fall apart, but then a guard captain, standing to one side, nodded to the guard. As Ray walked through the machine with his hidden microphone and tape recorder, the guard switched off the machine for a moment. None of the other visitors noticed anything out of the ordinary. The last thing the FBI wanted was for word to reach Louie that the guards had treated Ray any differently than any other visitor.

At the entrance to the visitors' room, Ray waited in line before a desk where guards checked visitors' authorization forms and identification. As Ray approached, a guard looked him over as if something wasn't right. Ray could see and hear inmates in the next room through an open door as the first visitors entered the visiting room. Any incident here and Louie would definitely hear about it.

But again, at the last second, the captain approached the guard and whispered in his ear. The guard glanced at Ray's paperwork and told him to leave his car keys and identification at the table. The guard handed him a claim ticket for his keys and Ray walked into the visiting room. He sat at a small, round metal table and waited. Joyous reunions erupted around him as inmates greeted wives, hugged children and embraced parents, brothers and sisters. Other reunions were far more sedate. Ray scanned the crowd, but did not see Louie. The minutes ticked by. Children grew bored with their visits and some couples with nothing left to say sat in silence. The longer he waited for Louie the more nervous Ray became. Had something gone wrong?

Just as Ray was about to give up, Louie sauntered into the visiting room. He spotted Ray and, as he approached, Ray flipped the switch in his pocket to start the tape recorder. The two men embraced. Ray hoped Louie wouldn't notice the wire running down his back under his shirt and coat.

"What's up, *Ese*?" Louie asked, using a slang Spanish word for friend. He hadn't felt the wire. "Long time no see."

As they sat at the metal table, Louie explained that a guard had only just told him that he had a visitor. He said he figured something must be important for Ray to want to come see him in prison, especially after what Ray had told him the last time they saw each other. Ray apologized about that, and said he really needed Louie's help. In fact, Louie was the only one he could trust to do the job. Louie was interested. Glancing around like a thief in a police station, Ray said he felt nervous in the prison and asked if they could talk outside. Louie said it must be really serious. After getting some food from the battered, grate-covered vending machines, they walked outside and down the chipped concrete steps to a patio. Louie had a microwaved burrito, a bag of chips and a soda, while Ray, too nervous to eat, just sipped a soda.

Ray told Louie he had a big problem and Ray stressed that Louie was the only one who could fix it. Ray moved in closer to make sure no one could overhear and mentioned "the thing" they had done in New York.

"Something came back and bit me in the ass," Ray said. "If I don't take care of the problem, my life will be on the line."

Louie looked grave as Ray explained that his people were pissed off at him. He reassured Louie that it had nothing to do with Louie, especially since they didn't even know Louie's identity. Ray's problem was related to the blond guy Louie had run into before he did his "thing" with De Noia, and who later followed the hit man down the stairs. Ray said the witness was giving his people a hard time.

"You mean blackmailing them?" Louie asked in disbelief. He thought he had made the hit for the Mafia. Who would dare blackmail La Cosa Nostra and, if anyone did, why were they still alive?

"Not exactly," Ray said. "He claims to know through some so-called source who ordered the hit, and he wants money to keep his mouth shut."

"Why don't they take him out?"

"Because they don't know who he is. He's hiding like a rat in a sewer and you're the only one who knows what the little ass-hole looks like. He told the police that he didn't see nothing and couldn't identify the shooter because it all happened so damn fast. So we know for sure he's not talking to the police, but he wants a payoff to continue his loss of memory."

"He's playing hardball with the mob?" Louie asked, still not believing anyone would be stupid enough to even attempt such a thing.

"In a way, yes. If they really wanted to, they could take him out. But if they did that, they'd probably take me out as well for being so stupid for not popping him right there and then after all he'd seen. I told my people I could fix it. I know where the prick lives and as soon as you get out I want you to take care of this guy. It's the only way my security is going to remain intact. You do remember what he looks like, right?"

"I think so, but what's to say they don't kill you after I do it and then come after me?"

"They can't. I never told them who you are. They already know you're solid and they were very impressed with your work. It's me they're pissed off at. I straighten this out and everything returns to normal. In fact, there are a few other things I want you to work on after we get rid of this situation."

Louie then turned to the most important issue; money. Ray said he would pay $100,000 with a guarantee that his people would never know Louie's identity. The heroin-addicted hit man could not believe the Mafia would agree to such a deal, but Ray said they had no choice. He stressed that time was of the utmost importance, but Louie said he wouldn't be out of prison for a few months.

"That's a pretty long time for these people, but I can try and convince them to wait. The point is you know I'm for real, Louie, and you know I'll give you top dollar."

"Yo, Homes, I already know that, I just don't want to end up with a bullet in my head after it's over."

"That ain't going to happen. The question is, can you pull it off?" Ray asked, fishing for evidence to put Louie in prison for the rest of his life.

"Of course I can. You already know that. I just have to be careful I don't step on the wrong toes. I know your people play for keeps, *Ese*."

"No one will ever know who you are."

Louie thought for a moment, but then his mind focused on only one thing: "A hundred thousand, huh?"

"Cash, and you know damn well I'll pay it. Like I said, there are a few other items I need you for and those can be worth a lot more than that."

"For real?"

"You do the job right, I'll be using you for a lot of heavy shit worth top dollar. But before we can even go there we've got to get rid of that kid. I already have two other jobs lined up, each of which could be worth over a hundred thousand each. The question is, can I count you in?"

"Hell, yeah, Homes. So long as I'm dealing only with you," Louie said, emphasizing the trust that was at the foundation of every criminal endeavor. "I don't want to meet them or even know who they are. No offense, but I know how those big boys play. I don't want to do the job then end up floating in some damn river."

Ray promised.

"Then you can count me in."

A guard announced that visiting hours were over. Ray and Louie embraced. Louie asked Ray to visit again, since his family and friends rarely made the hour-plus trip from Los Angeles to the prison. Ray promised he would try to visit again.

On the drive back to Los Angeles, Ray sat in the back of the Bronco, drained and exhausted. Garriola said they would need more to convict Louie. Ray said he knew that, but that he had wanted to get Louie talking freely before he shifted into a discussion of the De Noia thing. At least it was a first step.

Ray was writing a motion picture script in his home office one day in October 1992 when the telephone rang. It was Rocky Delamo. The Mafiosi had been released from jail the week before and wanted Ray to come over to his condo.

Ray tried to figure out why Rocky wanted to see him. His former boss would know that Ray couldn't do any jobs for him. Had Rocky decided to kill him? Ray knew about the squeeze play on Chippendales, and he was probably the only link between Rocky and Steve. What if Rocky feared the Feds would mistakenly link him to the De Noia murder through Ray?

Ray tried to beg off, saying he never knew when the Feds might stop by, but Rocky said it would only take half an hour and it was important. Ray said that if Rocky was planning on whacking him, he understood. He remembers saying, "Just put me in the front seat of the car, drive me into the desert and do the deed. All I ask is that I don't know when it's coming."

Rocky roared with laughter. He said if he had wanted to do that, it would have been done long ago. He promised no one was going to hurt Ray. He gave Ray his word.

Ray still debated whether to go, but realized he had no choice. If he ran, even to the Feds, his life wouldn't be worth two cents. The Mafia could kill him just as easily in prison as on the outside, and the witness protection program wasn't exactly as secure as Fort Knox. If Rocky was going to whack him, Ray knew, he would already be under the all-seeing eyes of Mafia soldiers.

Thirty minutes later, Ray reached Rocky's condo in Thousand Oaks northwest of Los Angeles in the San Fernando Valley. Ray drummed his fingers on his thighs as he stood at the open doorway, frozen with fear. If he entered, Rocky might shoot him as a burglar right in the hall. The door swung farther open and his old mentor stood there, grinning. Rocky made fun of Ray for not just coming in, since the door was open.

Ray walked in and sat in the chair closest to the door as he glanced at the dining room table laden from end to end with cakes, donuts, croissants, coffee, tea, and alcohol for Rocky's homecoming party. Crew members lounged around the room eating and drinking even as they closely watched Ray. Rocky brought Ray a cup of coffee, sat down and put his right hand over Ray's hands.

Rocky told Ray he was doing the right thing. Steve had let Ray rot in jail and would never have helped him. Ray said Steve had already paid Rocky a lot of money, but Rocky said it wasn't nearly enough for what Steve had put Ray through. Steve, Rocky said, was lucky they hadn't taken every dime the Chippendales czar had.

Ray gulped his coffee, letting the hot liquid course through his shaking body. He asked what would happen next; would he be allowed to walk out of the condo?

Rocky turned to his crew and laughed. "Will you fucking listen to this guy!" Rocky said he considered Ray a hero. Ray had done the right thing. He made a little money, Rocky made a little money, and the asshole—Steve—was going to get what he deserved. Rocky said it didn't get any better than that.

Rocky said Ray wasn't cut out for his line of work. Ray had a conscience and, to people like Rocky and his associates, that was dangerous. Rocky told Ray to finish the Banerjee thing and get on with his life.

Ray said he worried about being a marked man, for having left Rocky's employ and for having cooperated with the Feds, but Rocky blew up. He had ordered Ray to cooperate.

"You're no rat," Ray remembers Rocky roaring. Rocky threatened that if he ever heard anyone call Ray a rat, he would "rip his fucking eyes out."

Ray rose slowly, still not sure whether Rocky's words were just a way to put him at ease before the hammer fell.

"I appreciate all you've done for me, Rocky. I mean that."

They embraced.

Rocky asked if Ray needed any cash. Ray didn't want any money. He just wanted his life back.

Rocky said he could take care of Ray's little problem with Marty Bress. Ray could make "the bastard disappear" as his going-away gift. Ray was surprised Rocky knew about his problem with the bar owner, but he also realized that Rocky was letting him walk away alive because the Mafia boss knew Ray hadn't told the Feds a thing about Rocky or his crew.

Ray wanted to say yes to the offer about Bress, but declined. If anything happened to Marty, Ray would be the first one the Feds would, as Ray put it, "slam against the wall."

Ray looked over at the crew, some of whom he had known for 20 years, and said goodbye. None of them said a word. Rocky walked with Ray to the door, where they embraced again, and then Ray walked out the door. Ray kept thinking that any second they would drag him back inside to whack him. His legs almost gave out. He had never been so scared in his life. But nothing happened. Rocky had given him a pass. It was a gift Ray treasured for the rest of his life.

Chapter 20
Louie Done

Almost two months after his first visit, on December 10, 1992, Ray was back in the white Bronco with Garriola and Stefanek driving to the CRC in Norco to visit Louie again. Once again Ray carried a hidden mike and tape recorder with a switch in his pocket. Once again he was a nervous wreck.

Stefanek mentioned that it would probably be Ray's last chance to get Louie to talk. Ray didn't need to be told. Garriola added that if anything went wrong, they would all be in trouble. Ray snapped at the agents to get off his back.

Ray and Louie once again sat at the table they had used during Ray's first visit. After half an hour of small talk, Ray tried to shift the conversation toward the only subject he cared about: the De Noia murder. Ray asked why Louie hadn't popped the blond witness in the stairwell.

Louie said he almost did, but the guy stopped coming down. In another 10 seconds, he would have shot the guy.

Ray again explained that his "people" were giving him a hard time over it. He wished Louie had "done" the witness then and there, so no one could identify Louie.

Louie said the guy was so scared, he doubted he even remembered what Louie looked like.

Ray casually asked if De Noia seemed scared.

Louie said, not really. Louie said he walked into the office and De Noia was sitting behind his desk. Louie asked if he was Nick De Noia, and when the choreographer said, "Yes," Louie replied, "You're dead." Louie told Ray that De Noia kind of half stood up and smiled nervously, probably thinking it was a joke. Louie pulled out the gun and shot De Noia once in the face.

Ray asked whether Louie had been scared, even a little bit.

Louie said he hadn't had time to get scared. He knew it had to be done, so he did it. But he said he didn't want to talk about it anymore. It was over and done with.

Ray agreed. Louie didn't know how accurate his statement was; it was over and done with.

Ray said their big problem now was taking care of that "other nosey prick."

Louie said, "We'll see how long he lasts once I hit the bricks."

Ray patted Louie on the back and said, "Now that's what I want to hear, a man with a positive attitude."

The next day, drained from the previous day's meeting, Ray was watering his front lawn when the white Bronco screeched to a stop in his driveway. Garriola and Stefanek bolted out of the truck and ordered Ray into the house. They looked angry enough to kill him on the spot, although he was oblivious as to the cause of their anger.

Once inside, Stefanek pushed Ray onto the sofa and loomed over him as the agent shouted that Ray had sabotaged the operation. Stefanek roared that they had trusted him and he had repaid them by double-crossing them.

Ray was dumbfounded, wracking his mind to figure out what Stefanek was screaming about. Finally Ray figured it out; not a word of the conversation between Ray and Louie was on tape.

Ray swore he turned the machine on the moment Louie walked into the visiting room, but all the tape recorded was Ray and the agents talking on the drive out to the prison. It had been off the whole time Ray talked with Louie. Stefanek accused Ray of sabotaging the operation. Ray said he just screwed up. Nervous, he had turned the recorder on when he thought he was turning it off, and off when he thought he was turning it on.

Furious, Stefanek paced before Ray. Ray said he would just have to go back and try again. Stefanek was certain Louie would never talk about the murder again. It was over. Ray begged him for one more chance. Stefanek threatened to send Ray back to the MDC and work the case alone. Ray yelled right back at him. He had enough pressure on him without Stefanek's threats. Stefanek yelled that any pressure on Ray was self-inflicted.

Stefanek turned to Garriola. The partners grinned at each other.

"I think he's mad at us, Scott," Ray remembers Stefanek telling Garriola, who nodded. Stefanek put his hand on Ray's shoulder and told him to relax. They had just wanted to make sure Ray was on their side.

Ray would get one more chance to get Louie to talk.

Several nights later, at 11 o'clock, the case took yet another twist when Tammy Bressler, Strawberry's wife, called Barbara Colon. As Ray listened in on the other line and recorded the conversation, Tammy, who sounded drunk, railed against her husband, whom she thought the Feds had hidden somewhere in Ohio. Barbara asked why Tammy had told the FBI that Barbara had been harassing her. Tammy apologized and said she had been scared. She had not wanted Ray, whom the FBI said had Mafia connections, to hurt her or her children. Ray didn't follow her logic, but in any case it was the last time they ever heard from Tammy.

With the Christmas party for Barbara's hospital approaching, some of the doctors and nurses said they did not want Ray to attend. When Ray found out, he went ballistic. Even so, if Barbara wanted him to, he would stay home. Living up to his expectations that he had married a fighter, Barbara said she wanted to go with him. They went to the party and had a good time. Even so, his relationship with Barbara was deteriorating. Barbara now knew Ray for what he was, a small-time thug who had worked for the Mafia, threatening and hurting people, arranging arsons and, finally, conspiring to murder five people, with one resulting in a homicide. She would never feel the same way about him and he could not blame her for it. Yet, in spite of all of that, he later said, she was still willing to give of herself, to love and forgive him for all he had done. Ray later wrote that the enormity of what he had done brought on a dark feeling of self-hatred. He did not feel worthy of her, so he was the one who kept his distance. She would go to hug him and he would avoid her embrace. He would turn his check to her kisses. He knew that by withdrawing into a cocoon of self-loathing he would end up losing the only person he had ever truly loved. It was the only punishment, he later wrote, that his conscience could devise for his mortal sins.

On December 24, 1992, Ray once again sat waiting to visit Louie at the CRC in Norco. He felt the pressure of the moment, compounded by the foul moods of Stefanek and Garriola, who were missing Christmas Eve with their families. Ray had no idea what he was going to say to Louie. He had to get Louie to confess to the murder on tape. Louie would get suspicious if Ray kept visiting to talk about "the De Noia thing." This would be Ray's last chance.

Louie strolled into the visiting room and waved happily at Ray. It was cool in the desert and Ray held his jacket tight, apparently against the cold, but really to steady his shaking hands. They sat outside in the desert chill at their usual table. Ray decided to go for broke right away.

"My people are really starting to bust my balls about this fucking blond fag," he said as the FBI taped every word. "This is serious. They're about ready to cut my fucking balls off." He hoped Louie would attribute Ray's nervousness to fear of the Mafia and not to apprehension about getting Louie to talk.

Louie said they would have to wait until he got out.

"Maybe we can work out a plan so as soon as you're out we can get the fucking thing over with," Ray said. "The man's gotta be whacked. These people are serious and after all this time, I still don't know all the details. You've got to talk to me Louie, so at least I know what happened and can answer their questions without looking like a fool." Ray leaned in and whispered to

Louie, "Let's backtrack and see where the fuck we went wrong, so we don't make the same mistake again."

"Yo, Homes," Louie said, angry, "I didn't make no mistakes. Hell, I had to almost beg for you to give up the damn-ass gun so I could take care of business."

"I know that Louie, but you left a fucking witness alive."

"Stop right there, *Ese*. No one ever said anything about doing in that faggot."

"I know, but at the time I didn't realize just how important that blond fag would turn out to be. Now I wish the fucker had kept coming down the stairs."

"What's the difference? We already agreed I'd take care of him once I hit the bricks. Your people know where he is, don't they?"

"No fucking way! If they knew that they wouldn't need me. I'm the only one who has that information and I want to keep it that way. Do you remember what he looks like? Tell me when you first saw him."

"C'mon, Homes, I've already told you that."

"Tell me again. I want to have it straight in my head, so I know exactly how to deal with him when the time comes."

"Look, Homes, I really don't feel comfortable talking about this kind of stuff, especially in here."

"All I'm asking you is what the damn guy looked like. My fucking life is in your hands. The more I know about this guy and what happened, the more prepared I am if I'm asked for any details."

"Why the fuck do you need details?"

"You think my people are stupid? You're talking about the big boys here. They have contacts everywhere, including the police department. If I tell them something that's not even close to the police report, they'll know I'm fucking lying. They may not know who you are, but they know I was supposed to be there to make sure it went down right."

Louie glanced around to make sure no one was within earshot and whispered, "Yo, Homes, it's like I said before, once I was on the 15th floor I walked into this one office and saw the fag."

"You remember his face?"

"Hell, yeah. I'm good on shit like that. He was blond, about 25 or so. I asked him if he was De Noia. He said De Noia's office was next door."

"That was it?"

"Hell, no! I went to the restroom first and then walked into De Noia's office. He was alone, sitting at his desk. I asked him if he was Nick De Noia. He said, 'Yes' and that's when I pulled out the gun and told him 'You're dead.'"

"Holy shit. I bet he must've shit his pants when you said that."

"Not really. At first I think he thought it was a joke or something."

"A joke?"

"Yeah, cause he kind of smiled, until he saw me aim the gun at his head. That's when he knew I was there to take care of business."

"So that was it, huh?"

"Damn right that was it. I shot him in the face and then that's all, that's all I saw. I saw a little red dot on his face and I saw him going down."

"A red dot? What do you mean a red dot?"

"Where the bullet went in."

"You must've been scared as hell after that."

"I didn't have time to get scared, Homes. I jammed down the stairs. That's when that blond motherfucker started chasing me trying to play hero."

"I wish he would've kept following you so you could've taken him out."

"I would've too, if the motherfucker hadn't stopped."

"You damn sure pulled it off sweet."

"I told you I was there to take care of business."

"Yeah, that you did."

Louie laughed. "Shit! I remember how you were so scared after I got back into the car you could hardly drive. That's why I wanted to keep the gun. Shit, Homes, if we had got caught you're talking life without."

"No shit?"

"Hell, yeah; murder for hire. We both would've been sharing a cell for the rest of our lives."

The FBI taped every word. Now Louie was truly done.

Even though the FBI had what it needed on Louie, they did not act, yet. They wanted to complete the case against Steve before the Chippendales owner learned that his hit man had been arrested and charged with the De Noia murder. Unfortunately, Gilberto Rivera Lopez, prison number E90294, was due to be a free man just two weeks later. The FBI could not afford to let him walk the streets. There was no telling what he would do to Ray when he learned there would be no more jobs and no more money.

On January 7, 1993, Louie enjoyed all of two seconds of freedom. He walked out of the Norco facility and into the arms of two waiting INS agents, who arrested him. He was sentenced to 21 months in federal prison at Allenwood, PA, for being a convicted felon and an illegal alien. He probably assumed that Ray would continue to send him money and gifts as he served his new sentence. He was wrong. The FBI had all it needed. Louie soon learned that his golden goose had flown the coop. Louie was on his own and would soon be facing far more prison time than just 21 months.

In March 1993, the FBI tried to match Louie's fingerprints with those found at the De Noia murder scene. Unfortunately, the prints from the scene were not good enough to match. A photo-array with Louie in position number four was shown to witnesses, but no one identified Louie as the man who had murdered Nick De Noia. Therefore, Ray's testimony would be crucial to the case against Louie.

More than a year later, the initial interviewing conducted by the New York police, supplemented by Ray's information, allowed NYPD Detectives Richard Briecke and Michael Geddes, who had retired but still wanted to be involved, to interview Louie at the Federal Correction Facility in Big Springs, Texas. Louie had been moved to Texas, and Geddes and Briecke flew to the Lone Star State to try to close the case. The low-security facility was midway between Dallas and El Paso, just east of the southeast corner of New Mexico. With about 20,000 people, Big Springs was the setting for the opening scenes of *Midnight Cowboy*, representing the tiny, dusty town that Jon Voight's character desperately wants to escape from to go to New York.

Late in the afternoon of April 4, 1994, the two NYPD detectives arrived in Big Springs. The prison authorities told them it would be best to wait until the next morning to talk to Louie Lopez. Geddes disagreed. He wanted to talk to Lopez right away. Geddes got his way.

The US Attorney's and FBI agents involved with the case believed that Geddes would only be able to obtain a negative confession (Louie claiming he did not murder De Noia). True to the prediction, when Geddes started the interview at 6:30 p.m. Louie denied any involvement in De Noia's murder. Undeterred, Geddes carefully walked Louie through what had happened that day in precise detail. Geddes described how Ray and Louie had arrived in New York, rented a car and drove into Manhattan. How they parked at a Burger King just down from De Noia's office building. How Louie ate his burger and fries at the fast-food restaurant. Geddes described how Louie took the elevator up to De Noia's office, talked to Mott and went into the bathroom. Geddes was even able to tell Louie that he had left his Burger King soda cup in the bathroom before he returned to De Noia's office to murder the choreographer. Then Geddes described how Louie escaped down the stairs and out a service entrance. Geddes also knew from a witness that Louie had turned left down the street to hurry back to Ray waiting in the rental car.

Louie was amazed. Geddes vast number of small details convinced Louie that someone had rolled on him. Since the police knew so much, Louie decided he might as well cooperate. He made a "lengthy and detailed confession," which Louie later signed as a written statement. There were small discrepancies between what Ray had told the FBI and Louie's statement; Louie denied ever waving down at Ray from the building's stairwell and said the "soda cup in the crime scene photo was not his." The facts at the core of their stories, however, matched. The crucial conclusion was clear; on April 7, 1987 in Manhattan, Gilberto Rivera "Louie" Lopez murdered Nicholas "Nick" John De Noia.

How had the money he was paid to murder Nick De Noia benefited the murderer? Louie said he spent "the entire $25,000 on heroin and a few debts within a short time."

And remorse? By the time he confessed, almost seven years after the murder, Louie could not even remember for certain his victim's name, "I remember it as Nick or Dick."

Chapter 21
Europe

By January 1993, Steve thought Ray had fled to Europe. Stefanek and Garriola worried that Steve might hire private investigators to make sure Ray was no longer in the United States. Worse, Steve might put a contract out on his old friend, so the agents ordered Ray to remain out of sight. Still believing Steve had some semblance of friendship for him, Ray couldn't believe his old friend would put a hit out on him. Even so, he was ready. He carried a .25 automatic tucked in his pants when he was at home. Stefanek did not like it when Ray showed him the gun. Ray told him not to worry. He would only use it if someone started shooting at him.

The FBI agents had little hope they could ever convince their bosses, let alone the US Attorney's to allow Ray to go to Europe to meet Steve. At the end of January 1993, however, the Justice Department told a shocked Ray that he was going to Europe. The FBI gave him a passport with a fictitious name to show Steve when the time came.

On January 28, 1993, the FBI had Ray send Steve a note by messenger in an envelope marked, "Steve Only! Personal!!!" The note read, "Dear Steve, By the time you receive this letter I'll already be doing the show overseas. I'll be calling you soon, so you can bring the show to me. Please, Steve, don't let me down. Ciao."

Ray, Garriola, Stefanek, and an FBI tech agent flew to Italy. In Rome, Ray and the FBI agents met with the Italian police. The Italians thought there was a strong possibility that Steve would try and have Ray murdered once he knew where Ray was hiding. They wanted to put him in jail for his own protection when he was not working the case. Garriola convinced them that it would not work that way, since Steve would check on Ray's living arrangements. Instead, the FBI rented a one-bedroom apartment in the heart of Rome, where Ray was supposedly living on the run.

The FBI had Ray try calling Steve from Rome, but they were unable to connect. On February 3, Ray wrote Steve again as ungrammatical and misspelled as before; "Dear Mr. Banagee, Per our conversation and agreements several months ago, I am faxing you this letter to let you know that I am starting a new production in Rome, and therefore, am very interested in you bringing your show to Rome. It is most urgent that I discuss this matter with you personally. I called you at home from Rome, but somehow lost the connection. When I tried again the phone was busy all night. I was first told that you were on your way to Europe." Ray then gave Steve a phone and a fax number for him in Rome, and said he wanted to meet in Rome. "Since I am now fully committed to this European production indefinitely and therefore unable to return to the US at this time. Please seize this business opportunity immediately so that our business can benefit the both of us."

Ray remembered that he and the three agents were having breakfast in the hotel restaurant one morning when Stefanek said between bites of pastry, "I seriously doubt we'll ever hear from him."

"Here we go again," Ray said, dropping his knife and fork with a clatter. He was tired of Stefanek's negative attitude. "Has your wife ever wanted to shoot you?"

"All the time," Stefanek said with a grin, "but I'm the guy with the gun."

"When's her birthday?"

Even as the agents and Ray discussed whether to send another more threatening fax to Steve, a reply arrived. Steve said he would be in Europe in a few days.

"You see, gentleman," Ray said, "Patience is a virtue."

"He's not here yet," Stefanek said.

Ray turned to Garriola and asked, "Is there a black market in Italy?"

"Sure, why?"

"I really need to buy a gun."

On February 4, Ray, using the code name Dan Davenport, called Steve on a taped line. To Ray's surprise, Steve took his call, but told Ray to fax any correspondence to one of Steve's friends, Dave Osborne,* who lived in England. Osborne would forward Ray's messages to Steve.

Realizing that Steve wanted no direct contact with Ray, the FBI agents wondered how they were ever going to arrange a meeting between Ray and Steve. Ray believed he had to convince Steve to trust him, which meant convincing Steve that seeing Ray was in Steve's best interest. As long as Ray was free, in Steve's mind, the club owner was in the clear. But the only way to ensure Ray remained a free man was for Steve to give Ray enough money to continue his life on the run. To ensure Ray had the money to stay out of the FBI's clutches, Ray believed that Steve would meet him.

By fax, Steve said he would be staying at the Ramada Renaissance Hotel in Amsterdam, Holland, from February 6 through 10. He asked Ray to contact him at the hotel. On February 6 at 7:27 p.m. Ray called Steve in Amsterdam. The FBI taped the call. Sounding upset, Ray immediately asked why Steve had told Osborne about Ray and where he was hiding. Steve said not to worry, but Ray emphasized that he was on the run and couldn't afford any missteps. Having just told Ray not to worry, Steve then said he didn't want to talk on the phone because he didn't know who might be listening. Ray said no one was listening, although his words did little to reassure the suspicious Chippendales owner. Ray returned to the subject of Osborne, but Steve said his friend was just a secretary, a "nobody" who knew nothing.

"You sure?" Ray asked, trying to sound as scared and cautious as a man on the run from the law.

Steve then said that Ray should not have called him, even though, as Ray pointed out, Steve had asked Ray to call him. Steve repeated that he did not want to talk on the phone. Ray shook his head, not following Steve's logic. Ray asked the key question, "When are you gonna get your butt down here?"

Steve answered out of left field by asking Ray where he was staying, at a Ramada or a Hilton? Ray said both were far too American. If he stayed at such a hotel, the authorities would find him in a minute. He said he was staying in a small hotel in central Rome. Changing course again, Steve said he didn't like where Ray was calling from.

"What are you talking about?" Ray asked, trying to follow the disjointed conversation.

Steve changed course yet again and explained his plan to travel to Rome. He said he could fly to Zurich and then drive to Italy. The problem was that he didn't think the Italians would let him cross the border. If they refused him entry, he said, he would let Ray know where he was and they could arrange to meet somewhere else. Ray said that would be alright but told Steve not to tell anyone else their plans. He then told Steve that he was not going to see anyone, except Steve. Ray didn't want to meet some stranger who turned out to be a hit man, nor did he want to deal with Steve through an intermediary, which would make it next to impossible to prove that the club owner was involved in the murder of De Noia and the conspiracy against the Adonis leaders.

Steve said, "I'm the only guy who's coming."

Steve then worried about someone tapping his telephone. Ray said that if the authorities were tapping Steve's phone, they were tapping his, and if they were tapping his, then the Feds would have already arrested him. Ray told his old friend to relax and not to worry. He urged Steve to just come and see him, adding that he hoped Steve would have something for him: money.

Steve said, "It's taken care of."

He then chastised Ray for calling him in the United States a few days before. Steve feared the call had allowed the Feds to trace where Ray was calling from and, therefore, where he was hiding. Ray promised not to call Steve again in Los Angeles, but the club owner urged Ray to move, since the Feds probably already knew he was hiding in Rome. Ray agreed, although, he said, all he wanted to do right now was meet Steve and settle things, which meant getting some money. Ray stressed that once they met, he wouldn't have to bother Steve for a long time. Steve said he would come through and told Ray to call him tomorrow.

The next day, February 7, at about 7 p.m., Ray called Steve's hotel in Amsterdam from a taped line in Garriola's room while Stefanek and Garriola looked on. Steve was paged and answered the telephone in the hotel's lobby. Steve promised he would be in Italy the next day. Ray gave a thumbs-up to the two agents.

Steve, however, quickly complicated the arranged meeting with a plan as complex as a space shuttle launch. Steve wanted Ray to travel to several cities by train and then take a limousine across the border to pick up Steve and bring him back into Italy. After the call, Garriola and Stefanek rejected the plan because it had Ray running all over Italy.

The next day Ray called Steve back in Amsterdam. Ray tried to arrange a meeting, but the plan changed repeatedly for one reason or another in a cat and mouse game as the two men each sought control of the situation. At one point Steve offered a plan that would have made the investigation drag on indefinitely, if not scuttle it entirely. He wanted to send Ray money via Federal Express. Ray scrambled to kill the idea. If Steve FedExed the money, there would be no way for Ray to get Steve ever to talk about the murder conspiracies. Ray finally convinced Steve to drop the FedEx plan. Because he had an Indian passport, Steve thought he would have to wait 30 days for a visa to enter Italy. Ray had to convince him to at least try to come to Italy. Steve put his chances at 50/50 of entering Italy and again asked why Ray would not prefer to have "it" — the money — sent to him by mail or FedEx.

"No, no, no," Ray said. "That's too risky."

Steve said it always worked. Feeling the case slipping away, Ray lost his temper and said, "I go to New York, London, and fucking Canada for you, and now you can't even come here?"

Steve said Ray hadn't gone anywhere for him. Ray asked if Steve could at least meet him in Milan. Garriola grabbed a pad and scribbled a note to Ray: 'Damn it! Make him come to Rome!'

Ray threw up his hands in despair and shook his head. If he pushed too hard Steve might call the whole thing off.

Steve suddenly asked where Ray was calling from. Ray said Rome, but Steve meant precisely where. He feared Ray was calling from his room, which the authorities might have bugged. Ray couldn't believe Steve's level of suspicion, but promised always in the future to call from a pay telephone. Then they returned to a discussion of the FedEx plan, which Ray again vetoed. He said they had to talk in person. He needed guarantees.

Steve screamed, "Don't talk about it!"

"But you know we've got to meet."

Steve said he had made reservations at the Ramada Renaissance near Zurich airport for February 10. Could they meet there? Ray said he probably could.

Steve asked for the name of a hotel near where Ray was calling from. He wanted Ray to call him with the number of a phone at the hotel's front desk. Then Steve would call Ray back at the hotel desk at seven.

After he hung up, Ray faced the angry FBI agents. They were upset that Ray had even hinted he might meet Steve in Zurich. Ray said he had no choice. Otherwise, Steve was going to send the money via FedEx and, if he did that, they would never get a meeting.

Ray, Garriola and Stefanek hurried over to a nearby hotel. Ray gave his name to the desk clerk, got the phone number and called Steve from a pay phone in the lobby to give him the number. When Steve called back, Garriola and Stefanek taped the call. After another exhausting verbal jousting match, the partners in crime finally agreed to meet in Zurich.

Garriola called US Attorney Sally Meloch and convinced her that they would have to go to Zurich to meet Steve. It might be easier anyway, Garriola argued, since the Italian authorities were not as cooperative as the FBI had hoped.

The next day, Ray, Garriola, Stefanek, and the tech agent flew to Zurich. Swiss detectives met them at the airport. They choose a hotel, the City, near the train station to make it appear as if Ray had taken the train from Rome and stopped at the first hotel he saw. Stefanek took a room at a different hotel, since he had met Banerjee several years before, when Steve had contacted the FBI about John Gotti's Mafia crew trying to muscle in on the New York Chippendales. Stefanek had met Steve several times during the course of the investigation. Nothing came of the complaint, but Stefanek did not want to risk Steve recognizing him.

It is illegal for any foreign agency to tape record a suspect in Switzerland. Once a Swiss judged signed an order, however, the local police were authorized to tape the suspect and could then make a copy of the tape for the other country's authorities. Given Steve's alleged criminal activities, the local police had no trouble persuading a judge to issue the order. The Swiss police drilled a hole in the baseboard under the sink in Ray's hotel room and installed a microphone, running the wire into the adjacent room. The FBI had the rooms on either side of Ray; Garriola on the left, the tech agent on the right. They would storm into the room if Steve threatened Ray. Since Stefanek did not want to be seen by Steve, he would work with the surveillance team. The Swiss police already had men at the airport waiting for Steve.

The Swiss also threaded a bug through the hood of Ray's jacket, so they could listen in on, and tape, any conversation Ray had with Steve outside the hotel room. Given Steve's past inclination to search him with the utmost thoroughness, Ray opposed putting a bug in his coat. Garriola told Ray to relax, especially since Steve had not found the wire at their previous meeting.

"Only because I almost had the damn thing sewn into my balls," Ray recalls saying.

Even so, the bug stayed in his coat.

Ten Swiss police followed Steve after his KLM flight from Amsterdam landed at 12:05 p.m. on February 10. The Swiss had checked the name of every person on the plane to confirm that Steve was coming alone and not bringing someone to kill Ray.

Steve rented a Mercedes at Zurich-Kloten Airport and drove the short distance to the Ramada Renaissance hotel. The police already had men inside watching Steve. The Swiss had chosen the three most likely hotels in which the club owner might stay and had placed men in each one as desk clerks, as well as deploying teams to watch each hotel. The FBI agents were impressed by the preparations and diligence of the Swiss. The police masquerading as desk clerks also had one added benefit; they would ensure Steve would be placed in a room that had an empty room on either side from where the police could insert bugs into his room and tape his conversations.

It was time. As Garriola and Stefanek looked on, Ray, as Dan Davenport, called Steve's hotel and asked for his room. Steve sounded cautious, weighing every word as if his freedom depended on it as Ray tried to confirm their 7:30 dinner meeting to discuss the possibility of a Chippendales dance troupe performing at his fictional club. Steve tried to back out, explaining that he would be in Zurich for only two days and he was quite busy. Steve suggested discussing the issue via fax.

Ray countered that he would only be in Zurich until tomorrow, when he was leaving for several months supposedly to supervise a new club he was building in Sydney, Australia. Ray wanted Steve to think he was about to leave for distant shores, far from the reach of the law and far enough from Steve not to demand any more money. Ray said he only needed a few minutes to discuss certain matters that he would rather not discuss on the phone. There was a long pause as Ray and the FBI agents waited anxiously for Steve's answer.

"I'll meet you in the lobby of the Hilton Hotel Zurich at 7:45."

Finally Steve had agreed to a meeting.

Since he was supposed to be an experienced fugitive, Ray had to have Swiss currency for drinks, dinner and a cab. Garriola exchanged Ray's money.

"This was supposed to be my expense money," Ray remembers moaning as he handed all his US cash to Garriola in exchange for far less Swiss currency, since the agent had little local currency.

"So order cheap, Paley," Garriola said with a laugh.

The Swiss police would let the FBI and Ray know if Steve left his hotel room or made any telephone calls before the planned evening meeting in case Steve called someone to murder Ray. He did neither.

At 7:15 Ray took a cab alone to the meeting in case Steve had someone watching to make sure Ray arrived alone at the Hilton Hotel Zurich, which was near the airport on the Hohenbuhlstrasse. Seven stories, the white hotel was built in a gentle S-shape, with alpine landscaping stretching out behind it. The hotel was shielded from an adjacent freeway by a row of majestic trees. Ray wore the coat with the bug in it, a long scarf against the cold, and a phony mustache. His hair was tinted gray.

Ray was nervous. If he could not get Steve to incriminate himself, he feared the government would consider their agreement void and send him to prison for decades.

As Garriola and the head of the Swiss police team watched Ray from an unmarked police car across the street, Ray entered the hotel and sat in a lounge chair in the lobby. His eyes flicked over everyone who entered, but Steve did not appear. The meeting time of 7:45 came and passed. As the Swiss undercover police watched from their positions behind the main desk, the valet station and several other discrete locations, Ray began to wonder if something had gone wrong. He waited, his anxiety growing.

Then Ray was shocked to see Garriola and the lead Swiss detective walk through the front door. What were they doing? Steve was liable to show up any second.

Something was wrong. The Swiss police had reported that Steve was sitting in the lobby of his hotel, the Ramada Renaissance, and showed no sign of leaving. Ray called Steve at the Ramada and, after Steve was paged, asked him why he was still at his hotel. The Chippendales owner did not answer and, instead, asked Ray to come meet at the Ramada instead.

"I can't do that," Ray said. "I mean, I'm already here, man. You've got to come here. I've been running all over the damn place for you. Why can't you just come and see me? Jesus Christ!"

"I'm not going anywhere. You catch a cab and come over here."

"No, no! You catch a cab." Ray lost his temper. "If you don't come, I'm going to make your life fucking miserable, you understand me?"

"No! Do what you gotta do, but I can't come!"

"Your life is going to be miserable, count on it."

"It's already miserable."

In desperation, Ray finally agreed to meet in the Ramada's coffee shop.

"Alright, it's settled," Ray said, "but I ain't going to no room with you."

"You don't have too. Did you rent a room?"

The question, asked seemingly out of the blue, confused Ray. He said he rented a room before he could figure out why Steve had even asked the question.

"Why did you rent a room? I thought you were just going to see me and leave," Steve asked, his suspicions mounting.

"I got here at two in the morning. What the hell was I supposed to do, walk the streets until we met?"

Steve then offered to go to the Hilton, as originally planned, but by this point Ray did not care. He just wanted to meet somewhere, anywhere. "The Ramada is fine."

"If they're watching, they would know we're meeting here at the Ramada, not at the Hilton," Steve said, supporting his choice of meeting places. "I have a car. I'll drive over there and the minute I get there, we'll get in the car right away."

"I'm not getting in a car with you, man."

"Okay, okay. I'll meet you at the Hilton's coffee shop."

After Ray hung up, Garriola asked Ray if he thought Steve would show up.

Ray said if Steve didn't, he would go and hammer on Steve's God-damn door, because "one way or another that prick is going to see me."

Ray went downstairs to the coffee shop. Garriola and the Swiss police deployed their men to cover the area. Police officers were stationed in the lobby, lounge and coffee shop, while another group of undercover officers waited outside for Steve to arrive. Ray waited in the coffee shop. His anxiety rising by the minute, he waited 5 minutes, 10 minutes, 15 minutes, 20 minutes, 25 minutes. Steve still had not arrived. Had Steve seen something and been frightened off? Was the case dead?

Chapter 22
Dance with the Devil

On the evening of February 10, 1993, after months of attempting to arrange a meeting, Ray finally spotted Steve at the entrance to the Hilton Hotel in Zurich. The club owner wore a long, dark coat and carried a briefcase. They embraced and Ray said, "You made it. For a while there, I didn't think you'd show."

"C'mon, man," Steve said. "You're like a brother to me. I just had to make sure everything was on the up and up."

They sat at Ray's booth and ordered drinks and dinner.

"I almost didn't recognize you with that mustache and all," Steve said, admiring Ray's disguise. "And your clothes; you actually look like a European. How long have you been in Italy?"

"A few months. I have a little apartment in Rome."

"Did you have any trouble getting across the border?"

"Not at all. They didn't even stamp my passport," Ray said preemptively, in case Steve asked to see it and noticed the absence of an Italian custom's stamp.

Steve said Americans could cross borders so easily. He complained that with his Indian passport the Italians would not even let him into the country.

The waiter arrived with their drinks and food. As soon as the waiter withdrew, Steve asked, "So, did you come alone?"

"Here we go again. C'mon, Steve, we're in Switzerland for God's sake."

Steve stood, leaned across the table and patted Ray down.

"If you're that uncomfortable we can always go into the restroom and play strip show again," Ray said.

"Why bother? It's probably under your skin."

"Where the hell did you ever get an idea like that?"

"Don't laugh. I heard the FBI can do things like that."

"In the movies maybe. Steve, I don't want to insult you, especially since it's your money that's going to help keep me a free man, but that's the dumbest thing I've ever heard." Ray explained that there would be nowhere to put the microphone. It had to receive and it could not do that under someone's skin.

"So how's business?" Ray asked, trying to bring the conversation around to the Adonis murder plot and the De Noia murder.

"I'm making a living. How long are you planning to stay in Italy?"

Ray took off his jacket and laid it across the back of the booth. Across the lobby, Garriola wondered what the hell Ray was doing. The bug was in the jacket. If it was too far from Steve they would not record a single word.

"I don't know," Ray told Steve. "I was thinking of trying Spain."

"They're looking for you, huh?"

"Hell yeah, I'm already on the FBI's wanted list. Why don't you have your asshole attorney check that out? I can never go back."

Garriola attracted the waiter's attention, who was an undercover cop, and told him to ask Steve and Ray to move to the bar area. Garriola hoped Ray would put his jacket back on to ensure that the conversation was taped. The waiter told Ray and Steve that the restaurant was expecting a large party and needed the booth. The pair moved to the cocktail lounge. While Steve and

Ray talked in low voices, a piano player performed over the hum of conversation in the busy bar.

After an hour of futilely attempting to guide the conversation to the De Noia murder, Ray said, "That fucking piano player is driving me nuts. I can't even hear myself think." He was afraid the bug in his jacket would not pick up their conversation amid the noisy bar even if he did finally manage to get Steve to incriminate himself.

Steve said, "I still can't believe how you changed your whole look."

"I'm a European now. You should come over to my room and take a look at this Italian-cut suit I got that's out of this world." Maybe in his room, Steve would be more talkative.

"Maybe I'll come over a little later," Steve said, still as cautious as a man walking a tightrope in hockey skates. "So what happened in October [during Ray's court hearings]?"

Ray explained that the government had not wanted to give him any discovery information for his trial.

Steve said, "I knew right off the bat you should get the trial started, then plead guilty in exchange for a better deal."

"That's what I tried. They wanted me to cooperate, but I couldn't. I didn't want your name coming up. If your name was mentioned, then the De Noia thing would've been brought up. But then I started getting sick and after almost a year I made bail."

"I would have given you some money, but I couldn't take the chance they would trace the source of the money."

"I see what you mean," Ray said, although he thought Steve just lacked the guts to send him money for his defense. This was no time, however, to start an argument.

"I had the money. I was dying to give you the fucking money, you know, but there was no way I could give it to anybody. I gave it to your wife….If you were out on bail I would have thrown the money somewhere. You could've kept it and told them you had it saved under your mattress."

"My wife wouldn't take it."

"I know."

"So they gave you bail because of your kidneys?"

"Yeah, but they had me wear that monitor around my ankle."

"I'm sure they were watching you even after they took the monitor off."

"They weren't watching me or I would have never got out of the country."

"The FBI always watches you. They make you believe there's nothing going on and you're free and clear, but they're watching."

"If they were watching me as close as you say they were, they would've never let me leave the damn country. And if they thought you were involved, the same goes for you."

Steve frowned and Ray feared he had blown it.

"What?" Ray asked, fearing the answer. Was it all over?

"You're losing your mustache."

Ray felt his upper lip, where his false mustache was slipping down. He pulled it off and put it in his pocket.

"For all I know," Steve said, "the FBI is watching us right now, especially that agent, Stefanek."

"How do you know an FBI agent?"

Steve told Ray about the Mafia's attempt to muscle in on the New York Chippendales and his meetings with Stefanek. "I would have been better off giving the Mafia the damn club as much money as I ended up giving them anyway, thanks to you."

"Why would you think this Stefanek guy is watching you?"

"With my luck he's probably on vacation with his family in Zurich right now."

"I keep telling you there's no way the FBI are watching you. They still don't know who hired me and they aren't ever going to find out. I'm here, remember?"

"Maybe for now, but eventually they're going to put two and two together and they're going to come after me."

"They can suspect all they want, but the bottom line is they've got to prove a case against you and they have no case."

"Not now, but that doesn't mean they're not trying. They arrested you, didn't they?"

"True, but they still didn't find out who hired me. Even if they suspected you, which I'm sure they don't, they're a long way from getting anywhere near you. You're in the clear. Let's not even talk about it anymore. I'm in Europe now. They're not going to find me."

But Steve was not going to let his suspicions rest in peace. "You have your fake passport, right?"

"Of course I do."

"It really worked, huh?"

"I paid $10,000 for the damn thing. It better work."

"You can go back to the United States without any problem?"

"Why not? But I'm not going back, so I'll never find out." Ray decided to try and change the direction of the conversation, which appeared to be going nowhere. "So what are you going to do?"

"I have to go to Geneva and get some money."

"You don't have the money now?" Ray asked, suddenly worried. Combined with the tape of their conversation, the money would make the case against Steve airtight. "There's no problem, is there?"

"No, no problem. I'll give you some money so you can have enough until we can meet again. How much do you have now? Twenty, thirty thousand?"

"What, are you crazy? No way am I going to walk around with that kind of money in my pocket. I'll get jumped or arrested for sure. I have about $700."

"How much do you have in Rome?"

"About $3,800, something like that."

"That's pretty good. Come on, let's go to your hotel room."

"You're gonna drive, right?"

"I don't know. Maybe I shouldn't go there."

Ray saw the operation unraveling. He had to keep Steve talking and get the money. "Now that you're here you're not even going to stop by and see me?"

Steve finally relented and agreed to come to Ray's hotel room. Not wanting to ride alone in Steve's car, Ray caught a cab at about 8:30 back to his hotel. As he sat in the cab, he felt as if he had just played a marathon tournament of poker with a master of the game. Worse, he had a long way to go yet.

Garriola and the Swiss police shadowed Steve on his drive through Zurich as Swiss detectives took up positions around and throughout Ray's hotel. As Ray entered his room, the FBI tech agent burst out of the adjoining room, grabbed Ray's jacket and deftly removed the wire. The FBI no longer needed it, since Ray's room was bugged. Now there was no way Steve would find it. The agent retreated to his room. Ray collapsed onto the bed and closed his eyes.

Outside, Steve parked a half block from the hotel. A small, five-story, three-star hotel, the hotel City was on a corner of the legendary Bahnhofstrasse in the heart of Zurich's financial district. An urban hotel, it had no grounds, but featured a quiet rooftop terrace and old, tall trees along the broad sidewalk in front of the building.

Garriola parked a half block from Steve, who still sat in his car. The minutes passed and Garriola wondered if Steve had decided against going to Ray's room. Finally, apparently having decided the hotel was not being watched, Steve slowly got out of his car and walked into the hotel. Garriola wondered what Steve had expected to see during his long inspection of the hotel; a phalanx of agents with "FBI" emblazoned in neon yellow across their chests?

Ray had almost fallen asleep when Steve knocked at the door. Ray let him in. Steve said he couldn't stay long. Ray grabbed a cigarette from the bedside table. He asked for a light, but Steve didn't have one and told Ray to go downstairs for matches.

Ray knew Steve wanted him out of the room so he could search for bugs. Ray had believed the Swiss when they said Steve would never find the bugs in the room, but he did not want to take any chances. Ray said that when he ordered a beer he would ask them to bring up matches. He offered to order Steve a beer, but the Indian declined and again told Ray to go downstairs to get a beer and matches. They went back and forth on the issue before Ray settled it by calling room service and placing the order.

Steve sat in a chair by the curtained window and said the room was like a place he had lived in while he was in London. He asked about how many clothes Ray had brought, where his wife's picture was, and a host of other questions which, Ray knew, were attempts to catch him in a statement that did not fit his story of being a fugitive.

Steve announced that he did not want anyone to see him. Ray said no one was going to see him, but Steve said the bellboy who brought the beer might be an FBI agent. Ray told him to relax. They were in Europe, far beyond the reach of the FBI. Steve asked if Ray could hear people talking in the adjacent rooms. Ray reassured him that the walls were solid. No one would overhear them.

The bellboy delivered two beers and the matches. After he left, Ray walked over and, to prove how thick and soundproof the walls were, pounded on the wall. Even so, Steve was still nervous.

"The fucking FBI are probably right in the next room," Steve said, not knowing he was doubly right: the FBI was not only in the next room, they were in both of the adjacent rooms.

Acting like a fugitive drowning his sorrows in beer and tired of reassuring the nervous club owner, Ray did not soothe Steve's anxieties this time.

Steve asked when the hotel closed its front doors. Ray asked why a hotel would ever close its doors, but Steve said the small ones often did and, his suspicion increasing, asked why Ray didn't know that detail.

"Why would I know that?" Ray asked, thinking fast. "In my situation, the last fucking thing I'm going to do is go prancing around in the middle of the God-damn night."

Steve returned to the subject of the bellboy, wondering if he had got a good look at Steve. Ray said the bellboy hadn't even looked at him. Steve was sure the bellboy was an FBI plant, but Ray said the Bureau's agents could not operate outside the United States. Steve disagreed and they debated the jurisdictional authority of the FBI.

In the depths of the pointless argument, the telephone rang. Ray's heart stopped; who could possibly be calling? Steve grabbed his briefcase and was headed for the door as Ray picked up the phone. He motioned for Steve to sit back down. Reluctantly the club owner sat down, clutching his briefcase to his chest as Ray acted as if the call was a wrong number. It was Dale Mitchell calling from the FBI office in Los Angeles. He had just put Ray's life at risk, but Ray could not say or do anything about it—at least for now.

After he hung up, Ray said, "If I thought for one damn moment something wasn't right, I'd be the first to get the hell out of here, along with your damn briefcase, which I sure hope has my money in it."

As the night waned, they spent hours talking about the FBI, life on the run, simple codes to use on the phone when they talked in the future, and all manner of trivial things. As exhaustion and sleep crept up on Ray like a tantalizing fog, Steve finally asked about the De Noia case.

"They never found the gun, huh?"

"No," Ray said. "I had it destroyed."

"If they had someone to testify that a certain gun was used and then they checked the bullet that was found, they could connect the two."

"Yeah, but the gun was destroyed."

"What else does anybody have? Does anybody know anything else?"

"Nothing as far as you're concerned. I never mentioned you to anyone."

"Does anyone know that the gun came from Los Angeles, went to New York, then went back to LA?"

"Hell, no! The only thing my brother-in-law [Billy Barnes] knows is that I told him to destroy the gun. I don't know what the hell he did with it, but I can tell you they'll never find the gun."

[The FBI transcript contradicts Ray's later claim that he gave the gun to Mike Alvarez to melt down.]

Steve's eyes went wide and he froze as he stared at the door into the adjoining room. "How come that door's unlocked? Those fucking guys can walk right in!" Steve was on his feet in an instant, ready to flee.

"Hey, relax!" Ray said as he stepped over and locked the door.

Steve reluctantly sat back down.

Ray said, "If they thought that you were involved, they would have arrested you."

"Well, they can't because they need a puzzle to fit. For them to arrest me, they need you. That's the thing they're waiting for—you."

"How could they get me?"

Steve worried that the Feds would break Ray, but Ray insisted that the Feds would never be able to do that.

"They're hoping some fucking thing will come up, with some guys," Steve said. "Some guys coming up saying, 'Yeah, I was part of the deal,' and turn you in."

"You mean like the hitter or something?"

"Whatever, yeah."

"But he hasn't been arrested."

"No, but they're hoping they can get him for something big."

"Yeah, but how can they? They don't even know who he is."

"Sometimes they bust somebody and make a deal with that guy. He turns you in for a shorter sentence."

"If they even thought at this point that you had anything to do with it, they would've arrested you."

"Yeah, but they need a little bit more though," Steve said. "You know one thing; look at that case of the [John] Gotti, right? This guy said he killed nineteen people. He said, 'Me and Gotti sat in the car and watched the guy get blown away.' But they never told who fired the shot, who killed the guy. But he still got convicted for it."

"Yeah, but you were in LA [when De Noia was murdered]."

"No, I know that. I know that."

"Well, how the fuck, I mean you weren't even in New York."

"I know that. I looked into all the law books. If you go tell 'em you did it, you point a finger at me, then they have a case to arrest me...Now they don't have any concrete here, it's a good case, but not concrete in the sense they don't have proof that I gave you the money. They don't have proof I bought the gun. They don't have proof I gave you his address or none of that kind of stuff. They don't have proof of all that stuff. But on the other hand, it's believable. You might tell your story, but I know one thing: you have a difficult time telling the truth, no way, you can't tell the fucking truth. I just pray they never catch you."

"I'm not about to give them the chance. If I ever do get caught, I'll be doing Fed time, because I damn sure don't want to do state time. I'd rather kill myself. Either way, I damn sure ain't going back. I'll tell ya, I didn't think I had enough guts to do it."

"I know. I almost did it myself."

"You were going to run?"

"I almost got on a plane to leave my family," Steve said. "I even said goodbye to my children, my wife—even my own wife—I was leaving the country."

"How could you leave the country? You got a business there."

"Freedom is worth more than a fucking business. I'm gonna miss my kids and wife, but….I'll get a new wife and new kids."

"You really thought like that?"

"I already booked my ticket. I was ready to go." Steve explained that he had selected a nice house in India. It was "better than being in jail….I already went there. I have my area picked out. Beautiful, a condominium overlooking the ocean, cars, chauffeur, you know. It's kind of tough to live with poor people, but you know, what can you do, you get used to it….A lot of wealthy people [in India] have a very good social life, people are very nice. A lot of friends, beautiful friends, you know. A party, everybody come in, a hundred people, fifty people, you know, all invite each other." He discussed changing his name and leading a quiet life.

Ray found it ironic that Steve had come from India, made a fortune, and was thinking of ending up right back where he started.

Steve took a drink and asked, "So how does it feel being away from your family?"

"I miss the hell out of my wife."

"Fuck your wife. Get yourself a new one. The only damn reason I even stay with my wife is my children. She's been a good wife and a wonderful mother, but she's a bitch. She always has to know everything. She checks my mail! That's why you should never write me direct. She looks at everything."

After four hours of talking, Ray said he was tired and Steve offered to let him take a nap, but Ray declined. Soon after, the microphone picked up the sound of snoring. The FBI agents and Swiss police next door realized that Ray had fallen asleep with Steve, a possible mortal threat to him, in the same room. Should they burst into the room?

The Swiss police said it was Garriola's call whether to enter Ray's room to ensure his informant's safety. The big FBI agent ran his hand through his hair and made his decision; wait and see what happened. They could be in the room in seconds if they heard Steve make a move against the sleeping Ray. The conversation thus far might convict Steve, but the FBI agent wanted to be certain they had the strongest possible case.

In Ray's room, Steve watched Ray for a few minutes, making sure his old friend was asleep. The club owner stood and slowly and quietly began searching Ray's belongings, the furniture and the room. When he had completed his thorough but fruitless search for a bug, Steve returned to his chair and continued his silent vigil over his old friend.

A half hour later, Ray woke up. Steve told him to go back to sleep if he wanted, but Ray felt refreshed. At least he knew that Steve probably had no plans to harm him, since the Indian had done nothing while he slept.

As he rubbed sleep from his eyes and stretched, Ray turned the conversation to the Mafiosi Steve supposedly knew. It turned out that Steve's Mafia connection was 84 years old.

Steve said, "If I would have spoken to him, man…"

"I'd be dead," Ray finished the thought.

"He was a big mobster guy, but he was always telling me to do things the legal way."

"You tell me this now?"

Steve said that Ray should have just paid Strawberry and told him that Steve had changed his mind. Then the FBI tape would have recorded Ray cancelling the contract.

"But he was already there [in England]," Ray said. Ray had been trying not to talk about the Adonis attempted murders on the theory that Steve would mention them if he did not. His strategy had finally paid off.

"That wouldn't have mattered, if you had told him the deal was off," Steve said. "Too bad I didn't tell you to give him the money and cancel the whole fucking thing."

"But he was already there, Steve."

"That doesn't matter. If you'd have said you're not doing it any more, no problem."

"So now you're saying that I should've just paid him for nothing?"

"Fuck yeah!"

"The problem with that is that he had already gone to England and he didn't contact me until he was already talking to the fucking Feds, so it damn sure wouldn't have done any good. The fucking guy turned me in."

"Why did he have to turn you in? He could have just said I don't want any part of this rather than turn somebody in. What the fuck did he gain by doing that?"

"He was playing both sides of the fence. He was going to do it, that I'm sure of. Then a couple of weeks go by and all of a sudden he calls me. Once he started talking, I knew right away what was going on. Then the Feds came by my house. That's when I went over to see you at your office, but you thought I was bullshitting you."

"It was too late by then."

"Maybe, maybe not. If I'd had a good attorney, Steve, it would have still been his word against mine. They would have had the tapes, but I would've at least had a damn good chance of beating the rap. It wasn't an open and shut case. Anybody can talk shit, but proving that I really meant for it to happen is another thing. I wish I could've stopped it, but I'm here now and that's the bottom line. If you knew the case like you say, you should've known that."

Steve then revealed that he had read the FBI report on Ray's arrest. Ray didn't believe that Steve could have seen FBI files, but Steve said a lawyer he knew had given him the report. Steve's attorneys had also kept him current with all the information on Ray's court appearances. Ray fought to contain his anxiety as he tried to determine just how much Steve knew.

The club owner said he had been worried when he learned that Ray's case had been sealed, since that meant the case was, he said, "under serious investigation." Ray countered that if Steve had known that, the club owner also should have known that he had not cooperated. Steve said he hadn't known that, although he did know that Ray's lawyer had wanted $40,000 up front as part of a $100,000 fee.

"Yeah," Ray said, realizing how closely Steve had monitored his case, "but I didn't have it and I didn't get any money from you. I had to fucking bleed you for it."

"I was dying to give you the money, but I was—"

"Then why didn't you give it to me?" Ray demanded, his anger rising at Steve's betrayal.

"I was afraid," Steve said, staring at the floor. He looked up at Ray and added, "Besides, who the fuck could I trust? I tried to give it to Barbara, but she didn't want it. It's not like you never got any money."

"What's the difference now? I gave the lawyer the money and he didn't do shit for me."

"I couldn't believe you couldn't get a better deal. Do you think your lawyer was told that you might also be involved in the other thing?"

"You mean the D thing?"

"Yeah."

"No. He never brought it up," Ray said carefully, not wanting to spoil the possibility that Steve would discuss the De Noia murder.

"But did the Feds?"

"Why? Do you think they thought that you were involved?"

"Sure they know I was involved. They're not stupid. They just don't have any proof yet, but they know."

"But the D case never came up."

"Not yet, but that's where the investigation is going. They're waiting and hoping that something comes up that will tie me to the case."

"You mean like the hitter or something?"

"Something like that."

"But he hasn't been arrested."

"No, but they're waiting to get him for something else; something big so that maybe he'll give you up as part of a deal."

"Even if he rats me out, Steve, he still doesn't know who you are."

"The Feds don't have anything concrete yet. They don't have any proof that I gave you the money, bought the gun with you, or that I gave you D's address or any information about D. I won't talk to anybody, so they don't have me on tape."

"I guess you're right. They would never believe me," Ray said, enjoying the irony that even as Steve said that he would never let anyone tape him, he was being taped. "But I'll tell you one thing, you really are one paranoid son-of-a-bitch, especially about the D thing, since no one ever even brought it up."

Steve said the Feds didn't mention it because they were waiting for someone to make a mistake. He was sure the FBI was investigating him for the D case. Steve even thought his wife suspected his involvement, as did his sister-in-law's husband, who was an FBI agent.

Ray said, "If he does, he probably doesn't say a word about it to his wife for fear she tells your wife."

Steve asked if Ray's wife, Barbara, knew about the thing with....

"With De Noia?" Ray asked.

"Don't even mention that word," Steve said. "But Barbara suspects?"

"No way! She don't know. How would she know about something like that?"

"People suspect. That's what my wife suspects. She hears the rumors."

"Irene actually told you that?"

"Not in so many words, but you know in different ways cause she knows I wouldn't talk about it. I wouldn't. They got to kill me first. They gotta literally put a gun to my head...and kill me. After they kill [me], I still won't say."

"But did she ever say you did have something to do with it?"

"In a roundabout way. But I didn't answer her, I walked off."

Returning to the FBI and their potential case, Ray said, "If they don't have the D, they ain't got shit. You know what I mean? They ain't got shit."

"They're working on the D though."

"They're not working on the D T, I mean," Ray said, laughing at his mistake. "They're not working on the D, 'cause if they had, if they thought they had the D, you wouldn't be here, Steve."

"I know they're still working on it. They're gonna crack it sooner or later."

"No, they won't. We'll put this to rest," Ray said. "Has anybody ever on the D approached you or said they suspected, besides Irene?"

"No, but they all suspect me. They never said anything.... They know I'm the one involved with it. They're sure."

"Thinking and proving are two very different things. How about that attorney friend of yours?"

"Nahin? I think he knows that I'm the guy who hired you to do the job. I know he'd turn me in, if he found out."

"You really think he would?"

"Honest people are different, man, they don't tolerate something like that," Steve said. "Does the US Government give the death penalty for something like that?"

Ray explained the Feds had the death penalty, but only for certain crimes and not for conspiracy to commit murder.

"That means that for the D case, I can't get the death penalty?"

"Well, if it's any consolation, you're not gonna get the death penalty."

Their talk turned to Strawberry.

"I wish you had fucking hit the guy in London, then it would've been all over with," Steve said. "I mean I'm glad you didn't do it….Anyway, if I knew you were hiring somebody, I'd be dead against it. See you never told me the fucking truth, you told me the fucking Filipino guy, which—"

"Well, what am I gonna tell you?"

"You got some fucking blond, some, some blond hair fucking hillbilly. Fuck!"

"What do you mean blond? He wasn't blond."

"Whatever; some fucking Caucasian asshole."

Ray started laughing.

"I would never," Steve said. "I would of said no, if you can't do it, don't do it. Don't fucking do it. It's not worth it."

After briefly discussing the cancellation of the Dr. Sehdeva hit, Steve said, returning to the Adonis conspiracy, "I wish you would have told that guy, instead of cyanide, to go over there to choke him to death or something. It would be much easier for you, and then they wouldn't have got me for all this shit; cyanide and all that kind of crap, you know what I mean?"

Steve said he didn't think the FBI had a case against him for the plot against the Adonis troupe members.

Ray said, "If they even suspected you, they would have arrested you and got you to talk about me."

They then discussed the role of Billy Barnes. Steve hadn't known Billy was Ray's brother-in-law. Steve thought Billy had gone to the FBI, but Ray denied it. When Steve said Billy had told him that Billy and Ray had tried to go to Canada to kill Fullington, and that Billy was going to do the hit, Ray reacted strongly, probably because he knew the conversation was being recorded and wanted to keep his brother-in-law out of prison. "That's bullshit, because you wanna know something? He didn't know shit."

Then Steve backtracked. He said he didn't know Billy and had never spoken to him.

"The bottom line is it's over," Ray said. "Why do we keep talking about it? There's nothing I can do now, but run. At least you can go back to your business."

"Business? Why do you think I don't open another club? I don't even do that much business anymore because I don't feel safe. I feel like at any moment they're coming to get me and boom, it's all over."

Ray had a hard time feeling sorry for Steve, but said, "Give it time. It'll work out for you."

Steve still feared that Ray would cooperate with the Feds, but Ray said that if he was going to do that, he would have done it long ago. Ray stressed that the Feds didn't have a case against Steve, and that they only had a case against Ray because they had him on tape.

"They don't have me on tape and I want to keep it that way," Steve said, once again not realizing the irony of his statement. Steve again said that if the Feds ever got close, he would leave the country and desert his family. Ray pointed out that Steve would have to leave his business, but the Chippendales owner said his freedom was worth more than any business. Steve said that if they arrested him, he would kill himself.

"C'mon, Steve, you won't."

"Yes, I will. I couldn't take being in prison, plus shaming my family like that."

"If you kill yourself, you'd still be shaming your family."

"The big difference is that I wouldn't have been convicted of anything."

"But you'd be dead."

"But my children would at least have some honor."

"Let's not even talk about shit like that anymore. You're not going to get caught and you're not going to kill yourself. Go home to your family and live your life. I'll contact you in six or seven months."

Steve looked out the window. It was starting to get light. He said that he had better go. He opened his briefcase and tossed a stack of hundred-dollar bills onto the bed beside Ray. "There's $9,000. Count it."

Ray picked up the money and began to count, forcing his exhausted mind to concentrate. When he was finished, he had only counted $7,000. Steve told him to count it again. Ray counted again: $7,000. Steve insisted there was $9,000. Ray said he was not going to spend another five hours arguing. He took the money, whatever the amount, and tossed it on the bureau.

They walked out of the hotel into the cold, crisp morning air to Steve's rental car. Steve put his briefcase in the trunk and turned to Ray. "Take care of yourself and be careful. Remember, they'll be looking for you. One slip up and it's all over."

"I'll be alright," Ray said, thrown off by Steve's concern. Was it just because if Ray was caught, Steve's arrest would not be far off, or did it go deeper?

"Just make sure you stay cool," Ray said. "You're my only hope of staying free. I lose you and I'm fucked."

"I'm really sorry I didn't give you the money when I should have, but I made a lot of mistakes. The worst was getting you involved with all this crap over a lousy $7,000. Now look how much it's costing me, not to mention my freedom, if I ever get arrested."

"You won't. Now get the hell out of here, I'm tired as hell."

Steve hugged Ray. Just before he drove away, Steve said, "I wasn't lying when I said I always thought of you as a brother."

Chapter 23
Last Calls

Garriola congratulated Ray and Stefanek embraced him. Stefanek said it had been amazing. He had never thought Ray would be able to get the incredibly cautious Steve to say anything. Stefanek said breaking the case was all due to Ray.

Garriola collected the money, which would be checked for Steve's fingerprints, counted and used as evidence. The government determined that between November 1991 and February 1993, Steve gave Ray "in excess of a quarter of one million dollars in order to ensure the CI's [Confidential Informant] silence." The FBI also had records of cash withdrawals from Chippendales accounts ranging from $7,000 to $74,000, totaling $225,000, which they suspected had financed Steve's crimes. Ray would always disagree with the figure.

Stefanek called Mitchell in Los Angeles with the good news, but lost his temper with Mitchell about the call the LA agent had made to Ray's room during the meeting with Steve. Stefanek yelled that the call had put Ray in mortal danger and jeopardized the entire case.

Garriola called Meloch. Mitchell had been pressuring Meloch to jail Ray as soon as they landed in Los Angeles. Garriola argued that the case wasn't over, and that Ray had cooperated above and beyond the requirements of their plea agreement. He won the point. Ray would not return to the MDC. While Garriola and Stefanek worked out the details of the trip back to the City of Angels and obtaining a copy of the audio tapes from the Swiss, Ray went to bed.

Ray felt as if he had just shut his eyes when the telephone rang at 6 a.m. Jarred back to wakefulness, he reached for the phone.

"It's me, Steve."

"Hey," Ray said, trying to sound calm and relaxed even as he feared something had gone wrong. "Where are you?"

"On my way to Geneva. What are you doing?"

"Still sleeping. What's up?"

"I was thinking maybe you can meet me in Geneva, so we can hang out a while." Steve sounded like a lonely little boy searching for a friend.

"Geneva? That's far."

"Take a plane. It's a short trip. I'll give you another $50,000 so you'll be in good shape."

"Every time I get on a plane I'm taking a chance. Now that we have everything straightened out, just FedEx it to me."

"Suppose they intercept the package?"

"Better the package than me."

Steve suggested meeting in Spain or, possibly, Holland. Ray said he liked Spain, but in Holland his Puerto Rican complexion would stand out too much. But Ray said, "I'm fine now and I'm not going to bother you for a while. You have my word. Besides, I don't want to be anywhere near you when you're driving around Europe. We get stopped for some reason and they check me out, I'm fucked, and so are you if they put two and two together."

"I guess you're right."

"I'm going to take your advice. As soon as I get some rest I'm going to pick up my money in Italy and head for Spain."

"Once you're there, send me a coded letter like we talked about and I'll telex you where and when we can meet."

"Alright, take care of yourself."

"You too."

"Alright, I'll see you. Ciao."

At 6:48 a.m. Steve again called Ray to ask to meet. Ray once again declined. It was the last time Ray would ever speak to Steve.

On the flight home the next day, Stefanek and Garriola were jubilant. Ray was not. Although he was being treated as if he was a hero, he felt ashamed that he had betrayed a friend. No matter what justification the FBI agents, Rocky or even his own logic offered, he could not help but feel that he had lost any honor he may have once had. Part of him believed that the honorable thing for him to have done, would be to have just served whatever prison term he was given and let someone else or God punish Steve and Louie for their sins. He felt that, having betrayed his friend, he had sunk into an abyss of treachery. Even so, he knew that Steve was evil and had to be stopped. Justice had been served in a hotel room in Zurich.

After they returned from Europe, Stefanek and Garriola did not want to run the risk that someone might see Ray and tell Steve that Ray was not a fugitive in Europe. Until the FBI arrested Steve, Ray's presence in Los Angeles was a risk, so they sent Ray to New York several times to work with the detectives investigating the De Noia case.

In February 1993, a Grand Jury indicted Steve on racketeering, conspiracy and murder-for-hire charges. Charlie Parsons, special agent in charge of the Los Angeles FBI office said, "The basic theme of the new indictment is that anybody or anything that got in Banerjee's way, he would hire somebody to kill or burn the competitor."

In March 1993, during one of Ray's trips to New York, Barbara called. Rocky Delamo had died. Ray flew home for the funeral. He was concerned about the reaction of his former crew and other members of Rocky's organization, but nothing would have kept him from his former mentor's funeral. Even though they knew Ray had cooperated with the FBI, one of Rocky's crew told him at the funeral that they would honor Rocky's wish that Ray be left alone. Rocky's gift of life extended to Ray from beyond the grave.

Garriola and Stefanek were furious that Ray put himself at risk by attending the funeral. To keep him out of trouble, they put him to work with a red pen listening to each tape of his conversations with Louie and Steve, correcting the transcripts wherever the transcriber had erred.

In August 1993, Ray appeared before a Grand Jury in the Los Angeles Federal Courthouse to testify against Steve. Supported by the Zurich tapes, on August 31 Steve Banerjee was indicted for conspiracy, using interstate commerce facilities in the commission of murder-for-hire, and aiding and abetting, causing an act to be done.

On September 1, Stefanek told Ray that they would arrest Steve the next day. It was an example of how much the FBI agents now trusted Ray. He could easily have tipped off Steve. Stefanek warned Ray to stay alert in case Steve tried something. Ray carried a gun with him just in case, although he did not expect any trouble.

On September 2, Detective Michael Geddes retired in New York. The same day, a continent away, at 10:15 a.m. Steve Banerjee left his spacious home overlooking the beach in Playa del Rey. It was another beautiful morning in paradise, but Steve's paradise was about to end. He drove his Mercedes along Ocean Drive toward his office, followed at a discreet distance by two FBI agents in an unmarked car. Garriola, Stefanek and several other agents waited in cars at Steve's office. The Mercedes arrived, parked in front of the building and Steve got out. The agents rushed across the street. Holding their badges up, they closed in on a shocked Steve. Garriola and Stefanek had their guns holstered, but other agents, guns drawn, backed them up. Steve was ashen-faced as Stefanek cuffed him and Garriola read him his rights. Like Ray before him, the FBI took Steve to the MDC. The arrest made headlines in Los Angeles, New York and across the Atlantic in Britain.

Steve appeared before Judge Venetta S. Tassopulos for the Central District of California. Sally L. Meloch represented the government. Meloch strongly objected to bail. She argued that Steve met all three requirements for denying bail: he was a threat to himself, to the community, and was a flight risk. As evidence, she provided a transcript of the Zurich meeting, in which Steve said that if he was arrested, he would flee the country or commit suicide. The tapes also provided evidence that Steve had hired others to commit murder, which showed he was a threat to the community. Judge Tassopulos denied bail.

The trial was set for June 14, 1994. The trial was expected to last 30 days, with Swiss officers flying in to testify about Steve's Zurich meeting with Ray, and the FBI working with New Scotland Yard, who were collecting information about Strawberry and the Adonis troupe's movements in England. The Honorable Thomas J. Rea would preside in case CR-93-772, the United States of America vs. Somen "Steve" Banerjee.

In September 1993 the preliminaries began, with defense motions to suppress the Zurich tapes (denied) and to unseal the cases of Ray and Billy Barnes (granted). The defense was upset when they learned from the government that Louis Lopez was the same person as Gilberto Rivera Lopez. The government had been confused given Louie's penchant for using more than 20 aliases. The attorneys argued over copies of Steve's daily planner, which a Chippendales employee had taken from Steve's office without permission and apparently unbidden, and given to Garriola. The defense then alleged that while at the MDC Ray had attempted to convince other inmates to arrange the murder of Lynne "Strawberry" Bressler. Ray denied the accusation and refused to even meet Steve's attorney out of fear that if Steve learned where he was, the club owner would try to have him killed. The best of friends were now the worst of enemies.

In the harsh, concrete confines of the MDC, Steve's spirits sank. With the media coverage of his arrest, every inmate knew he was the millionaire owner of Chippendales, and in jail notoriety is a bad thing. Steve was terrified of his fellow inmates. Humiliated and scared, he cried repeatedly when he called his wife on the telephone or met her on visiting days. The other inmates considered him a crybaby and a pompous ass, which only isolated him more. Inmates taunted and threatened him. He only avoided being beaten up badly by the intervention of inmates, whom he paid for the use of their phone time.

Steve's attorneys could offer little, if any hope. As they reviewed the tapes from Zurich, there appeared to be no chink in the government's armored case. If he was convicted on all counts, Steve, 46, faced a prison term of up to 55 years and a fine of up to $1.5 million. Depressed and losing any hope that he could avoid spending the rest of his life in prison, Ray heard that Steve was put on a suicide watch.

While Steve struggled to survive in the MDC, Ray struggled to live at home. Someone would telephone and hang up when Ray answered. He was sure Barbara was having an affair, but lacked the mental energy to deal with it in any constructive way. She avoided him as much as possible, working longer hours, shopping for Christmas alone, and staying out of the house for long periods. They did not even attend the hospital's Christmas party. Barbara went alone. Ray later said he contemplated suicide.

As Ray struggled to maintain his emotional balance, the city's balance was thrown off. On January 17, 1994, at 4:31 a.m., the Northridge earthquake shook southern California. Ray's house suffered $83,000 in damage. Worse was to come for Ray. A few weeks after the quake, he suffered a mild heart attack. He was soon released from the hospital, but his health problems worsened as his kidneys caused him severe pain and he urinated blood. He had an infection in his right kidney and was taken to UCLA Medical Center. His situation worsened. When Stefanek and Garriola visited, the doctor told them Ray might not survive. Ray, however, pulled through. He was at home recuperating when his health, once again, deteriorated rapidly and he was rushed to the hospital. In an emergency operation, doctors removed his right kidney. After the operation, as he fought for life, Ray confessed to a Catholic priest about the arsons, attempted murders and the De Noia murder.

Steve's attorney had heard about Ray's illness and asked the judge to move the trial to a later date. The attorney was gambling that Ray would not survive long enough to appear at the trial. When Ray heard about it, he told the US Attorney's, "I'm not going anywhere."

Steve's attorney also investigated Ray in an attempt to shatter his credibility as a witness. A private investigator talked with Ray's former colleagues at the Palm Springs Police Department, his current neighbors, and his former neighbors at the Overland Palms apartments. The investigator also talked to people who had conducted business with Ray when he was with Hi-Spot Productions, as well as the staff and students who had met him when he taught traffic school. An investigator even tried to harvest any bad seeds from among Ray's drinking buddies at his favorite bar, the Sandpiper in Santa Clarita. Garriola and Stefanek had warned him Steve's lawyers would probably conduct just such an investigation, so Ray was not surprised when friends called to tell him that someone was asking questions about him. Luckily for Ray and the government's case, the PI found nothing to link Ray to Rocky Delamo, Leon Defina or his Mafia-associated crew—or maybe Ray's attorney, Jim Henderson, was right and Ray had no ties to the Mafia.

Steve made one last roll of the dice to avoid a conviction. In the summer of 1994, Henderson met one of his clients, Jack Rubinstein [who has since died], at the MDC. Rubinstein faced charges of carrying a concealed weapon and of drug possession with intent to sell.

Rubinstein said he had been talking to a "loaded...whining little fuck." He had convinced the other inmate that he could take care of some guy he wanted whacked. Rubinstein figured if he kept snowing the other inmate, it would be good for a few weeks' worth of free cigarettes and coffee.

Idly curious, Henderson asked what the guy was in for.

Rubinstein said it was related to Chippendales. Suddenly interested, Henderson mentioned Steve Banerjee. Rubinstein said it was the same guy. Rubinstein said he must have convinced the Chippendales mogul pretty damn good because Steve had offered Rubinstein $200,000 to have his so-called people take this guy out. The target's name: Ray Colon.

Henderson was skeptical, but Rubinstein convinced him he was telling the truth. Rubinstein made it clear he had never intended to do anything for Steve, but the key to Henderson was that the offer had been made. Henderson arranged for an ex-FBI agent he knew who was a private investigator and owned a bar in Las Vegas to play the part of a hit man. Henderson had Rubinstein arrange it so Steve could talk to his "hit man." Henderson reported it all to the FBI.

Rubinstein asked Steve to make a down payment for the hit. Soon after, Steve called his wife, Irene and, not telling her why, asked her deliver a $10,000 check (Henderson remembers it as far more) to an attorney's office on Ventura Boulevard. She thought the money was a retainer for another lawyer for Steve, but the attorney was actually a friend of Henderson's.

After dropping off the money, Irene called Steve to tell him she had run his errand. Steve told Irene he had changed his mind about hiring the other attorney. He asked her to retrieve the check and tear it up. She convinced the attorney to return the check and destroyed it without him even making a copy.

Since Steve might have hired other inmates to arrange Ray's murder, the FBI decided it would be safer to have their confidential information a continent away from Steve, so they sent Ray to New York. Steve faced more prison time than he would ever live to serve, so he was not charged with another murder-for-hire, but on July 8, 1994, the New York Manhattan Grand Jury charged him with one count of second degree murder in the death of Nicolas "Nick" De Noia.

After prolonged negotiation the government offered Steve's attorney, Barry Tarlow, a deal, but with a strict time deadline for acceptance. Steve said he heard about the offer on Tuesday and had until Friday, July 29, 1994 to sign. Steve said it would be the "gentlemanly thing" to give him more time to consider the plea offer. The government refused.

On July 29, Steve appeared in Federal Court for his plea hearing before US District Judge William J. Rea. Steve looked gaunt and pale, his usually lively manner subdued. The government presented its case and then, in his heavily-accented and ungrammatical English Steve told the judge, "I guess only the bad things that happened in my life is all here and there are many of the good things I have done. I have given thousands of people job. I have entertained millions of folks. I started with no money, work 18 hours a day, sweep the floors, work gasoline stations, work my way up, help many young American kids to see they can own their own business. Help them go to school, college. Nothing is said here. Only thing said here I have done these two terrible things wrong and I just want you to note that I have also done many, many things good and I have also helped with millions of dollars in the causes of women's breast cancer, AIDS, on and on and on....As I just heard everything said about me, I just didn't think it was me."

Steve then talked about the Red Onion arson: "At one time he [Ray] asked me that he can take care of this thing with Red Onion, and I have been a really busy guy and some of the time I did not believe this guy when he says something how true or how bad that is. How true—he was like a stand-up comic whom I known. So...one day we are in a conversation came up about different clubs and he said, 'I go to Red Onion once in a while. Maybe we ought to throw some Molotov cocktail there.' I said, 'I guess so.' And so I found out that somebody threw something through the window of Red Onion." But, Steve said, "I am sorry that I, someone like me even got involved with anything like that and I am glad no one got hurt or nothing happened. But I didn't mean it that way, what happened there. But I am really, really sorry and I take complete responsibility for that." He added, "I think I am guilty of the homicide and I take complete responsibility for it. And that is about all. And I am very, very sorry."

Steve repeated several times that he was willing to accept the plea to avoid costing the government $1 million to conduct a trial. For Steve, it always came down to money.

"I am kind of always outspoken," Steve said, possibly in an attempt to suggest that what he had asked Ray to do had been merely an exaggeration. It made no difference. Even his attorney, Tarlow, who graduated first in his class from Boston University Law School, had been practicing criminal law since 1966, often representing celebrities, and who was one of the leading authorities in the country in defending against Racketeer Influenced and Corrupt Organization (RICO) charges, could do little for Steve.

Under a plea bargain, Steve pled guilty to several charges related to the April 1987 murder-for-hire (second degree murder) of Nick De Noia and the 1984 attempted arson of the Red Onion, including solicitation, and charges under the RICO statutes, which characterized Chippendales as a criminal organization, with Steve willing to pay for arson and murder to prevent anyone from competing with his club. Steve would forfeit all of his interests in Chippendales and its related companies, which the previous year, according to the government, had grossed $18 million. The "vast majority" of the income was from the Chippendales tours. Steve would also pay a $500,000 fine and serve 26 years in prison with no possibility of parole. In 26 years, Steve Banerjee would be 74 years old.

The US Attorney's involved with the case, Sally Meloch and Steve Clymer, had called the De Noia family to request approval for the plea deal before they offered it to Steve. The attorneys told Val De Noia that the day Steve got out of prison, he would be deported to India, since he had never become a US citizen. Val believed Steve should not only lose his freedom but also all of his money since he only had all that money because of Nick. However, after hearing the details of the deal, Val said, "Speaking on behalf of my brothers and I, we'll accept that. I'd like for him to get the chair, but we know that isn't possible."

If he did not accept the deal, Steve would go to trial where he risked being sentenced to life in prison and even stiffer financial penalties. He said, "I am willing to make a deal here because I have nothing left." Sentencing was set for October 24, 1994, at 9:30 a.m. The seven year NYPD investigation and the four-year FBI investigation that had spanned two continents and involved dozens of US and European police officers, FBI agents, and witnesses was finally over.

At their last meeting, Steve told his wife Irene that he loved her and, when she raised the possibility of yet another legal tactic to avoid sentencing, he said it was over. His final words to her as MDC visiting hours ended, were, "Take care of the children."

On October 24, 1994, a guard on a routine two-hour check noticed something wrong in Unit 5 South, cell 546 or 507 (records vary): Steve's cell. The guard had trouble getting into the cell, since the door was partially blocked. The guard summoned help and guards used an air tank to batter open the door. Steve hung by a bed sheet from a hook on the wall against the door. MDC medical personnel and Los Angeles Fire Department paramedics attempted to revive him, but failed, pronouncing him dead at 4:35 a.m. Reonard McFadden, executive to the warden at the MDC, said, "Mr. Banerjee tied a piece of bed sheet around his neck, placed it on a wall-mounted jacket hanger and pulled down on it while he kneeled, causing the flow of air to be cut off; that caused his death." The autopsy determined that death was caused by "suicide by tracheal asphyxiation."

Steve was 48 years old.

On June 5, 1999, US Attorney Sally Meloch signed off on case CR-93-772-WJR, United States vs. Somen "Steve" Banerjee. On the form, the conviction box was checked and beside it was written "Died before sentencing."

Chapter 24
College and a Civil Suit

Nick De Noia's brother, Val, arrived in Los Angeles to attend Steve's sentencing with his brother, Lou, and nephew, Tom. Val had flown in later than the others and arrived at his hotel early the morning of the sentencing to find a message from Garriola waiting for him. Val called Garriola, who said he had good news and bad news. Val asked for the bad news first. Garriola said Steve was not going to be sentenced that morning. Val cursed, angry that something had gone wrong. Then Garriola told him the good news: Steve had committed suicide. Val later said, "We enjoyed that."

Early the morning after Steve's suicide, Stefanek called Ray with the news. Ray felt a deep sadness. A man he had known for almost 20 years, at one time a close friend, was dead and Ray had played a pivotal part in causing his death. Ray believed that Steve had changed. His pursuit of money and success had turned him into a monster. Ray, however, had never wanted Steve dead. If Steve was a monster deserving of death, Ray thought, then so was he.

The authorities ruled Steve's death a suicide, although some of his friends believed that he had been murdered. McFadden, the executive to the warden at the MDC, told the *Los Angeles Times*, "Banerjee, like every other inmate, had been interviewed by a staff psychologist. There was no indication he was suicidal." Sally Meloch later said she had no information that Banerjee was depressed. Others involved in the case also did not recall hearing that Steve was depressed. Ray, however, believed that Steve had been on and off suicide watch for months. The preponderance of the evidence suggests that Steve was not on suicide watch. Given Steve's arrogance, it seems likely that he never gave up hope until the very end, especially given his behavior in the last months of his life to allow his wife to retain control of his creation: Chippendales.

A news story reported that authorities found a note in an Indian language in the cell, although no such note appears in the case files. Steve's cellmate claimed never to have heard a thing, although as Garriola said, "Cellmates never hear anything." If Steve had been murdered, Ray thought there was a strong possibility that Rocky's organization had been involved, since, Ray said, Steve's cellmate had been a good friend of one of Rocky's soldiers. Or, the cellmate might have just been in the right place at the right time for those with a conspiratorial mindset. Ray later heard that Steve's cellmate, when he was brought to the MDC just days before Steve's suicide, raised a ruckus about being assigned to a room with an African-American and had then been assigned to Steve's room. MDC records, however, indicate that Steve was alone when he died. How reliable was Ray as a source of information? Often his information is at odds with several other sources. Whatever the truth, it was just one more confusing twist in the long and twisted life of Somen "Steve" Banerjee.

Steve left a legacy of a monumental legal battle. In the last months of his life, even as he fought the criminal charges against him, civil claimants lined up to seek financial compensation for his crimes. On March 30, 1994, Val De Noia and the estate of Nick De Noia brought suit in New York against Steve and Ray Colon. On July 14, 1994, Read "Scott" Schrotel, Stephen White and Adonis Management Co. filed a complaint against Steve, Easebe, Ray, and Billy Barnes.

Steve worked hard to ensure that none of the victims of his crimes would ever receive a penny of his money. On July 28, 1994, Steve and Irene signed a hastily written, one-page agreement rife with typos during one of her visits to the MDC. In the agreement, Steve transferred almost all of his assets to Irene, including 91 percent of Easebe, Inc., the Chippendales parent company, as well as two homes in Playa del Rey. (Bruce Nahin, in a thoughtful and generous gesture, had already given his 10 percent stake in the company to Irene for Steve's kids.) The Steve-Irene deal cancelled an existing pre-nuptial agreement, which stated that all such property was Steve's alone. The only compensation Steve received for the transfer was release from child-support obligations for his two children. The day after the couple signed the deal, Steve pled guilty.

On August 17, a judge approved the agreement. In their submissions, Steve and Irene stated that they "do not presently contemplate obtaining a judgment of dissolution of marriage, or legal separation." Soon after a judge approved the deal, Steve and Irene divorced.

Even before the July 28 agreement with Steve, Irene had been seeking to sell Easebe and its primary asset, Chippendales. In a July 1, 1994, letter from Nace Cohen and CLP, Ltd. to Irene, Cohen stated his intent to buy Easebe. In November 1993, Cohen had been introduced to Irene by his son-in-law, Mark Pakin, who had been a Chippendales employee for more than a decade. In November 1993, Cohen had started working as a 40-hour-a-week consultant at Chippendales. Just six months before the July 1, 1994 letter of interest, the company had been valued at $8 million. The letter offered to buy all of Easebe's assets, including Chippendales, for $2 million ($1 million in cash; $1 million promissory note), plus $100,000 a year to Irene for five years as a consultant, followed by $50,000 a year thereafter.

A second letter of interest dated August 11, 1994 and prepared at the same time as the Steve-Irene marital settlement gave Irene 15 percent ownership in CLP in exchange for a non-competition clause. This clause was asserted to have value even though Irene claimed to be selling Chippendales because she was "a single housewife" unfit to run such a company. The letter set the terms of a $1 million promissory note payable in less than 18 months, which made it extremely difficult for any creditors to ever collect. If the note was transferred involuntarily, such as if it was seized by creditors, the terms would change to a term of 10 years, with interest only payments until that date. Therefore, instead of getting $1 million in less than 18 months, a creditor would only receive $60,000 a year and none of the principle for 10 years. The August 11 letter also included an enhanced "consulting agreement": Irene would receive $100,000 a year for 25 years. The deal required her to work five hours a month, which worked out to an astronomical wage of $16,000 an hour. On top of the sweet consulting deal, Irene would receive a broker's commission for selling Easebe. Finally, there was a confidentiality clause, which was unusual in that neither the buyer nor the seller could reveal to anyone information about the terms of the transaction. Such information would be crucial to the civil litigants against Steve and Easebe.

Since it was requiring Steve to forfeit his company as part of the plea agreement, in August 1994 the government sought and received a temporary restraining order barring Irene from selling Easebe without the approval of the US Attorney's office. Apparently hoping the government would approve the sale, on October 3, 1994, Irene sold Chippendales to Nace Cohen and CLP, Ltd.

The October 3, 1994 deal was only slightly different from the July and August letters of intent. In the deal, CLP assumed $1.4 million of Chippendales' liabilities and offered $2 million in promissory notes, as well as paying $130,000 in legal fees and other incidentals. Irene was to receive $100,000 a year for 25 years. When defending the deal against government opposition, CLP's attorneys said it was a classic no-money down leveraged buyout. The attorneys argued that Easebe had no other sale alternatives and was facing a "perilous financial situation."

Whatever the true state of Easebe and Chippendales, the October 3 agreement was terrible for the civil litigants, should they ever win their suits. A long list of provisions in the sale agreement sought to keep creditors at bay. New provisions indemnified the buyer, Cohen and CLP, against claims by an earlier creditor by the name of Gerald Roberts against Easebe. In another provision, if Irene violated the consulting agreement or the non-competition clause, offsets would be applied against the promissory note owed to Easebe first. Therefore, Easebe, not Irene, would forfeit money owed it by CLP if Irene broke the deal. The agreement also made the security of the promissory note an illusion, since if CLP defaulted on the note, Cohen could claim various offsets that had to be arbitrated before a creditor could foreclose. Irene and Cohen also agreed that the bulk sales laws of California were inapplicable, so there would be no published notice to creditors of the terms, which otherwise would have been required. Furthermore, the agreement put three different liens on the Chippendales trademark (the most valuable part of the company). Creditors or the winners of any civil suit against Steve or Easebe would be fourth in line.

Based on the August 1994 restraining order, Janet Hudson, Chief of the Asset Forfeiture Section of the US Attorney's Office for the Central District of California, said she had "serious reservations" about the sale, since Easebe received almost nothing for its major asset, Chippendales. Hudson later said, "He [Steve] was trying very hard to avoid the forfeiture." She later wrote, "He engaged in fraudulent transfers to ensure that his assets would be passed to his wife rather than the government." After reviewing the deal, the US Attorney's office said the deal was a "fraud" on creditors and refused to approve the sale. Just two days after the October 3 deal was signed, it was dead. It looked as if White, Schrotel and the De Noia estate would have a chance to receive financial damages from Steve, Easebe and Chippendales if they won their case in court. Then everything changed.

On October 23, 1994, Steve committed suicide. Forfeiture can be criminal and/or civil. In criminal forfeiture, the forfeiture is part of punishment and is against a person, called *in personam*. A criminal forfeiture requires that the person involved be convicted before their assets or money can be forfeited. In a civil forfeiture, the government can take possession of assets even if there is no conviction. Civil forfeiture can be against a thing, called *in rem*. In such cases the burden is on the government to prove that the asset or money was used to facilitate a crime or are the proceeds of a crime. If a person who claims the asset can prove they did not know it was used for a crime or that it was the proceeds of a crime, they retain their asset. In many cases of civil forfeiture, however, no one comes forward. If police raid an unoccupied hotel room and find $20,000 in cash and drugs, the government can make a civil forfeiture case. The money is probably the result of criminal activity since the cash was found with drugs. If no one comes forward to claim the money, the government can then take ownership of the money. The forfeiture in such *in rem* cases is not part of any punishment.

Most laws that include forfeiture, such as most drug laws, include both civil and criminal forfeiture. Unfortunately for the government, the RICO laws do not have a civil forfeiture statute, only a criminal forfeiture statute. A criminal forfeiture can only be imposed as part of an individual's sentence. If an individual is never sentenced, then the criminal forfeiture cannot occur. Therefore, when Steve committed suicide before sentencing, the RICO statute related to criminal forfeiture of Chippendales no longer applied. Lacking a civil forfeiture provision in the RICO laws, the government could do nothing to stop Irene from selling Chippendales. Irene and Cohen then could, and did make their deal.

In the final November 10, 1994, deal there was yet another change in Irene's consulting provision. Irene was to receive $12,000 a year for five years and $2.5 million in a promissory note. Easebe/Chippendales did not receive a dime from the deal. Cohen wrote three checks: $130,000 to Irene's lawyers; $250,000 to Irene to buy her 15 percent share of CLP; and $200,000 to Irene for her "story rights." All Easebe's assets had been transferred to Cohen and CLP for money to Irene, the US Attorney's argued, "On every pretext other than for the purchase of the Easebe assets, leaving the company insolvent." Cohen immediately stopped paying on the promissory note to Easebe. Irene ignored the failure to pay.

In 11 months, via the marital transfer and the sale to CLP and Cohen, assets worth more than $8 million had been transferred from Steve to Irene, and then from Irene and Easebe to CLP and Nace Cohen. As the US Attorney's Office concluded, "The rape of the creditors was now complete."

In November 1994, in California, Read Schrotel, Stephen White and De Noia's estate filed a fraudulent transfer claim against Irene, Easebe and CLP. The civil case and disputes over the asset transfer dragged on for years. The battles over Steve's assets were a lawyer's dream: piles of money, multiple contending parties, and years of billable hours.

Finally in 1997, Schrotel and White, the intended victims of the cyanide murder plot, and the De Noia estate won a civil lawsuit asserting various tort claims, RICO and anti-trust violations, as well as fraudulent transfer against Steve's estate, Easebe and Chippendales. On February 21, a jury awarded De Noia's company, Unicorn Tales, $44.9 million, including $30.5 million in punitive damages. Schrotel and White were each awarded $2 million in emotional distress. Schrotel, White and Adonis were also awarded nearly $1.4 million in economic damages, $895,000 in damages on an anti-trust claim, and $1.2 million in damages from Steve Banerjee personally, as well as $9.5 million in punitive damages. Adonis Management was awarded $7.5 million in punitive damages. CLP Tours was not found responsible or liable. The transfer from Steve to Irene was ruled fraudulent, although the sale to CLP and Cohen was not. Irene appealed the ruling related to the fraudulent transfer, but the ruling was affirmed on September 9, 1998.

California civil code provides that a transfer made with the intent to hinder, delay or defraud any creditor or debtor constitutes a fraudulent transfer. The transfer of Chippendales from Steve to Irene and then to CLP both appeared to be fraudulent. A fraudulent transfer is indicated if the transferred assets were being threatened by legal action, which the assets of Steve and Chippendales clearly were, and were transferred to an insider. Legally, an insider is someone employed by one of the parties with access to information not available to the public. Mark Pakin had worked at Chippendales for more than a decade and had an eight percent share of CLP. Pakin's father-in-law, Nace Cohen worked at Chippendales for a year and a half before the sale. Irene, who received a 15 percent share in CLP after the sale, was married to the previous owner, Steve Banerjee. Pakin, Cohen and Irene all appeared to be insiders. Another indicator of a fraudulent transfer is if the value of the assets transferred was far in excess of the amount received for them, and the transfer leaves an individual or company basically insolvent. Steve transferred virtually all of his assets to Irene and after the deal with CLP, Easebe was left basically insolvent. A final indication that a transfer was fraudulent is if the details of the transfer are kept secret. Irene asked the court to seal the criminal file related to the case to ensure the secrecy of the deal.

Although the court found that the transfer from Steve to Irene was fraudulent, a ruling that appears to have been supported by the law, the transfer from Irene to Cohen and CLP was not found to be fraudulent, which appears to have been a legally questionable ruling. The jury may have so ruled because they were asked if "each" party to the sale acted with fraudulent intent, even though a transfer is fraudulent even if only one party (the buyer or the seller) intends to defraud. The jury instructions made Cohen's good faith relevant, yet it is irrelevant to proving fraud if Irene acted in bad faith. Furthermore, legally, Cohen had to prove good faith; it is not assumed. The jury was also told that actual payment is not required to give reasonably equivalent value, which probably misled the jury. Finally, the jury was given a list of eight indications or "badges" of fraud, which is often done, but was then also given a list of circumstances or signs of non-fraud, which is not usually done and was legally questionable. The eighth indication of non-fraud on the list was if a business would fail without the transfer. This indicator made it appear that Cohen was a "white knight" rescuing Easebe and Chippendales from looming bankruptcy, even though such a factor is irrelevant to a fraud case.

Even though the Steve-to-Irene transfer was ruled to be a fraud, the District Court did not void it and in a June 6, 1997 ruling offered no remedy to the plaintiffs, nor did the court award any damages. The plaintiffs appealed, but to no avail.

As of the writing of this book, the De Noia family, White, Schrotel, and Adonis have not collected a penny from Steve's estate, Irene or Easebe. Val later laughed when asked about their victory in court against Steve and Easebe. Referring to the award and the government's suspicion that Steve had salted away millions in Swiss bank accounts to hide from creditors, Val said, "Now all we have to do is go to Switzerland to collect it."

On March 8, 1994, Ray appeared in Federal Court for sentencing. Ray's cooperation and deteriorating health were balanced by the judge against his heinous crimes.

"With some reluctance, I will accept the plea agreement and do hereby sentence you to 30 months in federal prison," the judge said. Ray would receive psychiatric treatment during his sentence and would then be on three years of supervised release. The court ordered Ray to report by noon on March 13 to the Federal Prison Hospital in Springfield, Missouri.

Ray spent one last night at home. As he lay awake holding Barbara, he kept asking himself why now, when he was about to leave, did he show her the love and affection for which she had longed for so many years?

The next morning Stefanek and Garriola picked up Ray at 9 a.m. to take him to Missouri. Ray said a long goodbye to Barbara. The next day Ray sat in a cell in Springfield and began to pay his debt to society. His payments were about to increase substantially. A few months after he entered prison, Barbara filed for divorce after more than 20 years of marriage. While he was working the case against Louie and Steve, Ray had been the one unable to show his love for Barbara and now, when he finally could show his love, she had no love for him. She received permission from the court to sell their house, the house on which Ray had worked so long and hard.

Ray had far from learned to walk the straight and narrow. While in Springfield, in 1995 Ray was charged with using a phone with a co-conspirator to try to introduce drugs into the prison.

Ray served his entire term at Springfield.

The US Attorney's office offered Gilberto Rivera "Louie" Lopez a deal, but Louie's attorney advised his client against accepting it. With all the sensationalism around the O.J. Simpson trial in Los Angeles the summer before, Louie's attorney may have been seeking similar attention for his client with his ties to the Chippendales troupe and the murder of an Emmy award winning choreographer in Manhattan. Detective Geddes, who had returned from retirement to see the case through to the end, later said the attorney commented on the lack of media attention during the trial.

The case ran in New York from June 21 to July 18, 1996, with 17 days of trial and one day lost when Louie was too ill to appear. After the jury was sworn in, on June 26 the prosecution first called an "engineering technician," Marie Venticinque. She had extensive experience modeling crime scenes. Years before, she applied for a position with the DA's office and was told it was in the drafting unit. When she learned what the job really entailed, modeling crime scenes, she was quickly told she would never have to go to a crime scene herself, basing her work on photographs and police reports. She was involved with many cases, including the murder of John Lennon. She had started to create a model of the crime scene of the Dakota, the apartment building at 1 West 72nd Street, where in 1980 Mark David Chapman shot Lennon to death. "It was three-quarters finished when he pled guilty," she later told a reporter. At Louie's trial, she testified about the De Noia crime scene.

On July 8, 10 and 11, 1996, Ray appeared against Louie. Ray's testimony was crucial, since the witnesses in the building at the time of the murder had been of little help in identifying Louie. On October 16, 1992, the police showed a photo-array to one of the witnesses, Mott, with the murderer, "Louie" Lopez in the number three slot. Ray was also in the array. Mott did not recognize anyone. Val De Noia, Stefanek, Garriola, and the medical examiner also appeared to testify for the People. The defense only called one witness: "Louie" Lopez. On July 17 the defense summed up their case in an hour and forty-five minutes, followed by the People summing up over two hours and twenty minutes.

After the trial, with Val De Noia and his wife attending every day, Gilberto Rivera "Louie" Lopez was found guilty of the criminal use of a firearm in the first degree and the second-degree murder of Nick De Noia. Louie was sentenced on September 10, 1996. The judge could no longer impose the death penalty under New York law, even though, the judge said, Lopez deserved it. Lopez was sentenced to a maximum term of life and a minimum term of 25 years.

Even though Ray vehemently denied that his brother-in-law had been involved, William "Billy" Nelson Barnes, Jr., cut his own deal with the government. On May 10, 1993, he was sentenced to 51 months in prison and 3 years' probation. His cooperation had reduced his sentence, but he accompanied Ray on the abortive trip to Canada with Ray, traveled to Britain to learn about Adonis, and there was evidence he had given Strawberry $2,500 from Ray. Most damning of all, he had advance knowledge of the conspiracy to murder the Adonis members.

Mike Alvarez, the other arsonist, cooperated with the government for a reduced sentence. Errol Lynn "Strawberry" Bressler, who turned to the FBI instead of murdering the Adonis troupe members, served no time for his involvement in the conspiracy.

The De Noia family congratulated the NYPD and FBI on doing what Val De Noia called "a wonderful job," even as they mourned the loss of their beloved Nick. Mike Fullington, the choreographer and Steve's first Adonis target, died of complications of HIV/AIDS in 1991. Adonis targets Stephen White was hospitalized for anxiety, while a stress-ridden Read "Scott" Schrotel lost his job and filed for bankruptcy. Schrotel's marriage almost failed under the stress of thinking someone else might have been hired to kill him. Involvement in a murder, even tangentially, can sow a lifetime of suspicion. Decades later, several of the participants in the story were hesitant to discuss the case until they had verified the author's credentials for fear that someone might be trying to murder them.

Irene Banerjee died of breast cancer in the late 1990s. Barbara Colon is now a nurse manager in southern California. Bruce Nahin, having cut his ties with Chippendales, ensured that Nick De Noia's name lived on in his second son, Nicholas.

Scott Garriola still works as an FBI agent in Los Angeles. Andrew "Andy" Stefanek is retired, as is Detective Michael Geddes, who has his own small business in New York.

In the late 1980s the Chippendales dancers declined in popularity. In an October 27, 1990 *Saturday Night Live* skit, the buffed, Joffre-trained professional dancer and actor, Patrick Swayze staged a dance off against an overweight, rhythm-challenged, comedian Chris Farley before a panel of Chippendales recruiters. Chippendales had become the target of satire.

In 1995, Lou Perlman purchased Chippendales. He later said Chippendales gave him the idea for his band, the Backstreet Boys, which became phenomenally successful. In 2008 Perlman continued Chippendales' relationship with crime when he was sentenced to 25 years for charges related to running one of the biggest and longest Ponzi schemes in history.

After their low point in the late 1980s and early 1990s, the Chippendales rebounded. By 1997 they were back on a 60-city American "You Turn Me On Tour," while a second troupe toured Europe. Although the kiss-and-tips were long gone, women still packed arenas and clubs to see the buffed strippers. By the turn of the new century, the Chippendales began appearing as a headline show at the Rio in Las Vegas, even as they continued to stage tours around the world, and promote an active website as they sold calendars, posters and DVDs.

With Steve dead, Louie convicted and Ray's sentence served, the case was closed. His life shortened by complications from polycystic kidneys, Ray lived out the remainder of his life in a small apartment in San Bernardino, CA, with his mother and nephew. Ray said Steve "destroyed my honor" and "beat" me. "He was smarter than me, but in the end, I outsmarted him. I got him. I became a piece of shit, but he became dead."

After his death, based on their shared interest, many of Nick De Noia's possessions relating to television ended up at the home of his niece, Marie De Noia. Amazingly productive, Nick left behind stacks of scripts, concepts and ideas for shows and movies. Amongst it all, Marie found audiocassettes he used to tape subjects to gather information when he was developing new projects. Missing her beloved uncle, Marie sat down to listen to every one of the cassettes in hopes of hearing his voice one last time. The first voice she heard was not Nick's, nor was the second or the third. After several tapes she realized that Nick would give each subject a series of written questions and then tape their answers. Hoping against hope, on tape after tape she listened in vain for the sound of her uncle's voice, until at one point a subject started to ask Nick a question. Marie's hope soared, but then the subject said, "Oh, you don't want your voice on here, right." For once the extroverted Nick De Noia, who was always the center of attention, never said a word.

Author's Note

In 1997 I worked at a brokerage firm in Century City, California. A broker, Patrick MontesDeOca, who was also an actor and
producer, met Ray Colon at an acting class. As a form of thera-
py, Ray's psychiatrist suggested he write about his experiences with Steve Banerjee. Patrick gave me the result: a 900-page
script. Patrick asked if I wanted to revise the script and write
a book. It was a tall order. Motion picture scripts are about 120
pages. Ray had written a 15-hour epic.

After reading the script, I was intrigued. Ray and I arranged
to meet. When my parents heard about my plans to meet a button man (as my ex-crime reporter father called Ray, using underworld slang for a person who arranges a murder), my father
was excited as he relived his reporting days. My mother was
worried. I was meeting Ray alone. The thought of Ray hurting
me had never entered my mind. Maybe I was young and foolish, but I had also read his story.

Ray worked for Rocky as a button man, probably not killing
anyone, but certainly being present when force was used. To
Ray, such work was a job. Outside of his work for Rocky and

Steve, Ray was not a violent man. Violence for Ray was part of a job and did not seep into other facets of his life. There is no evidence, for example, that he ever physically abused any of his wives. In the hours I spent interviewing him I only once saw any sign of a temper, and never felt threatened. He had a low-key, relaxed personality. Like a cool professional gambler who methodically places his bets and, win or lose, is just doing his job, Ray perceived his work, whether as a police officer or as a button man, as just work. Legality did not appear to enter into the equation.

In his relationship with Steve, Ray always stressed that Steve had some sort of hold over him based on a combination of friendship and fear. Those elements were certainly present, but so was something else: Ray was always a dutiful soldier. He took orders, whether from his police superiors, Rocky or Steve, and always did what he was told to do.

Ray repeatedly emphasized that Steve never paid him. To most people, the issue would be of little importance. To Ray, the professional criminal, the point was crucial, even if it ignored the $7,000 Ray took for his first arson job and the $250,000 the FBI said Steve paid Ray. When I interviewed Ray, the only time he sounded angry was when he said that Steve had never paid him. The nature of the job did not seem to matter. Ray had done a job and Steve had welched on him.

Ray showed me photographs of his family on the wall of his mother's apartment. He smiled as he pointed out Rocky and his crew—a part of his extended family—in a photograph sitting on a picnic table in prison. Ray's world was so different from most Americans' lives, yet he spoke of it as if everyone would accept it as normal, possibly a reflection of the glorification of the Mafia in the media. To Ray, crimes for the Mafia seemed less evil than crimes for Steve. He willingly talked about criminal acts committed for Rocky, yet was careful to say he always delayed in carrying out Steve's criminal plans, as if hesitating negated some, if not all, of the responsibility for his crimes. In the end, however, Ray did what Steve wanted. Delay or not, Ray was a criminal who tried to arrange the murder of several men—and had one man murdered.

Ray's script was a mixture of truth and falsehood, with the difference still, after years of research, at times difficult to determine. I supplemented the information in the script with in-depth interviews with Ray and with more than two dozen individuals involved in the story, as well as extensive research into court transcripts and documents. The telephone conversations between Strawberry and Ray, for example, are from an FBI agent's summary of the conversations, which are in court records. The additional information added background and texture to the story drawn from Ray's script, as well as correcting many, although certainly not all, of the times Ray altered the story to mitigate his involvement. Besides having been a reporter, my father is a scientist and I was raised to seek the truth. I hope I have found most, if not all of it in the preceding pages. Each participant will have a different view of many of the happenings in this book, but I hope they will see that the central truth of what happened has been told.

Scot Macdonald
May 2014
Culver City, California

About the Authors

K. Scot Macdonald is the author of the novels, *The Shakespeare Drug, In Justice Found*, and *Mouse's Dream*, as well as two non-fiction books. Writing as Liam Shay, he also wrote *The Grizzly Extinction Plot*. He has also contributed to *The Writers' Journal, Funds for Writers, Animal Wellness, The Marine Corps Gazette, US Naval Institute Proceedings* and several other magazines and journals. He lives in California with his wife, daughter, and two Scottish terriers. To find out more about him, visit KScotMacdonald.com.

Patrick MontesDeOca is an actor, writer and producer. He helped bring the story behind the motion picture *Rudy* to the big screen and has appeared in dozens of television shows and motion pictures including *The Shield, Walker, Texas Ranger, Melrose Place* and *Dead Again*.

About Kerrera House Press

Kerrera House Press is an independent press dedicated to producing the books you keep. For more information about our books, please visit KerreraHousePress.com.

Reader Resources

For photographs related to the Chippendales murders, a reader's guide, and more about the story and writing of *Deadly Dance*, please visit KerreraHousePress.com.

CPSIA information can be obtained
at www.ICGtesting.com
Printed in the USA
LVHW040219310322
714851LV00015B/686

9 780991 665327